Ew, It's Beautiful

Also by Joshua Barkman

False Knees: An Illustrated Guide to Animal Behavior

Ew, It's Beautiful

A False Knees Comic Collection

Joshua Barkman

Andrews McMeel
PUBLISHING®

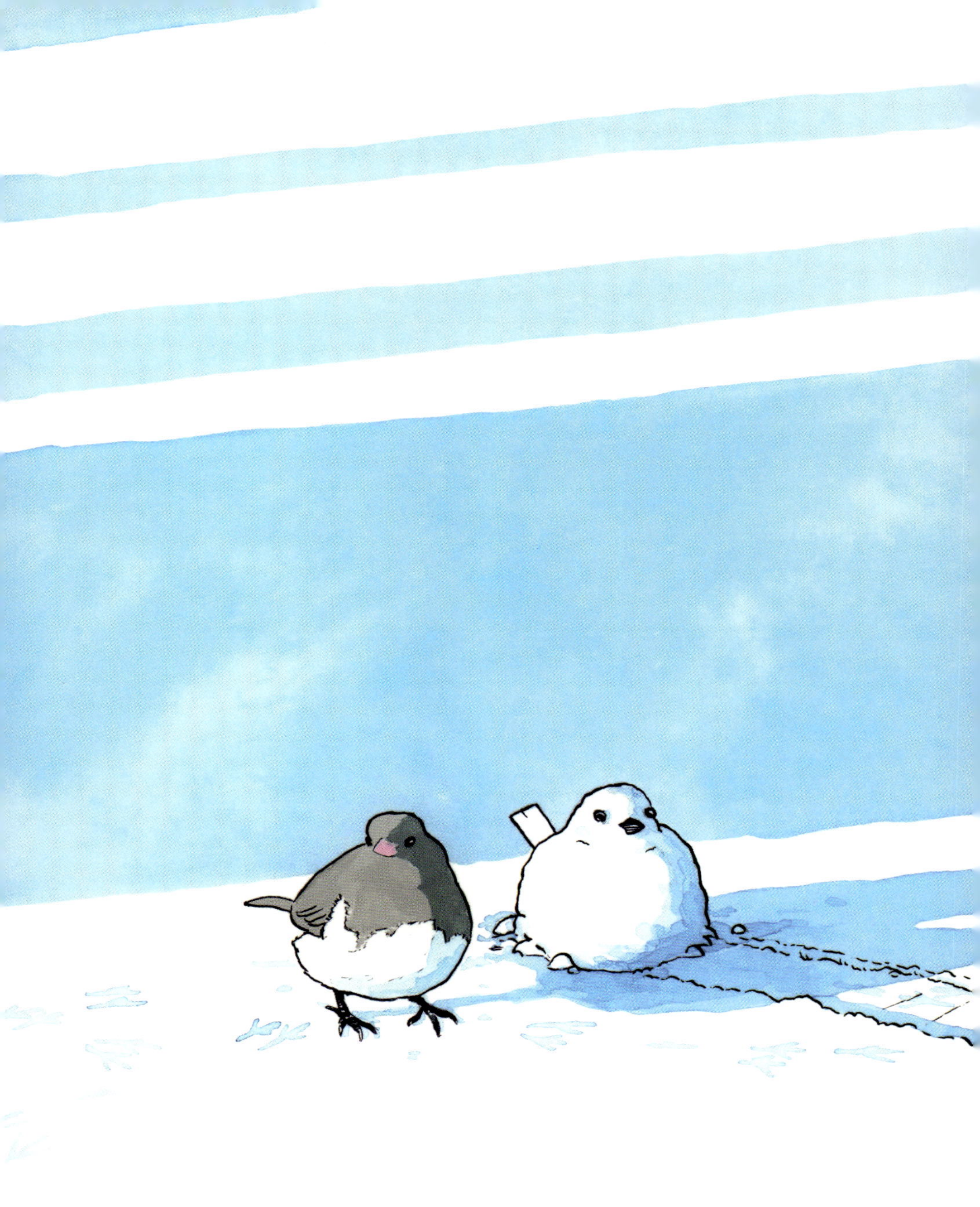

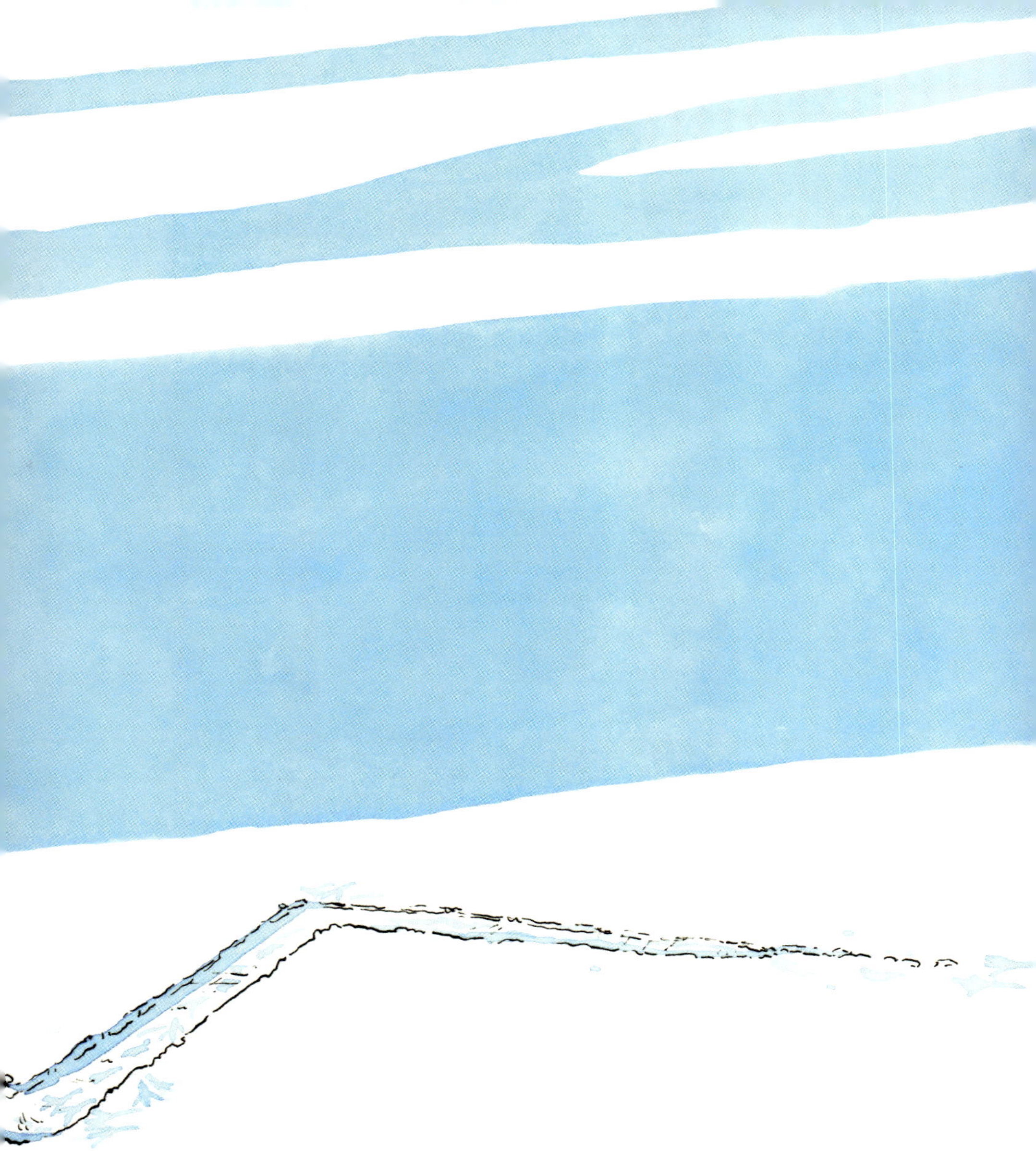

Winter

I GUESS I'M PRETTY CONTENT THESE DAYS...
I'M FEELING HEALTHY
GOT PLENTY TO EAT...
TIME TO STIR UP SOME UNNECESSARY BULLSHIT!

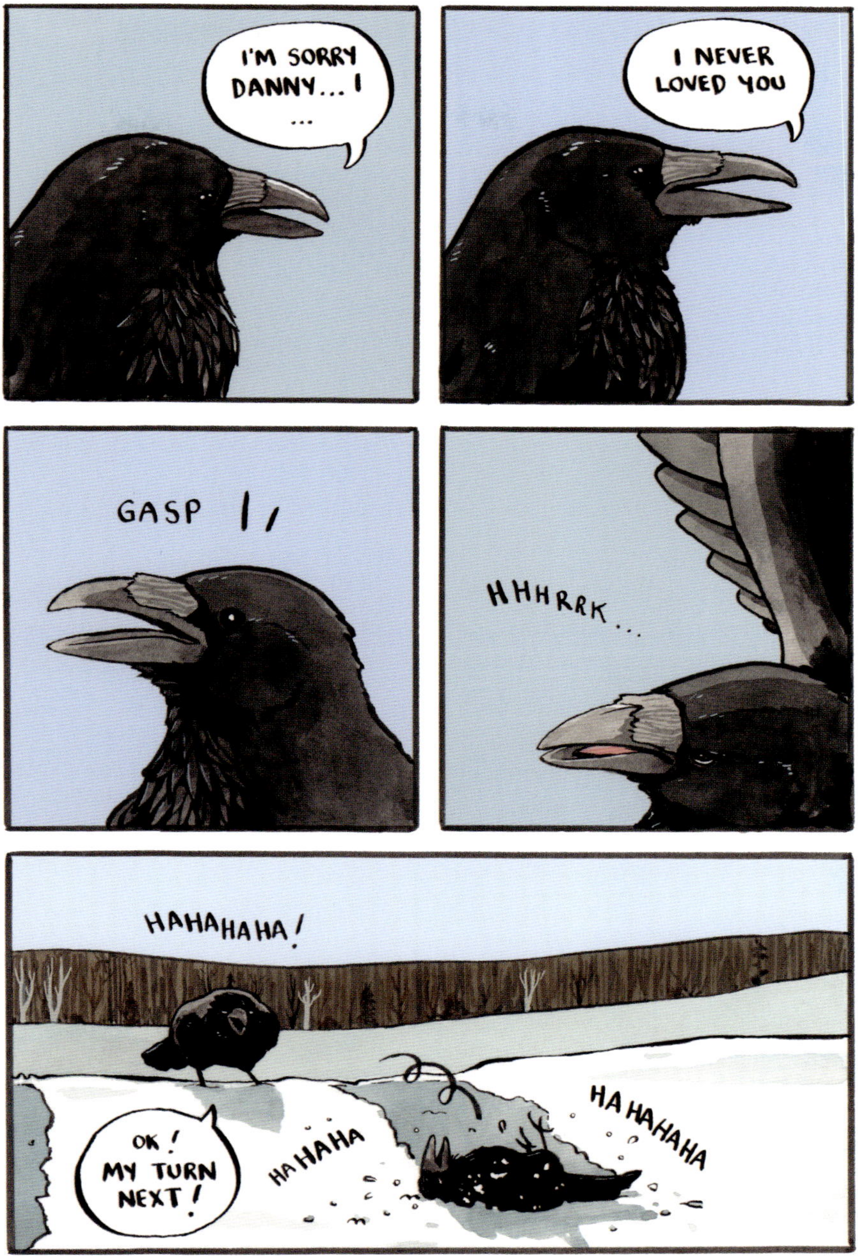
I'M SORRY DANNY... I ...
I NEVER LOVED YOU
GASP !!
HHHRRK...
HAHAHAHA!
OK! MY TURN NEXT!
HAHAHA
HAHAHAHAHA

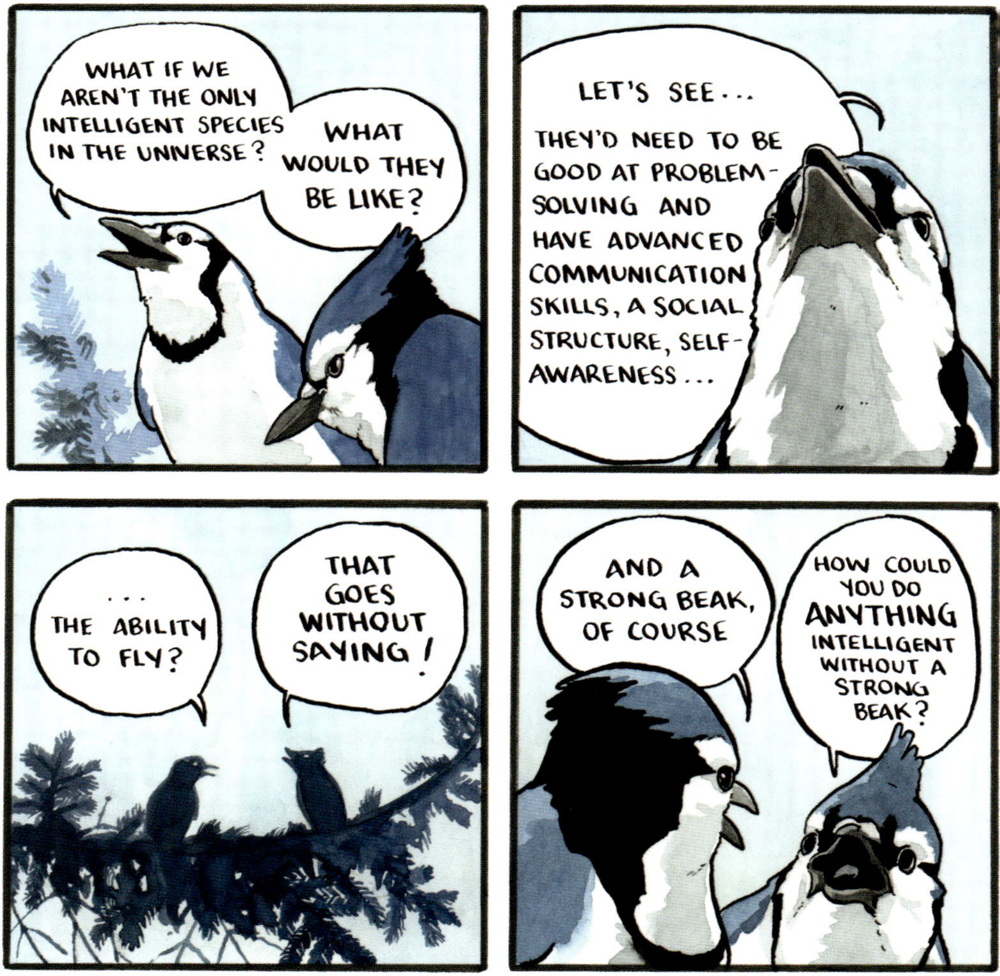
WHAT IF WE AREN'T THE ONLY INTELLIGENT SPECIES IN THE UNIVERSE?
WHAT WOULD THEY BE LIKE?
LET'S SEE...
THEY'D NEED TO BE GOOD AT PROBLEM-SOLVING AND HAVE ADVANCED COMMUNICATION SKILLS, A SOCIAL STRUCTURE, SELF-AWARENESS...
... THE ABILITY TO FLY?
THAT GOES WITHOUT SAYING!
AND A STRONG BEAK, OF COURSE
HOW COULD YOU DO ANYTHING INTELLIGENT WITHOUT A STRONG BEAK?

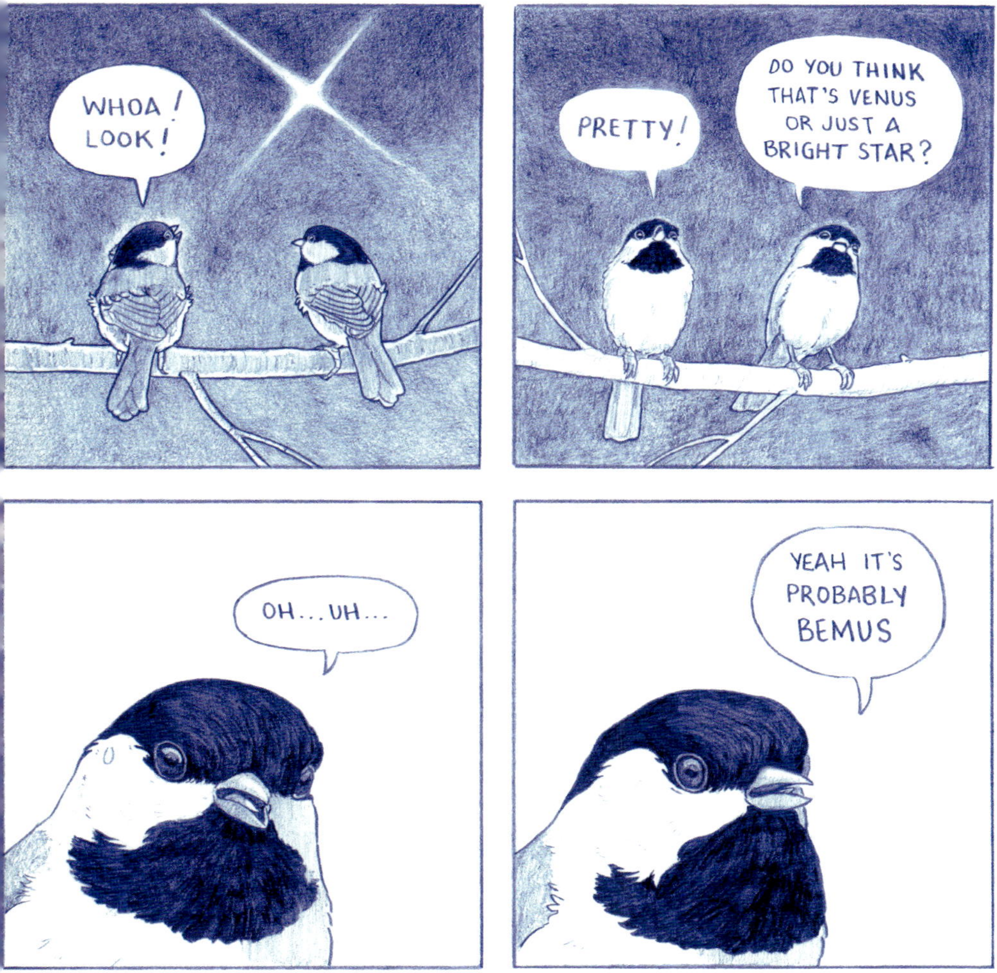
WHOA! LOOK!
PRETTY!
DO YOU THINK THAT'S VENUS OR JUST A BRIGHT STAR?
OH... UH...
YEAH IT'S PROBABLY BEMUS

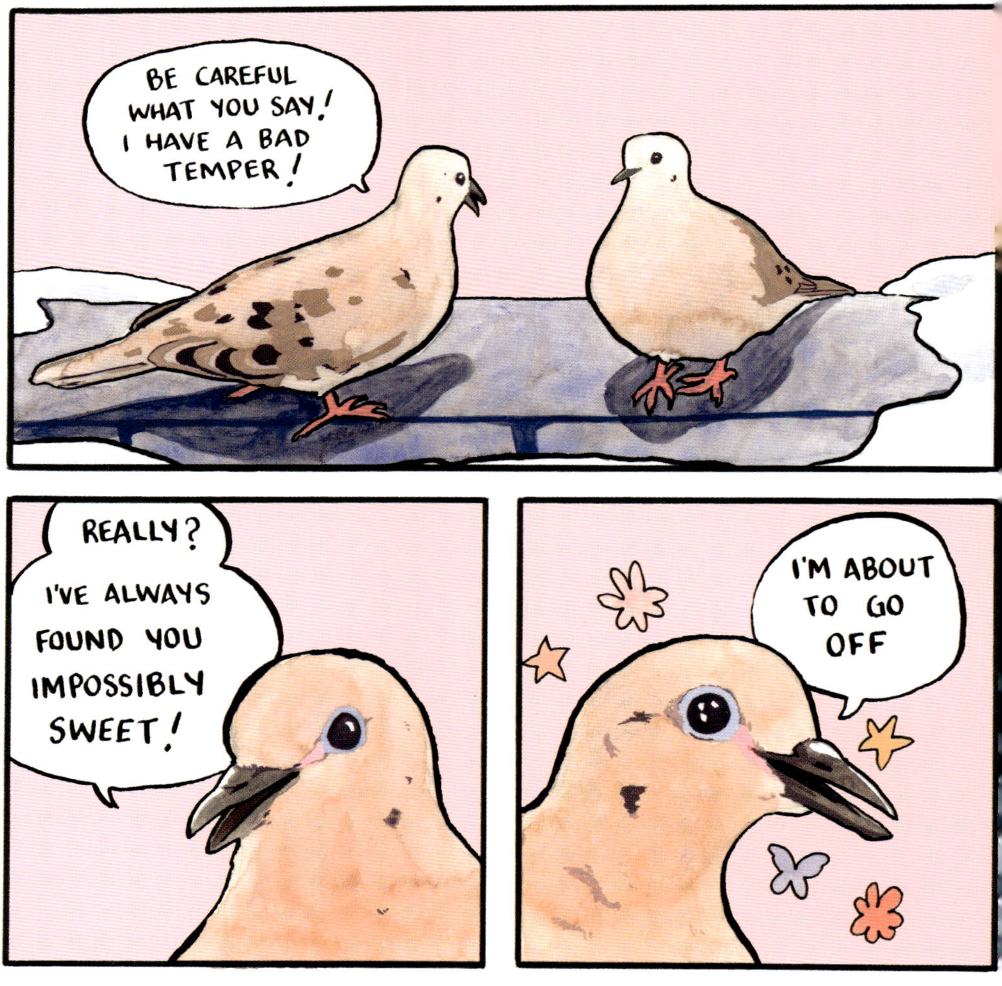
BE CAREFUL WHAT YOU SAY! I HAVE A BAD TEMPER!
REALLY?
I'VE ALWAYS FOUND YOU IMPOSSIBLY SWEET!
I'M ABOUT TO GO OFF

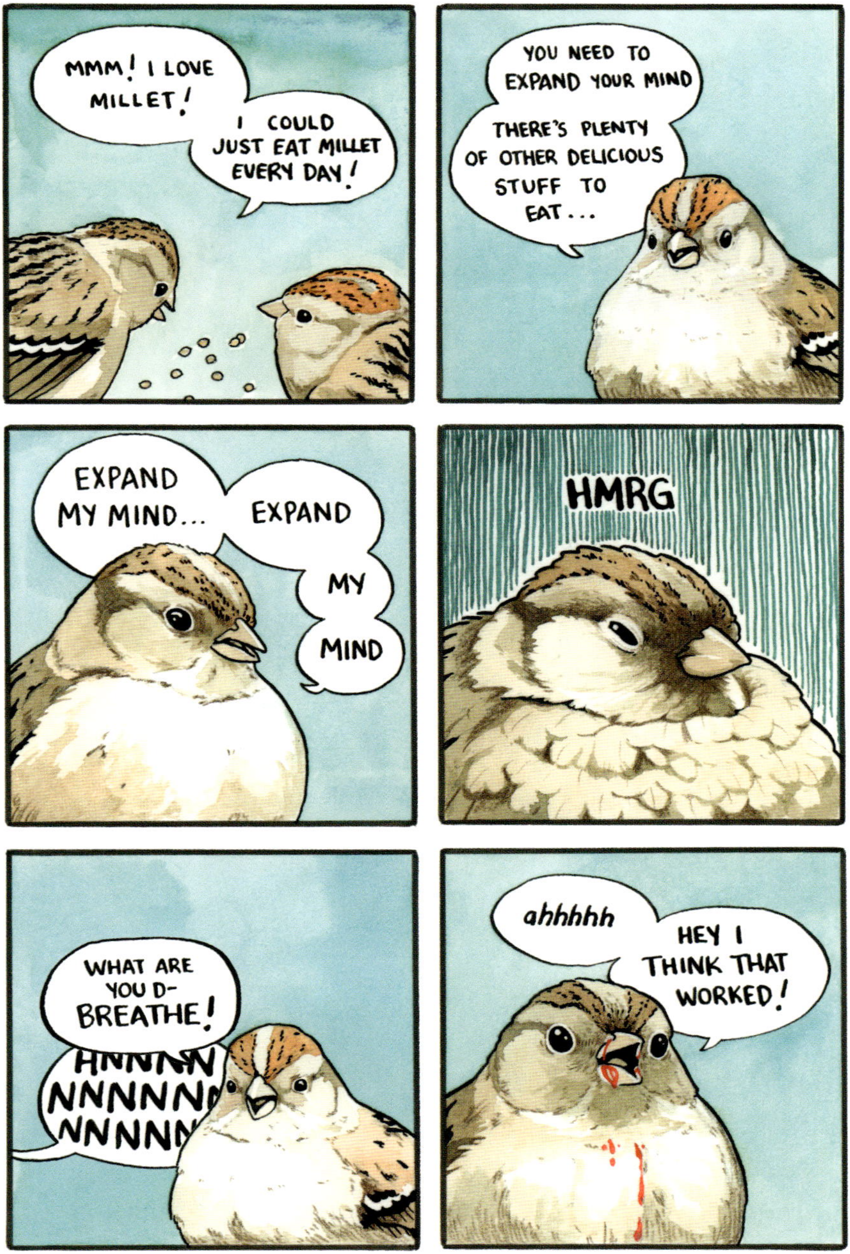
MMM! I LOVE MILLET!
I COULD JUST EAT MILLET EVERY DAY!
YOU NEED TO EXPAND YOUR MIND
THERE'S PLENTY OF OTHER DELICIOUS STUFF TO EAT...
EXPAND MY MIND...
EXPAND
MY
MIND
HMRG
WHAT ARE YOU D- BREATHE!
HNNNN NNNNN NNNNN
ahhhhh
HEY I THINK THAT WORKED!

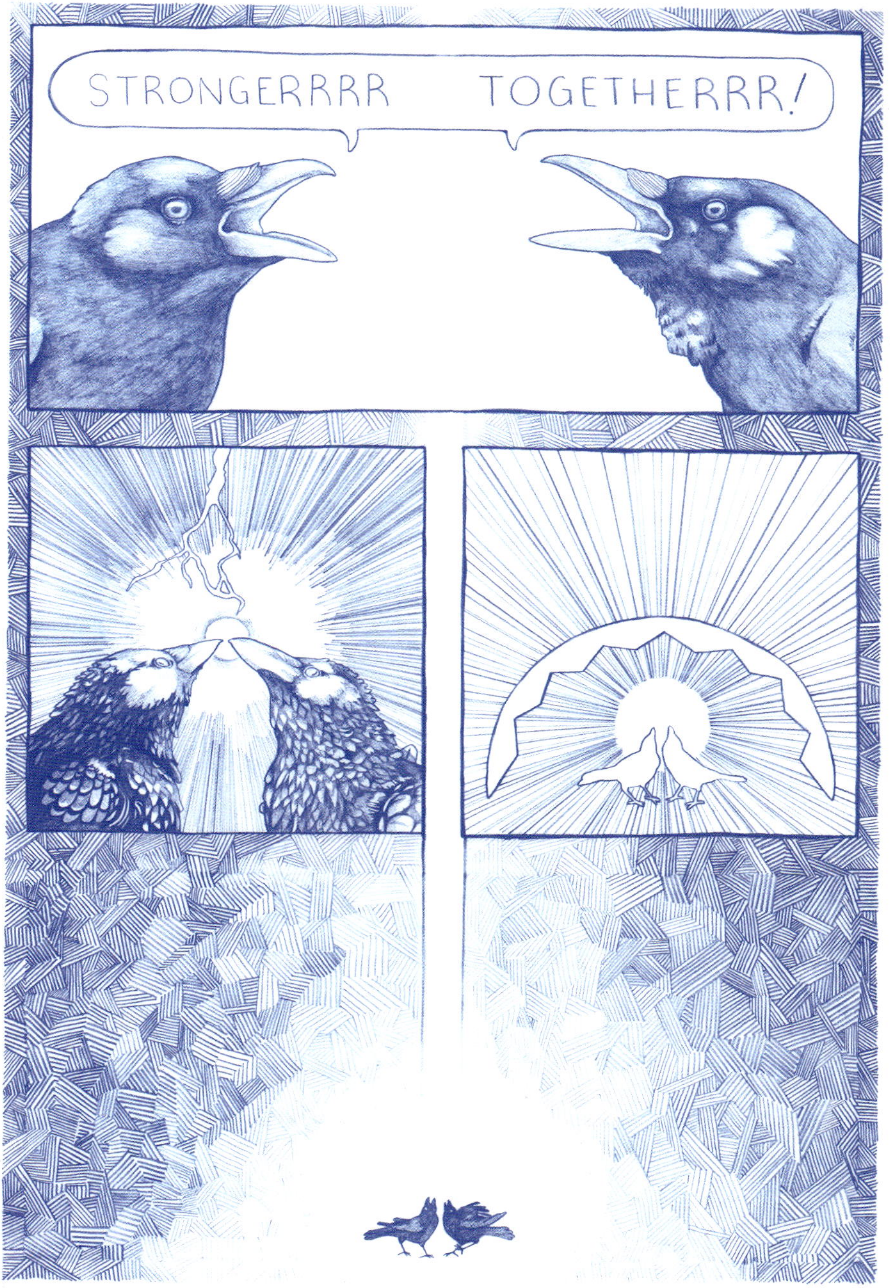
STRONGERRRR TOGETHERRR!

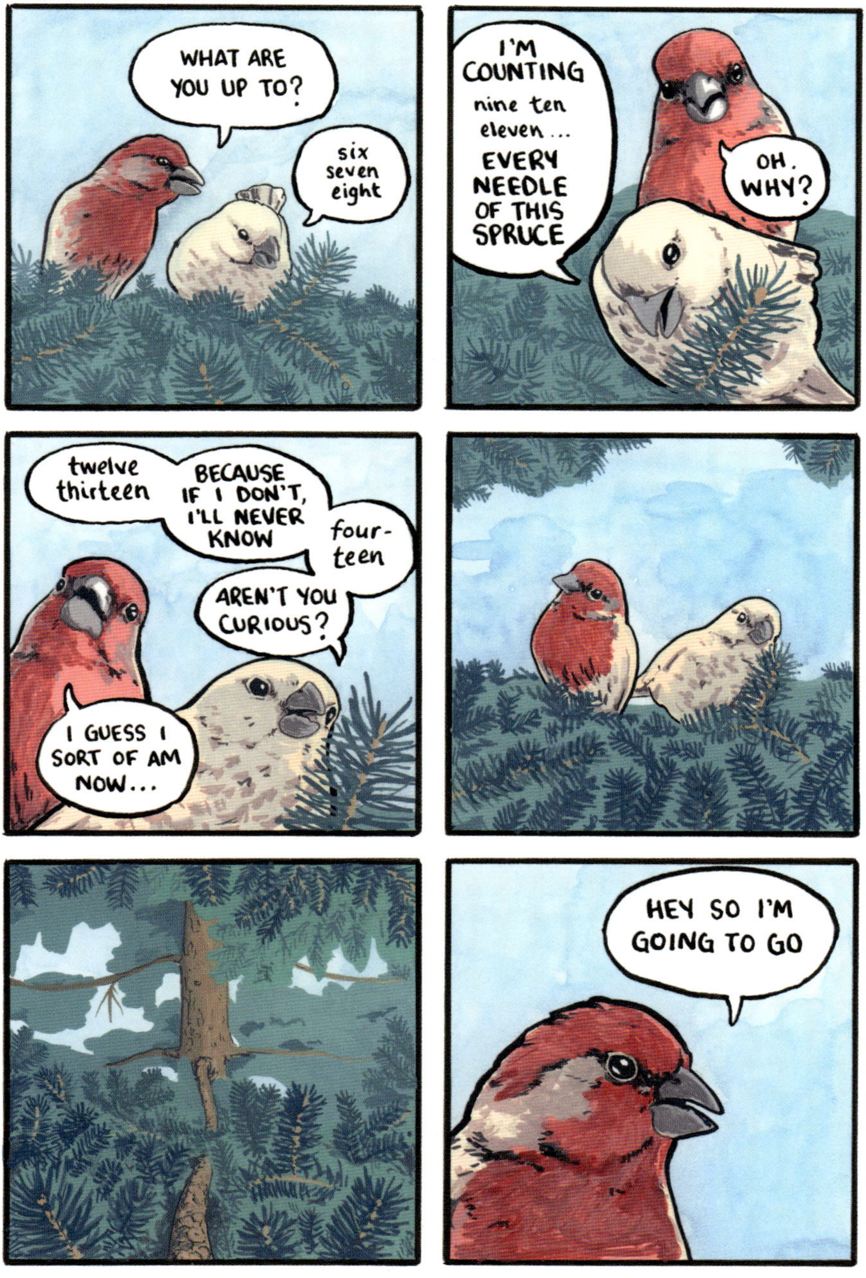
WHAT ARE YOU UP TO?
six seven eight
I'M COUNTING
nine ten eleven...
EVERY NEEDLE OF THIS SPRUCE
OH. WHY?
twelve thirteen
BECAUSE IF I DON'T, I'LL NEVER KNOW
four-teen
AREN'T YOU CURIOUS?
I GUESS I SORT OF AM NOW...
HEY SO I'M GOING TO GO

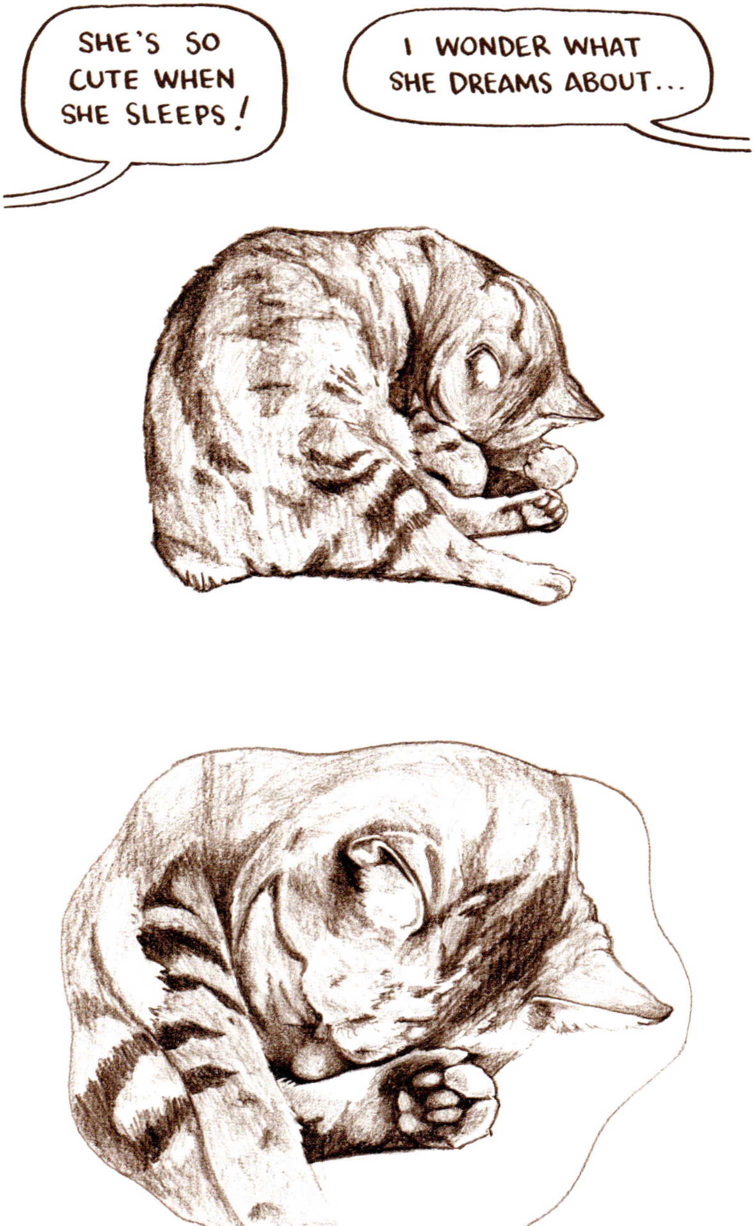
SHE'S SO CUTE WHEN SHE SLEEPS!
I WONDER WHAT SHE DREAMS ABOUT...

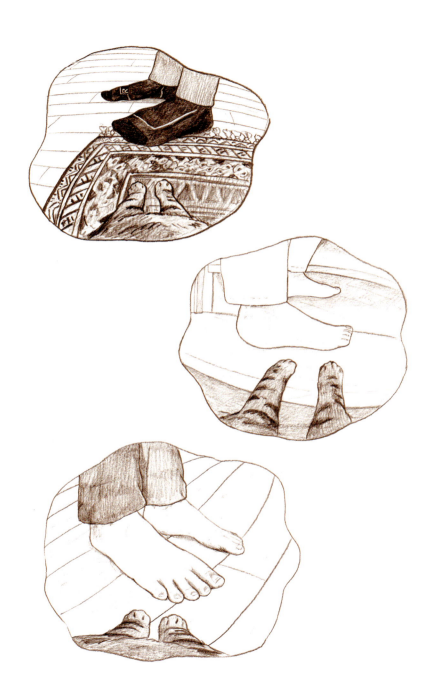

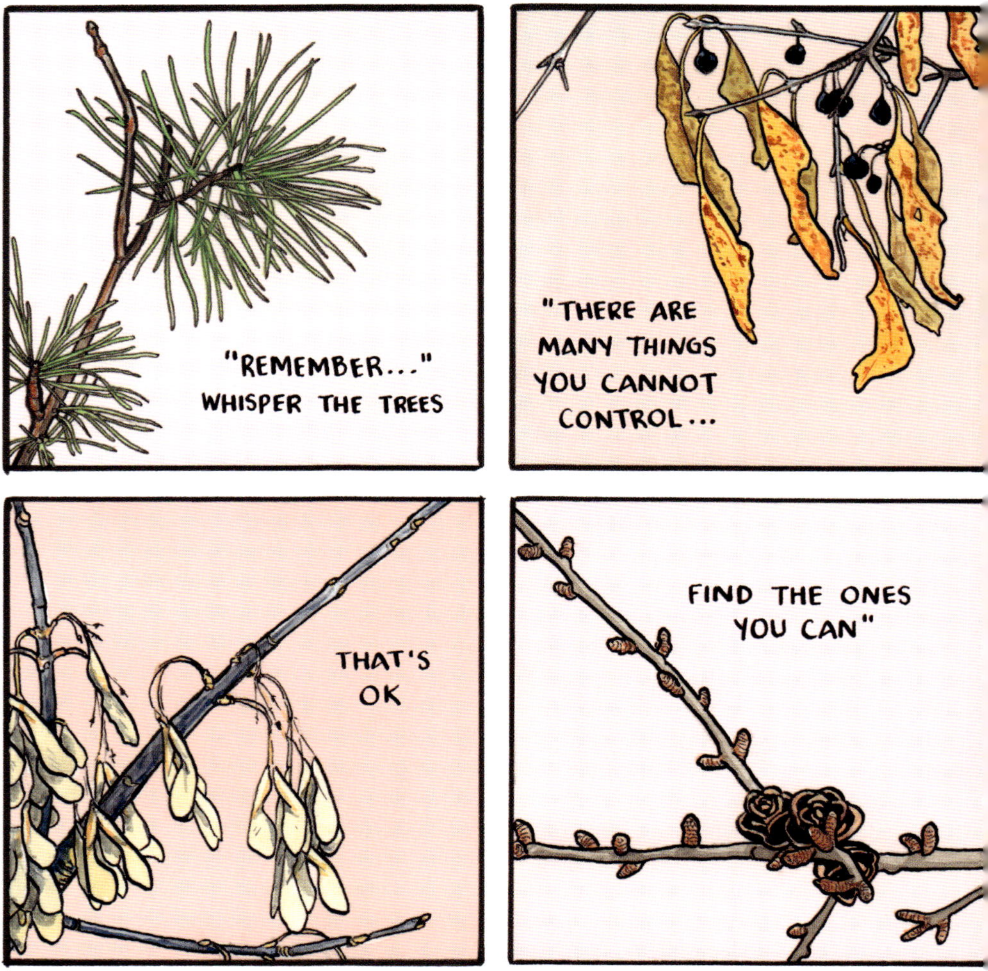
"REMEMBER..." WHISPER THE TREES
"THERE ARE MANY THINGS YOU CANNOT CONTROL...
THAT'S OK
FIND THE ONES YOU CAN"

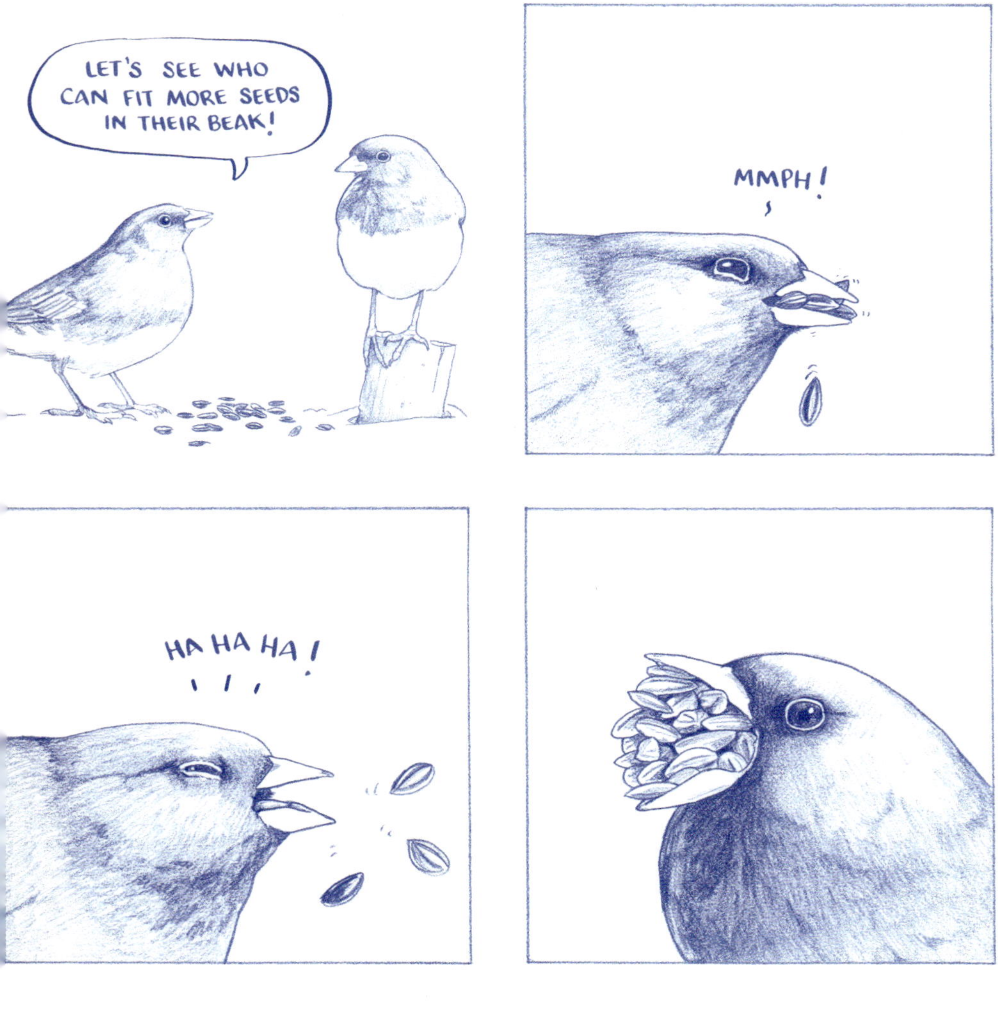
LET'S SEE WHO CAN FIT MORE SEEDS IN THEIR BEAK!
MMPH!
HA HA HA!

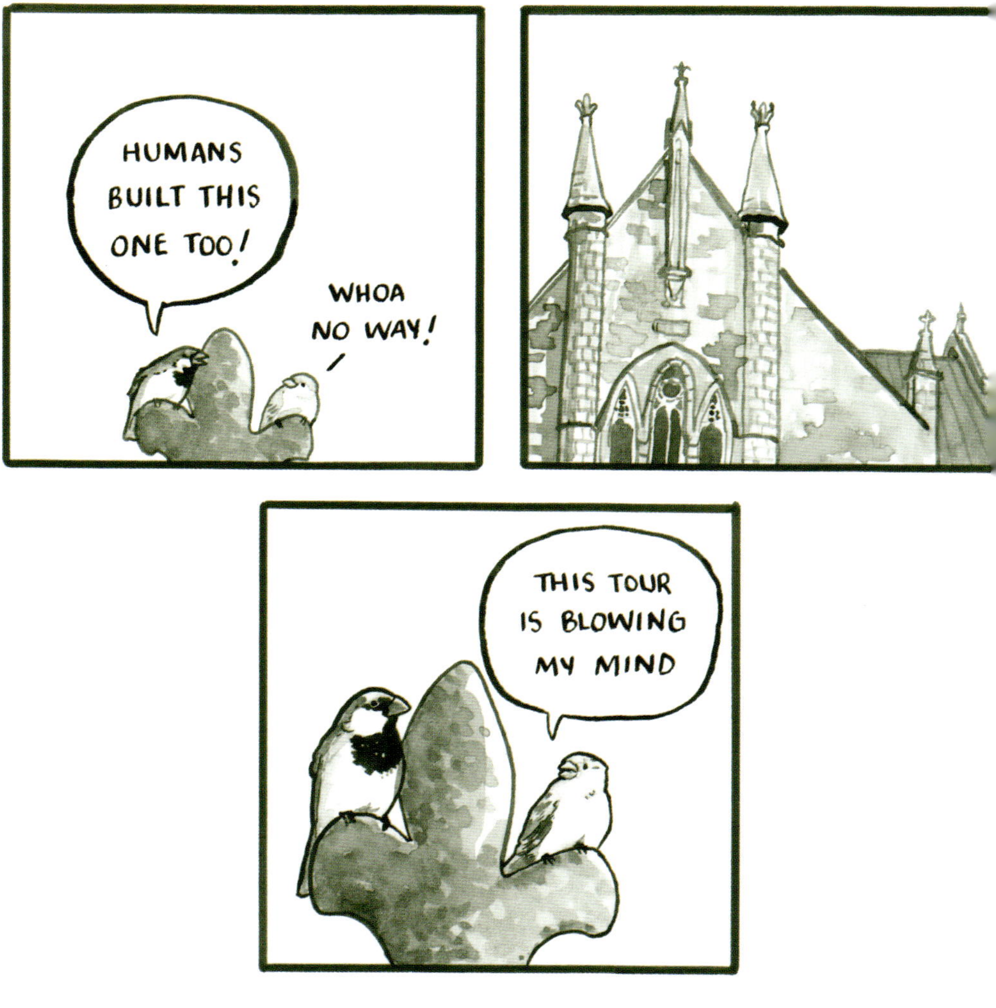
HUMANS BUILT THIS ONE TOO!
WHOA NO WAY!
THIS TOUR IS BLOWING MY MIND

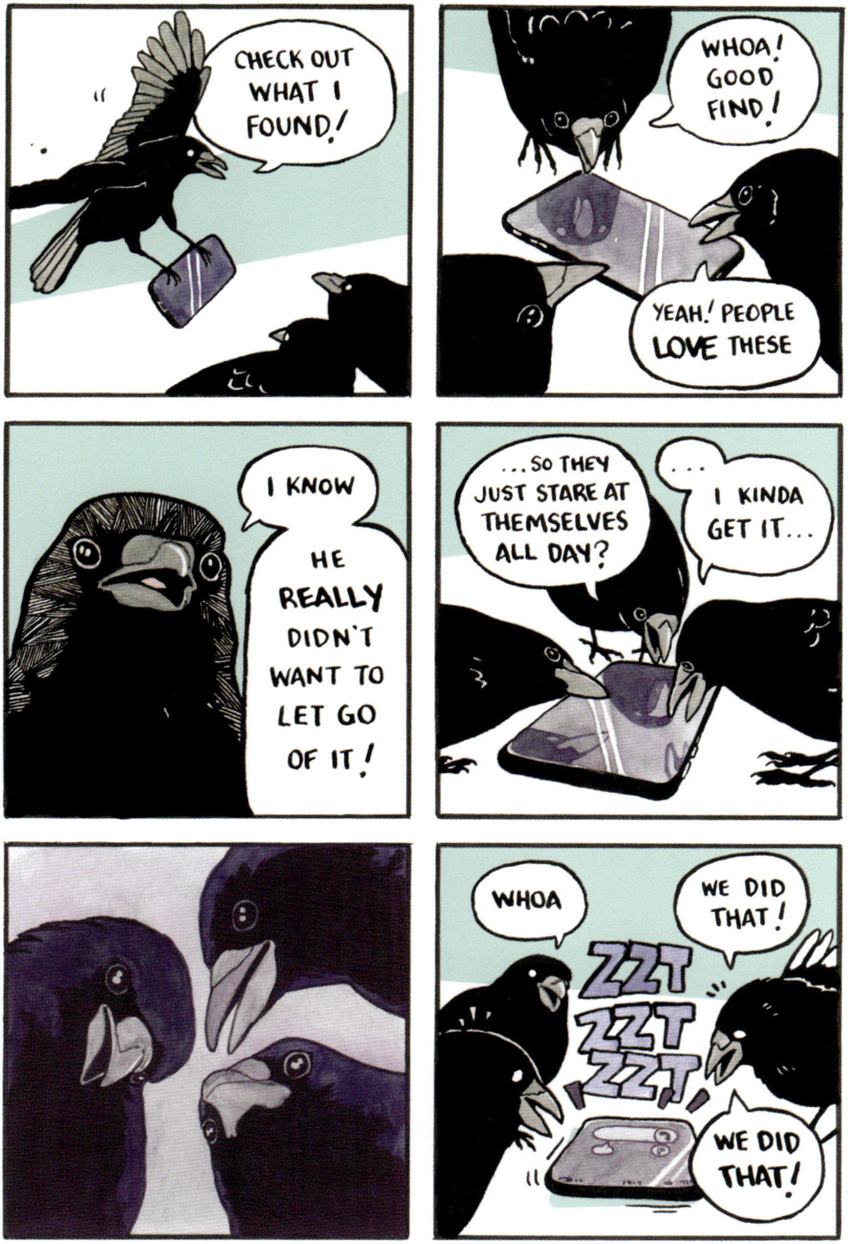
CHECK OUT WHAT I FOUND!
WHOA! GOOD FIND!
YEAH! PEOPLE LOVE THESE
I KNOW
HE REALLY DIDN'T WANT TO LET GO OF IT!
...SO THEY JUST STARE AT THEMSELVES ALL DAY?
...
I KINDA GET IT...
WHOA
WE DID THAT!
ZZT ZZT ZZT
WE DID THAT!

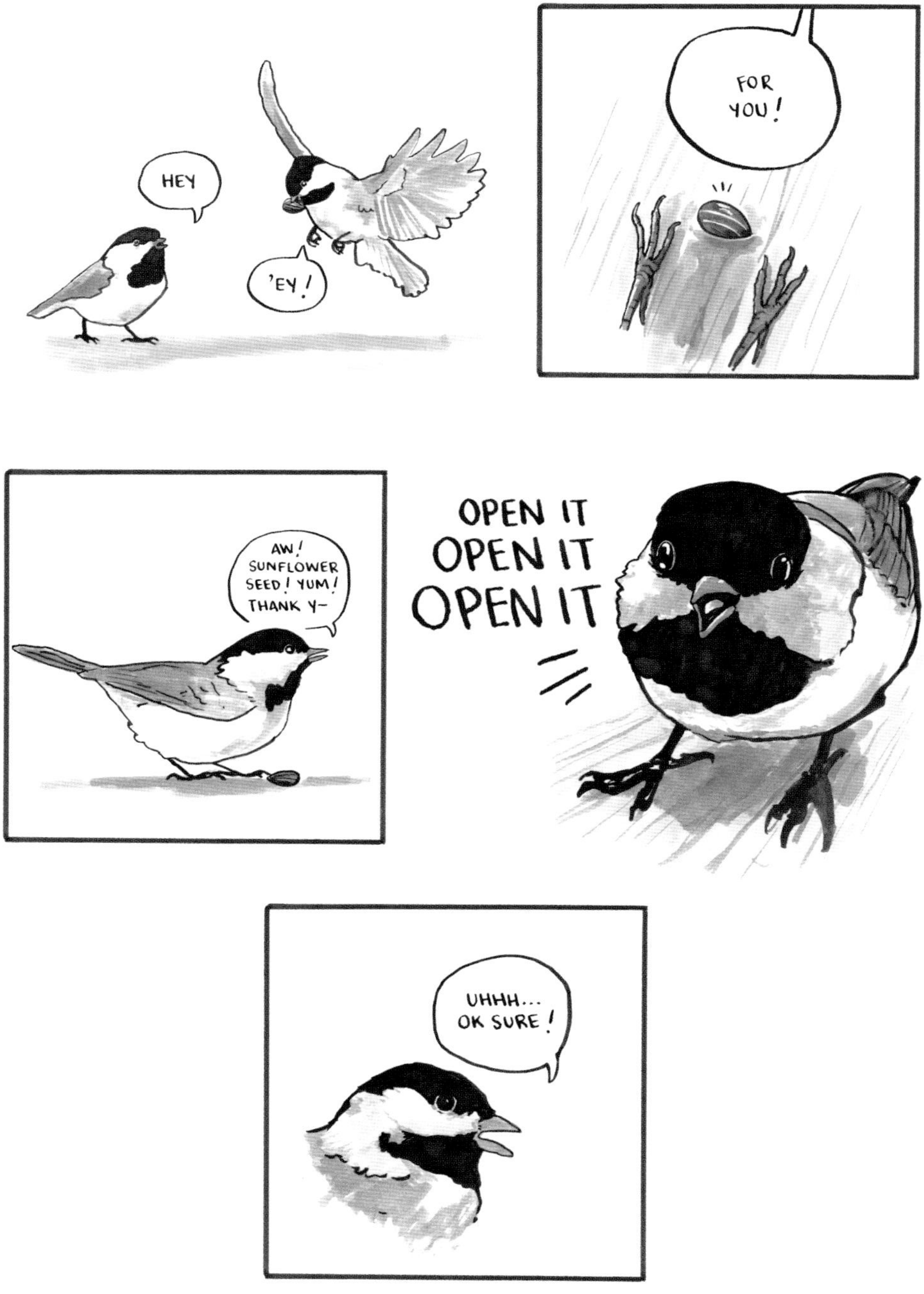
HEY
'EY!
FOR YOU!
AW! SUNFLOWER SEED! YUM! THANK Y–
OPEN IT OPEN IT OPEN IT
UHHH... OK SURE!

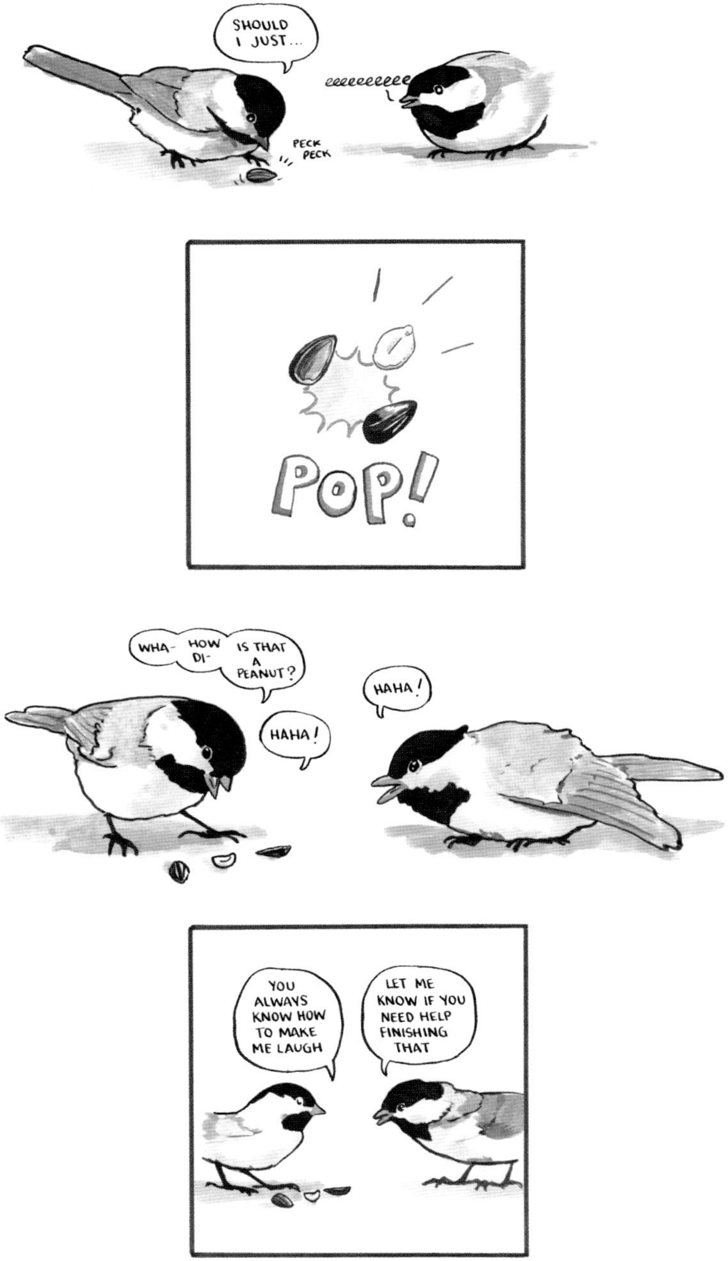
SHOULD I JUST...
eeeeeeeeee
PECK PECK
POP!
WHA-
HOW DI-
IS THAT A PEANUT?
HAHA!
HAHA!
YOU ALWAYS KNOW HOW TO MAKE ME LAUGH
LET ME KNOW IF YOU NEED HELP FINISHING THAT

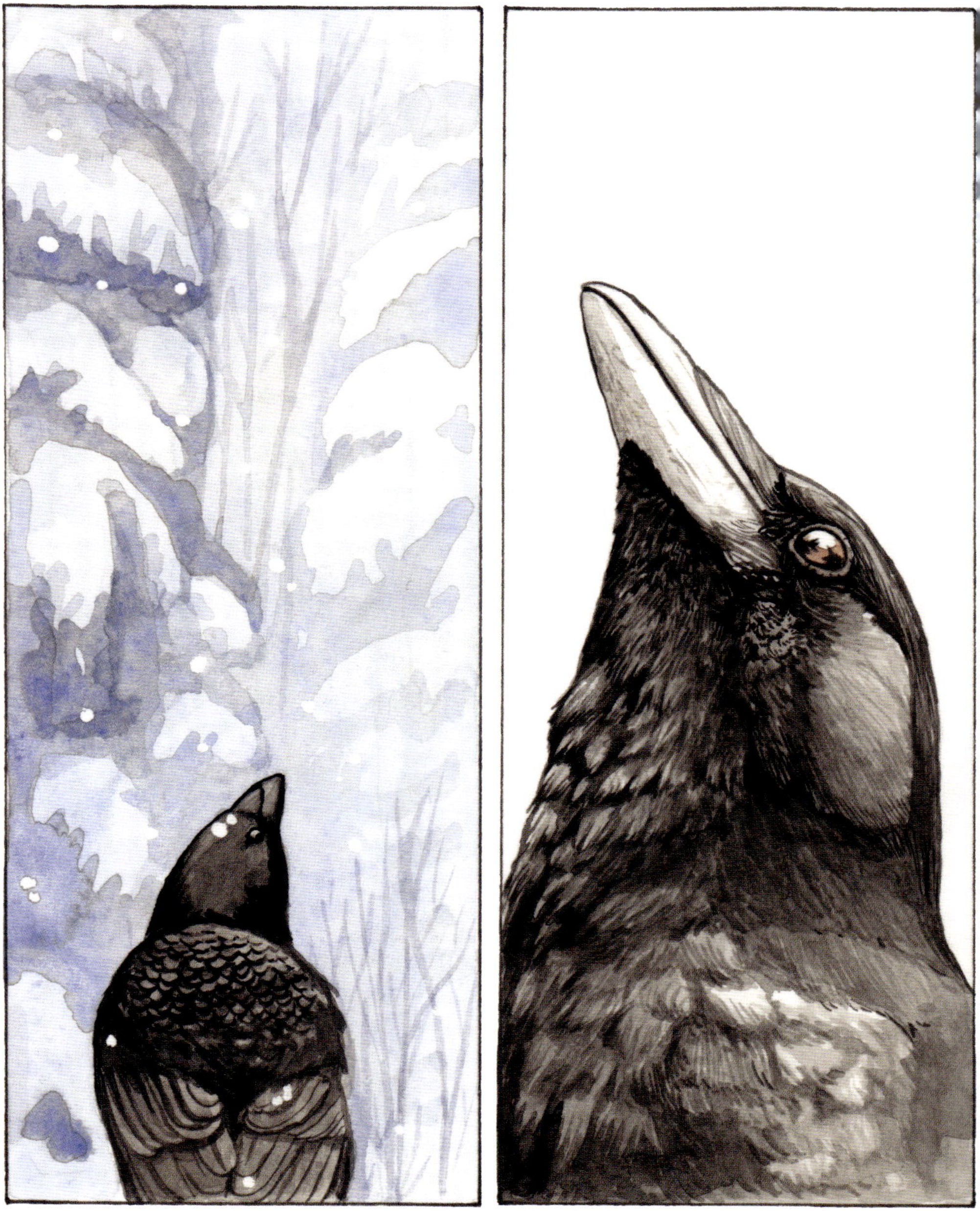

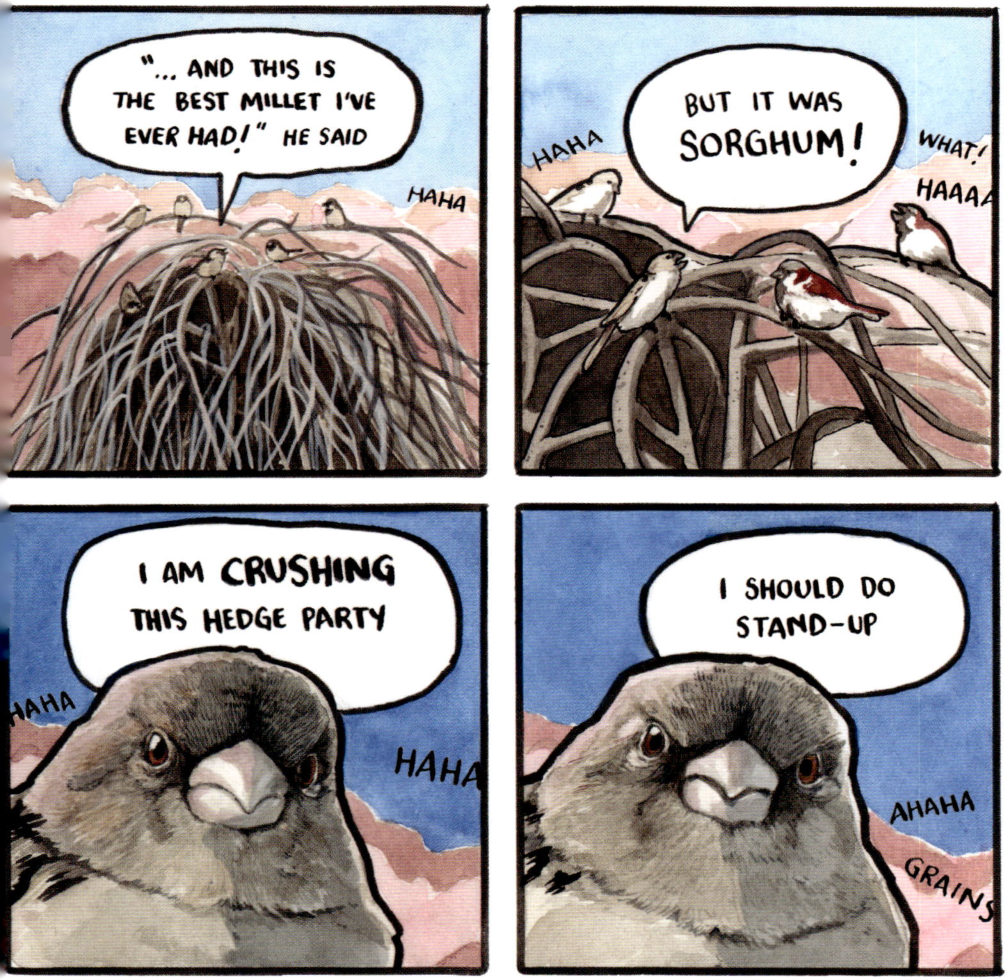
"... AND THIS IS THE BEST MILLET I'VE EVER HAD!" HE SAID
HAHA
HAHA
BUT IT WAS SORGHUM!
WHAT!
HAAAA
I AM CRUSHING THIS HEDGE PARTY
HAHA
HAHA
I SHOULD DO STAND-UP
AHAHA
GRAINS

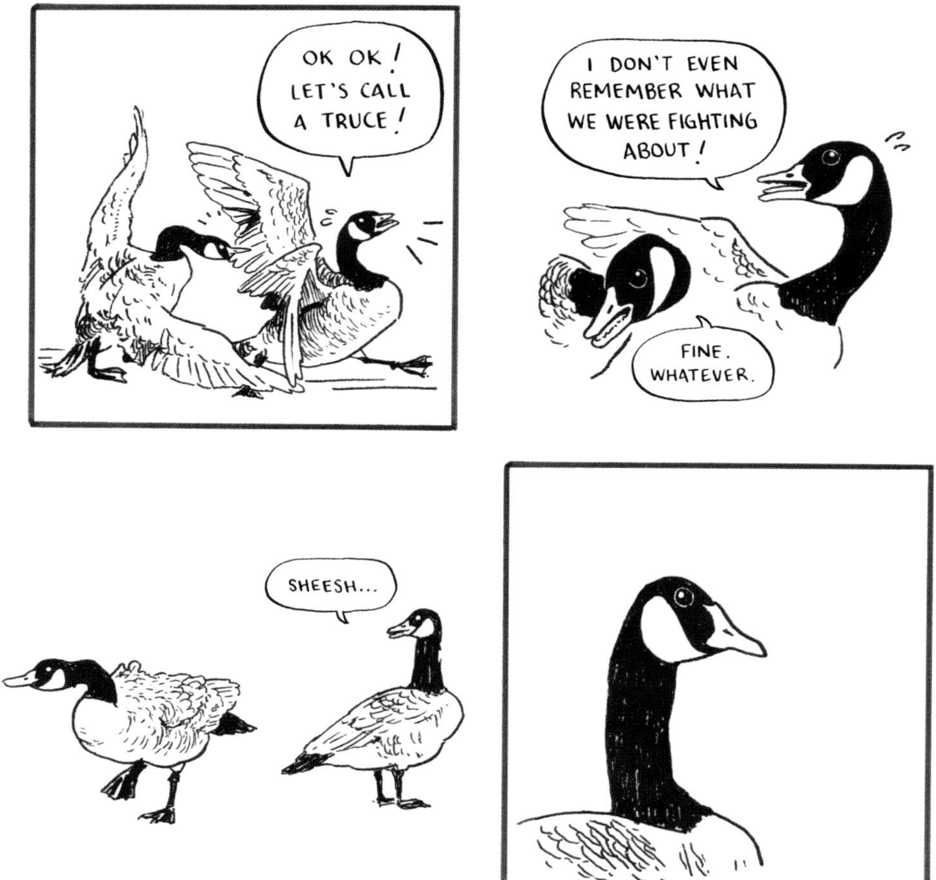
OK OK! LET'S CALL A TRUCE!
I DON'T EVEN REMEMBER WHAT WE WERE FIGHTING ABOUT!
FINE. WHATEVER.
SHEESH...

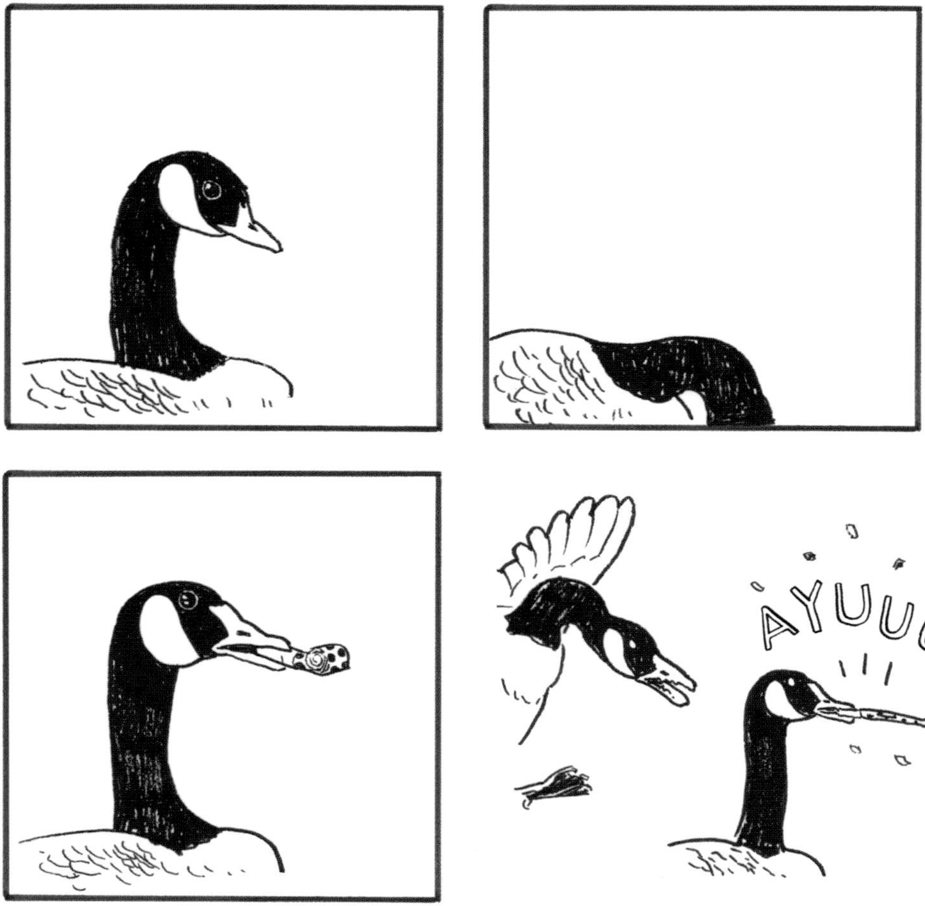
AYUUU!

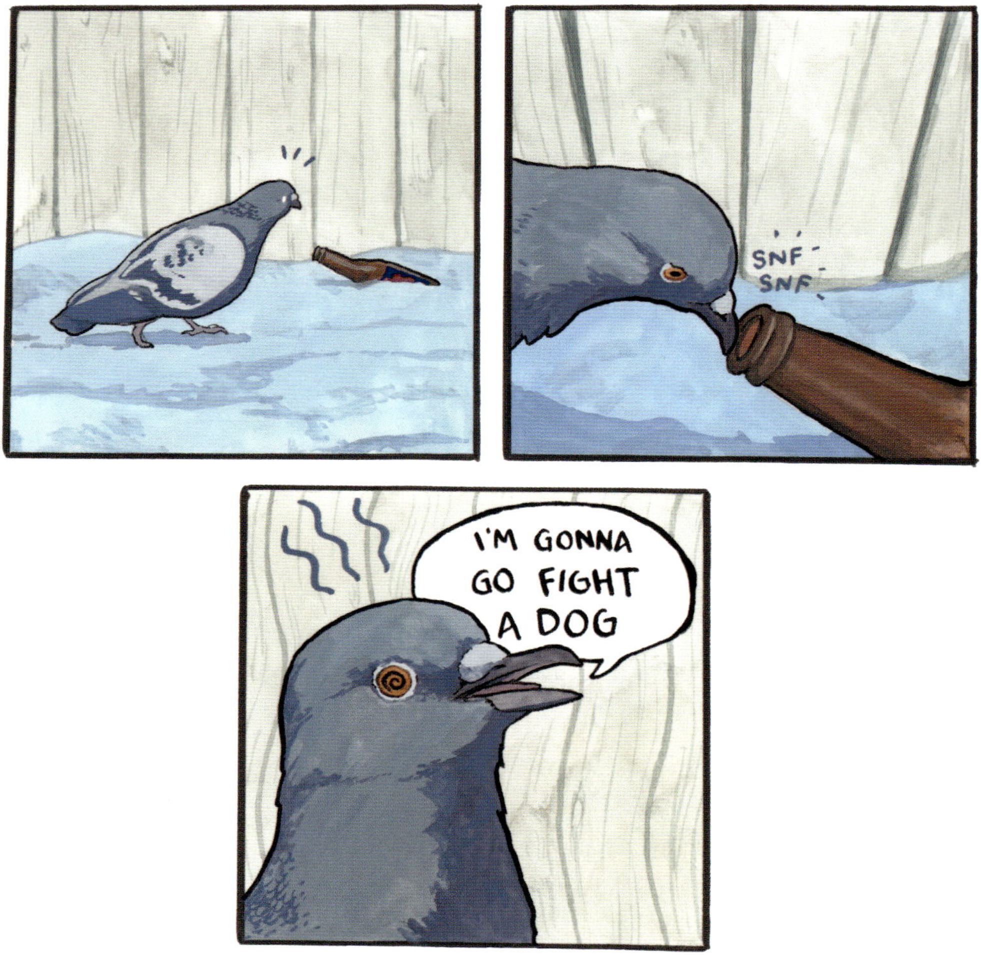
SNF
SNF
I'M GONNA GO FIGHT A DOG

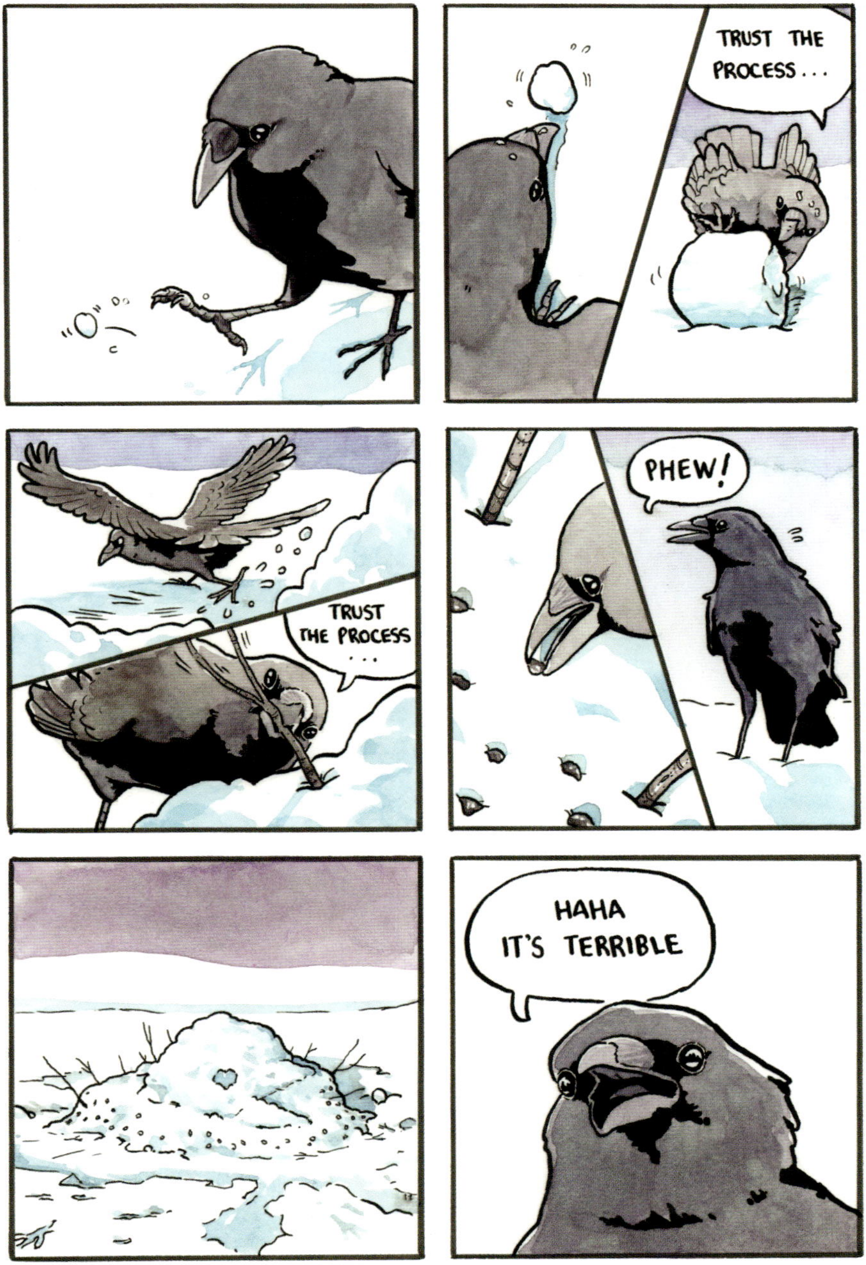
TRUST THE PROCESS...
TRUST THE PROCESS ...
PHEW!
HAHA IT'S TERRIBLE

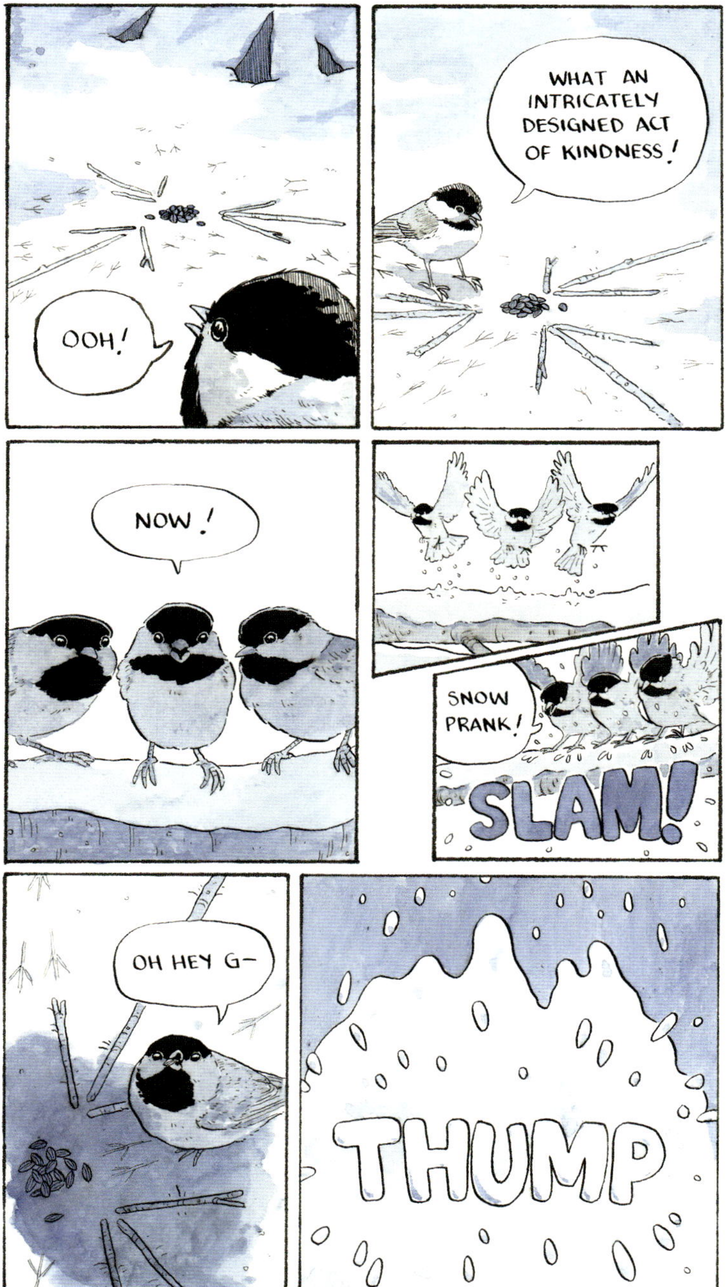
OOH!
WHAT AN INTRICATELY DESIGNED ACT OF KINDNESS!
NOW!
SNOW PRANK!
SLAM!
OH HEY G—
THUMP

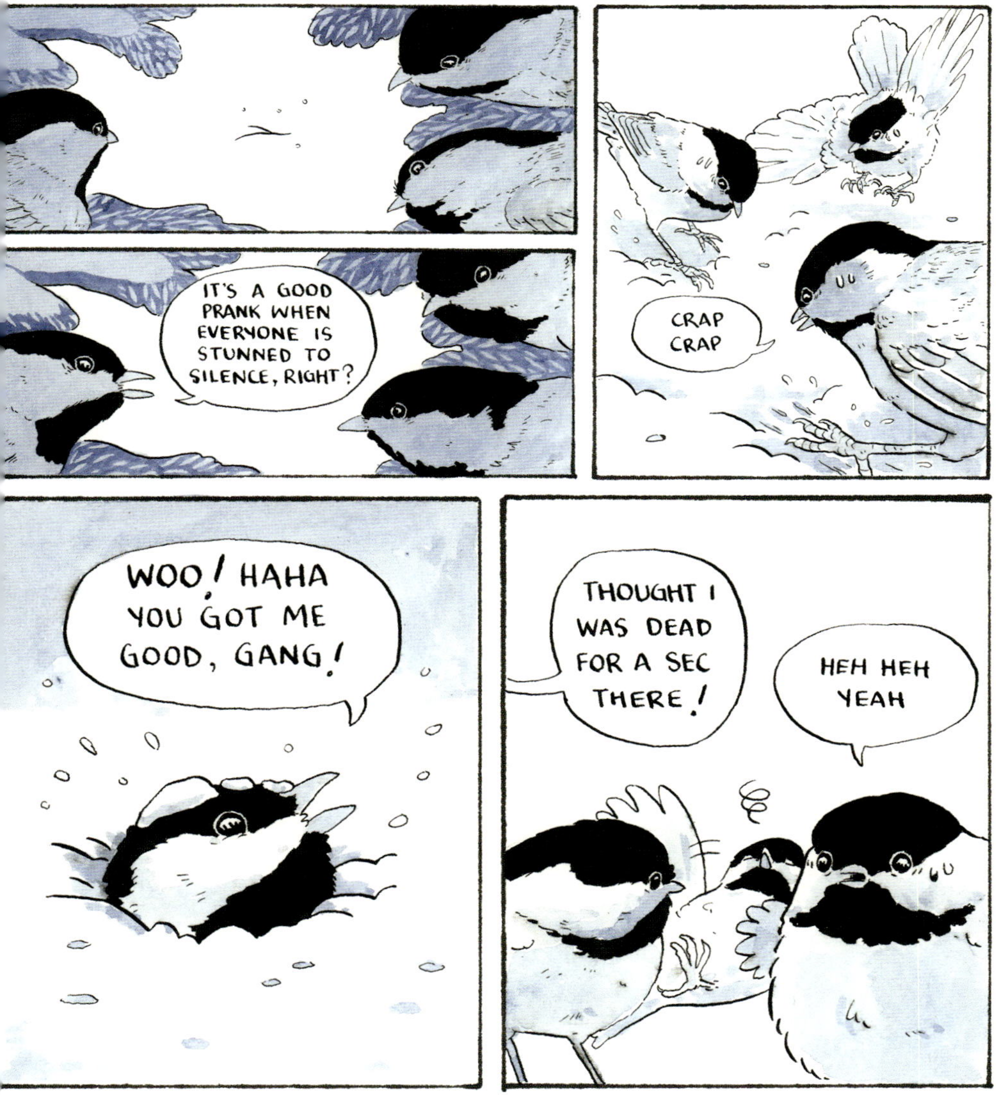
IT'S A GOOD PRANK WHEN EVERYONE IS STUNNED TO SILENCE, RIGHT?
CRAP CRAP
WOO! HAHA YOU GOT ME GOOD, GANG!
THOUGHT I WAS DEAD FOR A SEC THERE!
HEH HEH YEAH

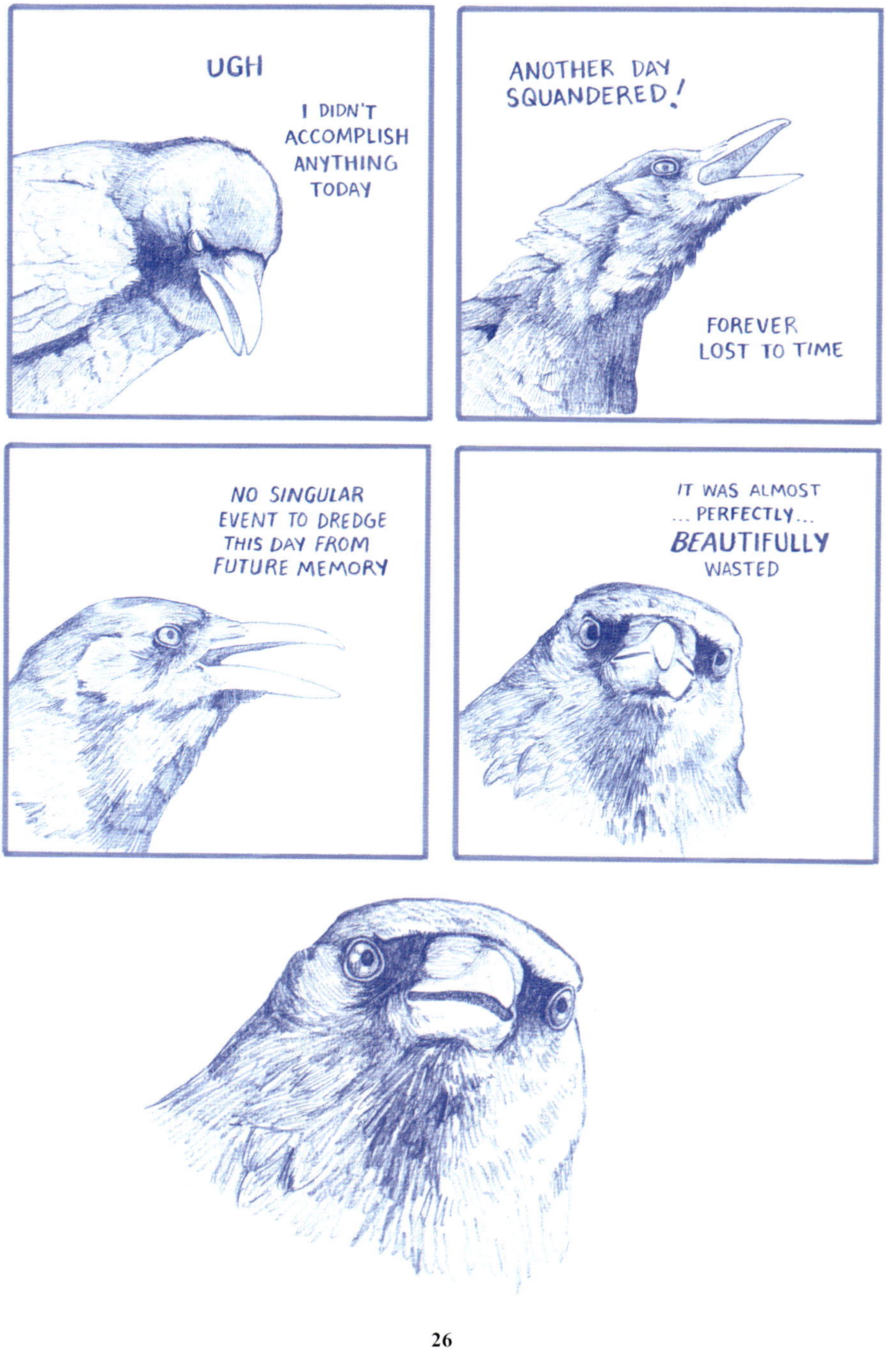

UGH
I DIDN'T ACCOMPLISH ANYTHING TODAY
ANOTHER DAY SQUANDERED!
FOREVER LOST TO TIME
NO SINGULAR EVENT TO DREDGE THIS DAY FROM FUTURE MEMORY
IT WAS ALMOST ... PERFECTLY... BEAUTIFULLY WASTED

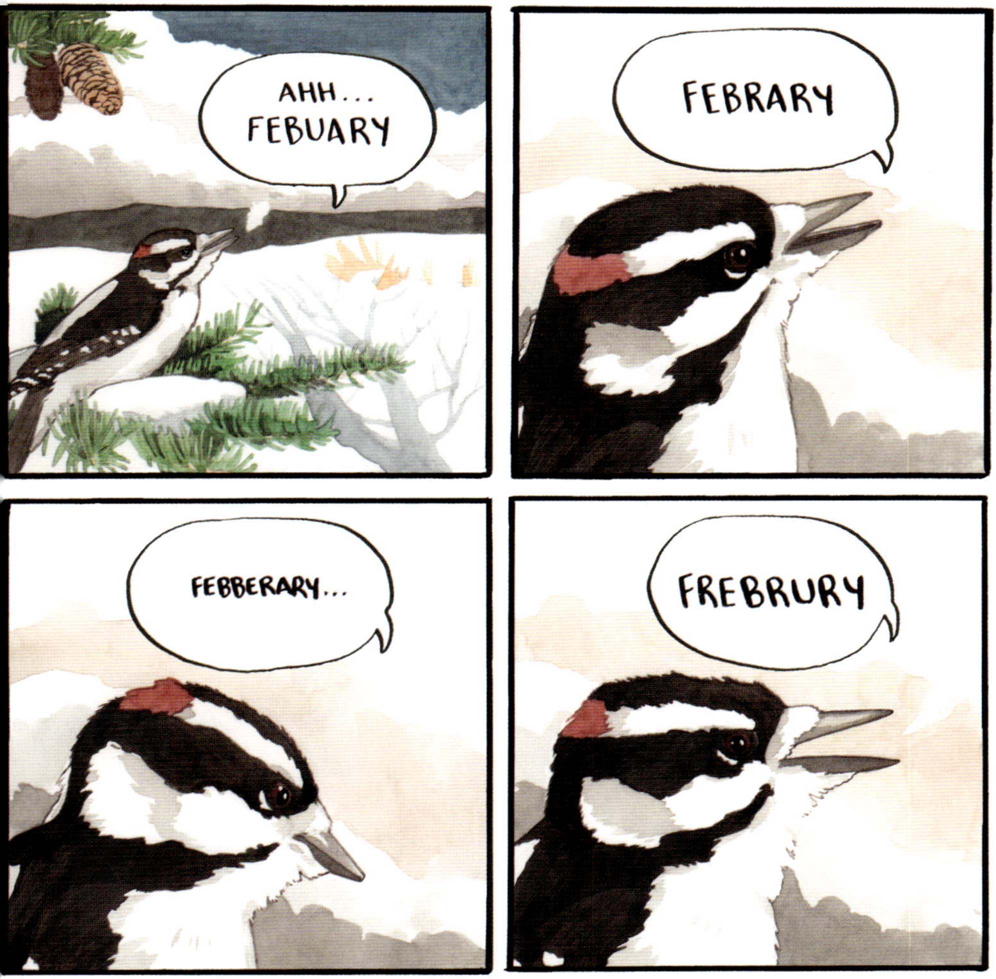
AHH... FEBUARY
FEBRARY
FEBBERARY...
FREBRURY

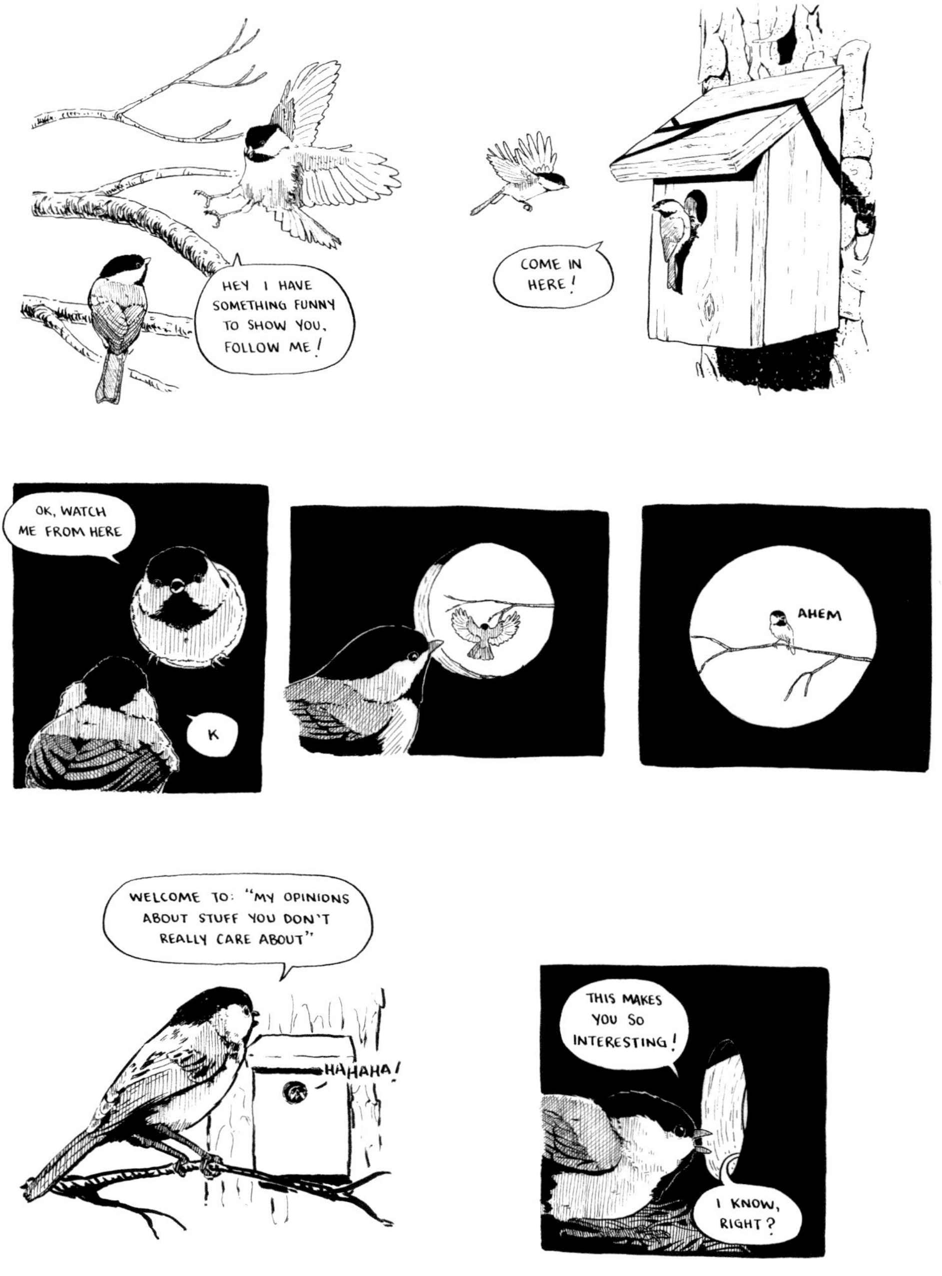
HEY I HAVE SOMETHING FUNNY TO SHOW YOU. FOLLOW ME!
COME IN HERE!
OK, WATCH ME FROM HERE
K
AHEM
WELCOME TO: "MY OPINIONS ABOUT STUFF YOU DON'T REALLY CARE ABOUT"
HAHAHA!
THIS MAKES YOU SO INTERESTING!
I KNOW, RIGHT?

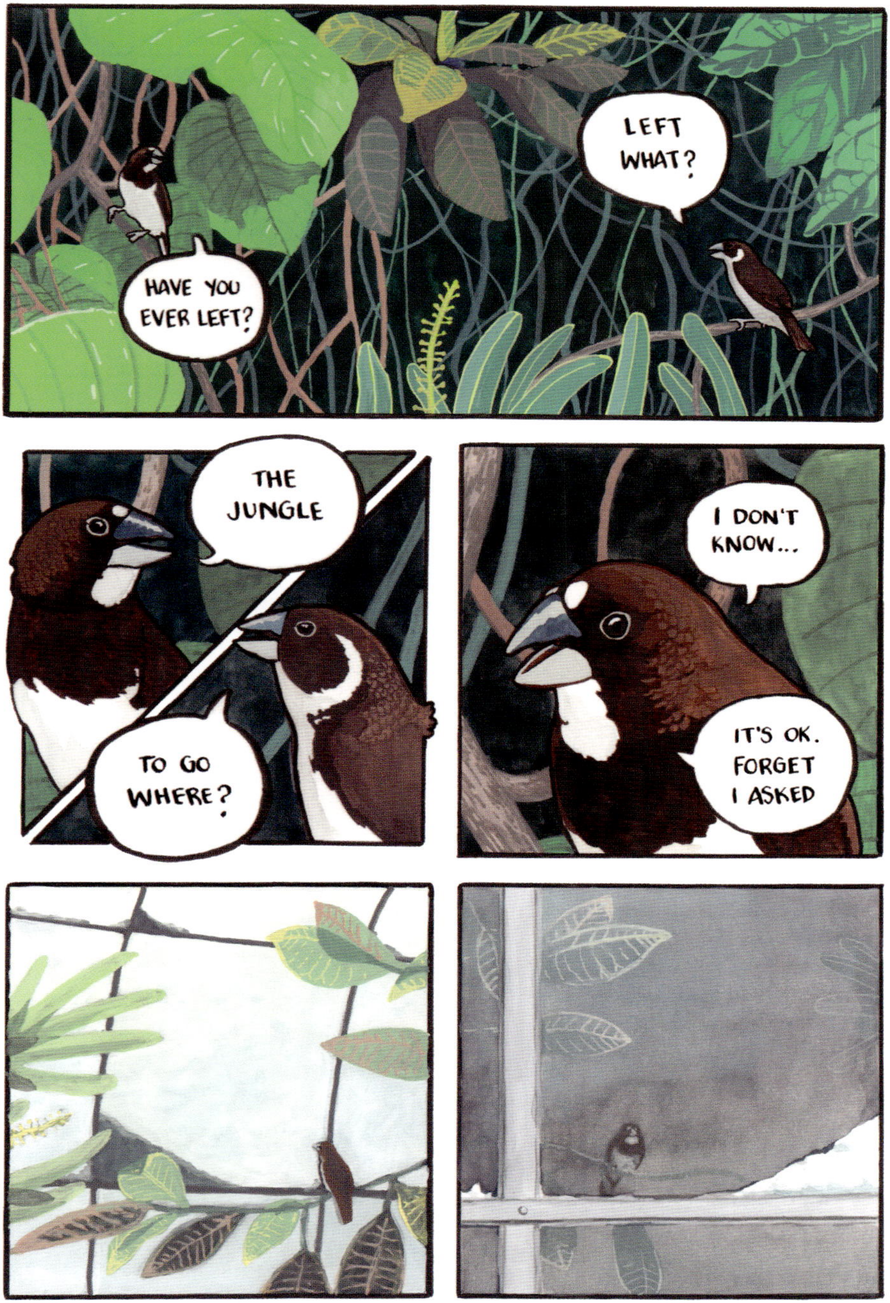
HAVE YOU EVER LEFT?
LEFT WHAT?
THE JUNGLE
TO GO WHERE?
I DON'T KNOW...
IT'S OK. FORGET I ASKED

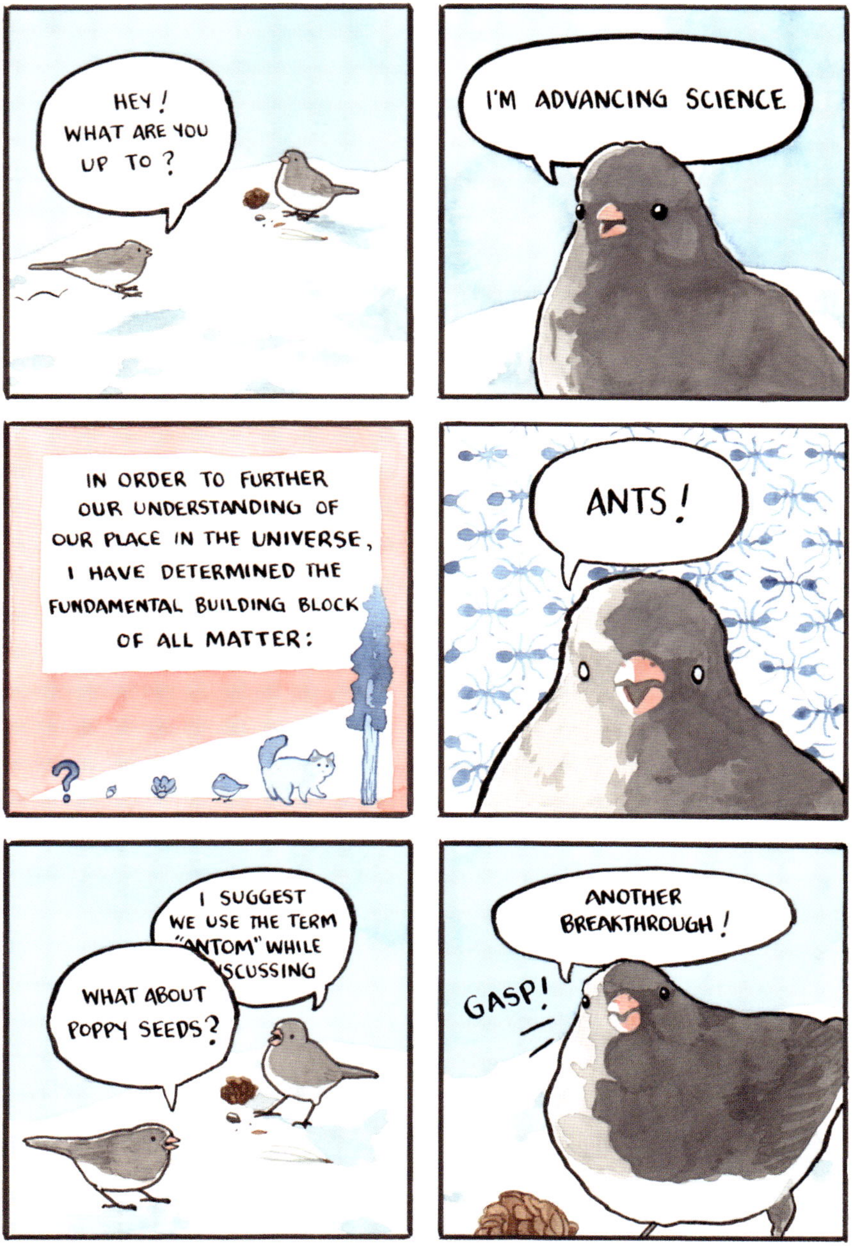
HEY! WHAT ARE YOU UP TO?
I'M ADVANCING SCIENCE
IN ORDER TO FURTHER OUR UNDERSTANDING OF OUR PLACE IN THE UNIVERSE, I HAVE DETERMINED THE FUNDAMENTAL BUILDING BLOCK OF ALL MATTER:
ANTS!
I SUGGEST WE USE THE TERM "ANTOM" WHILE
WHAT ABOUT POPPY SEEDS?
ANOTHER BREAKTHROUGH!
GASP!

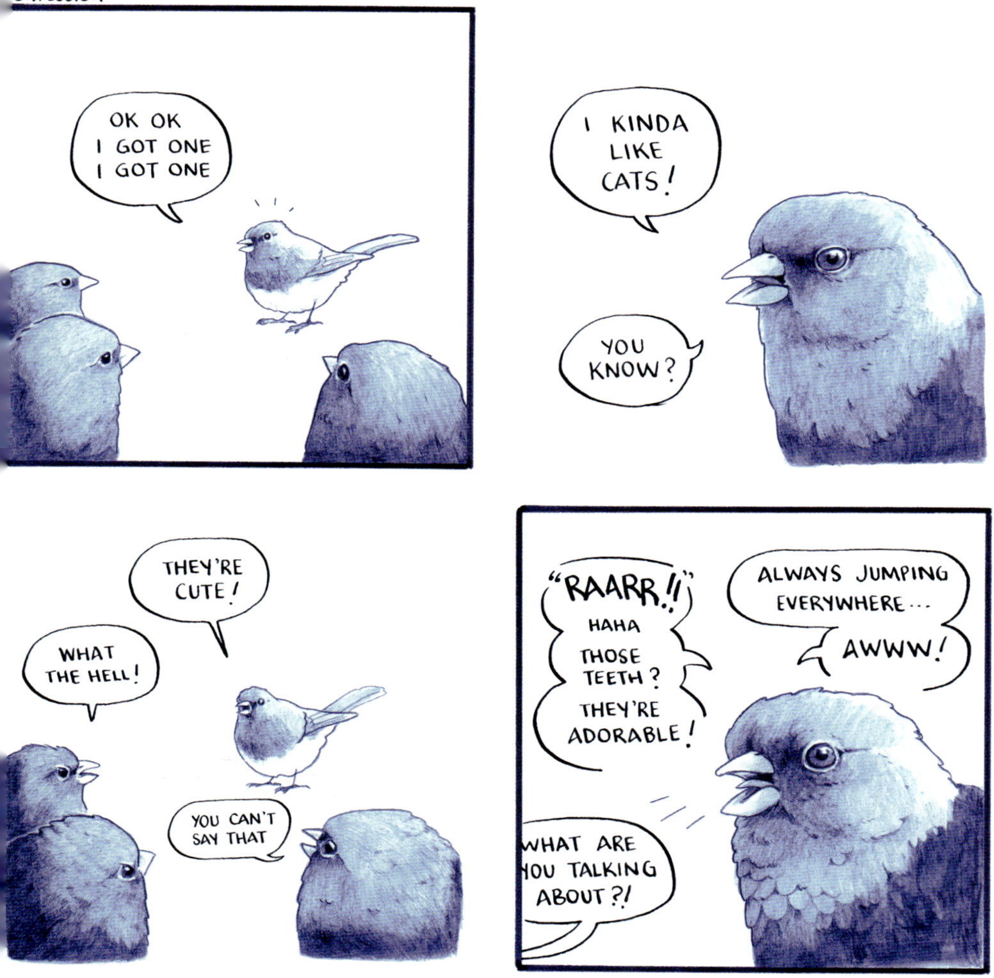
OK OK I GOT ONE I GOT ONE
I KINDA LIKE CATS!
YOU KNOW?
THEY'RE CUTE!
WHAT THE HELL!
YOU CAN'T SAY THAT
"RAARR!!" HAHA THOSE TEETH? THEY'RE ADORABLE!
ALWAYS JUMPING EVERYWHERE...
AWWW!
WHAT ARE YOU TALKING ABOUT?!

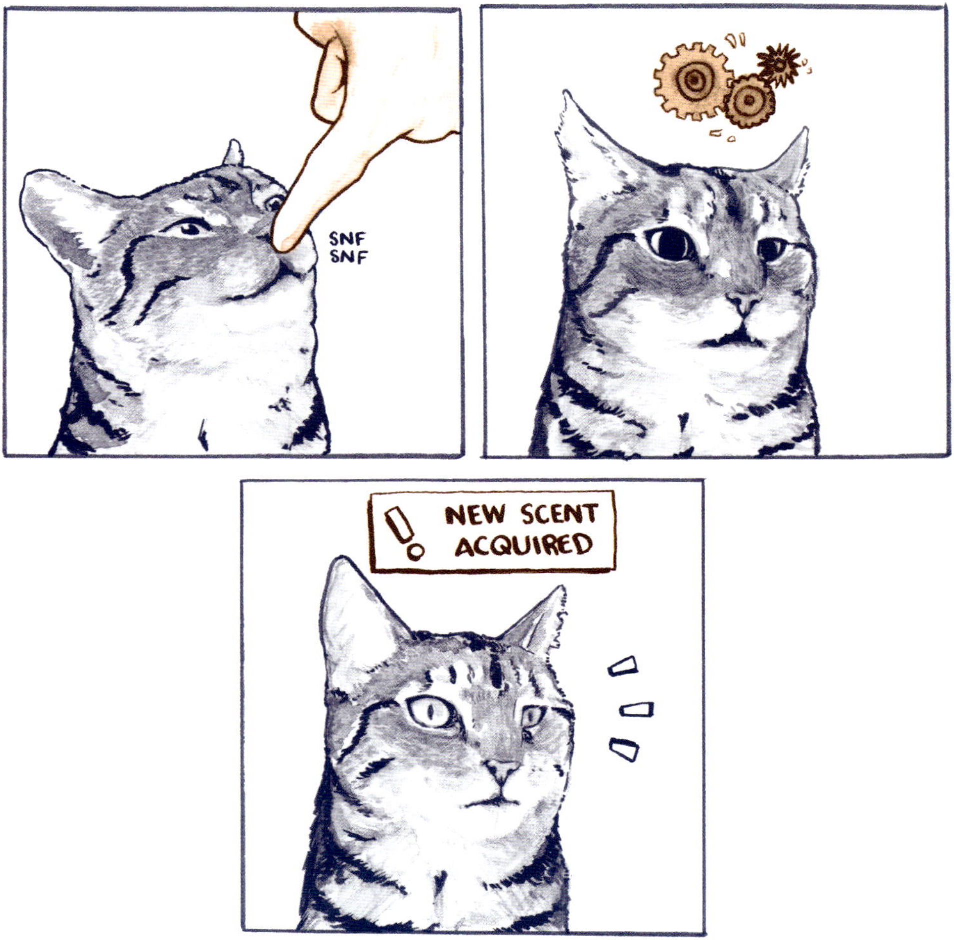
SNF
SNF
NEW SCENT
ACQUIRED

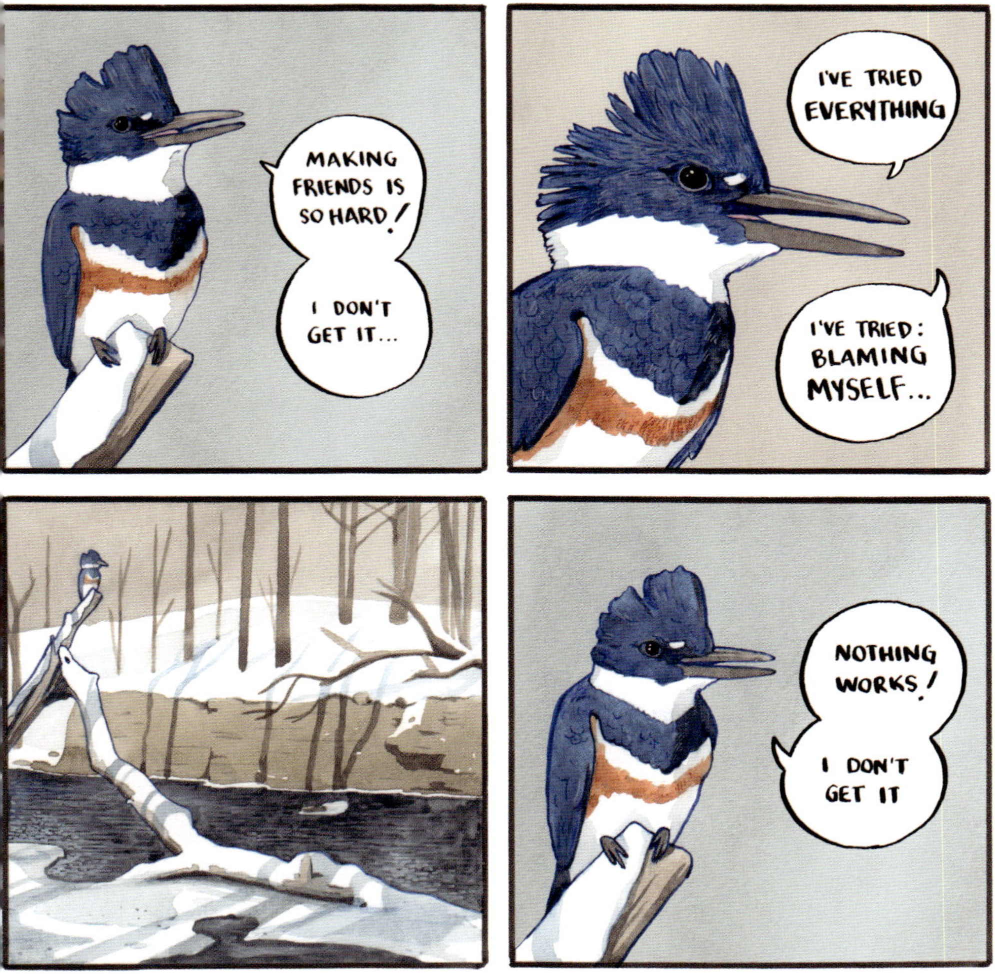
MAKING FRIENDS IS SO HARD!
I DON'T GET IT...
I'VE TRIED EVERYTHING
I'VE TRIED: BLAMING MYSELF...
NOTHING WORKS!
I DON'T GET IT

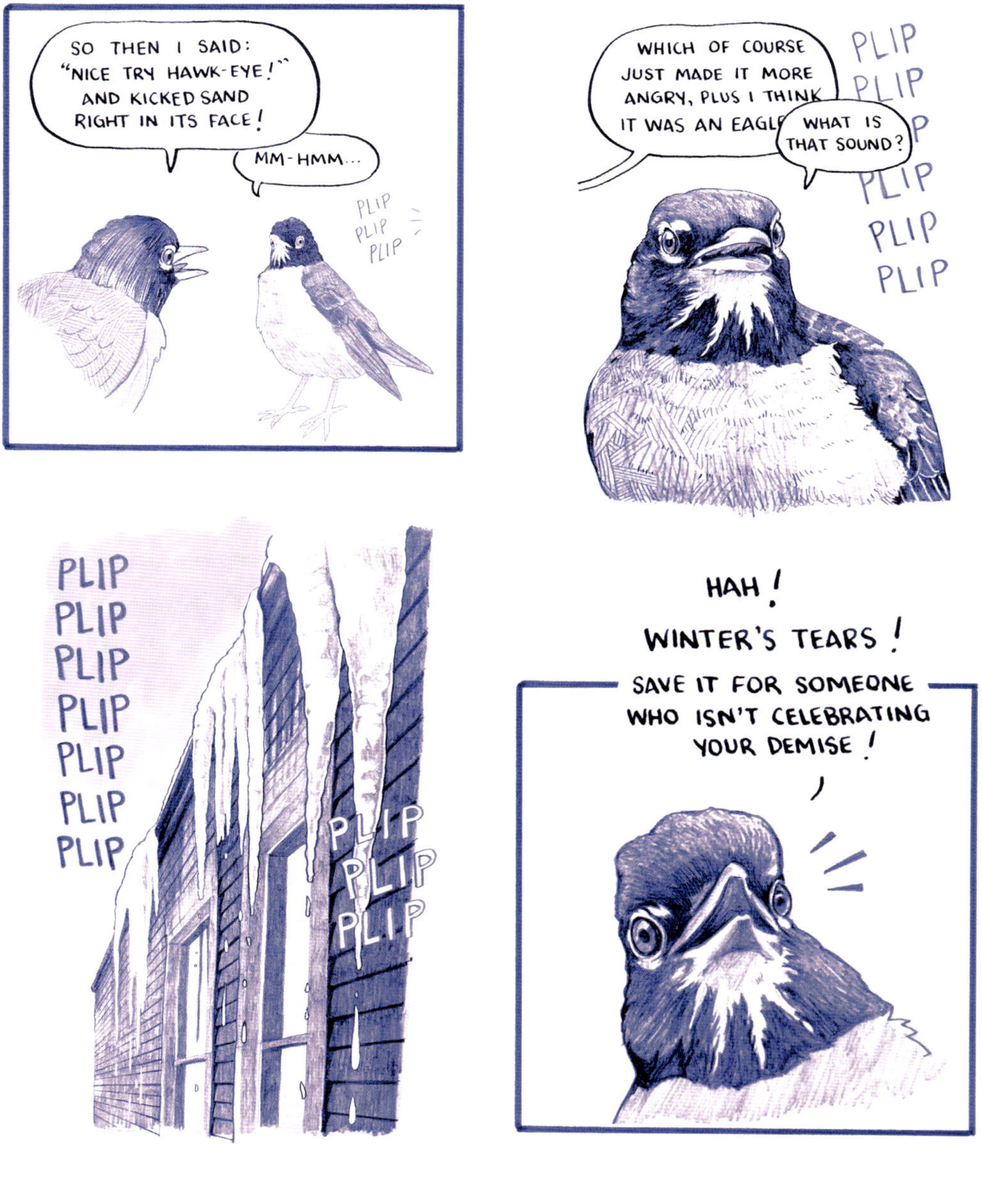
SO THEN I SAID: "NICE TRY HAWK-EYE!" AND KICKED SAND RIGHT IN ITS FACE!
MM-HMM...
PLIP PLIP PLIP
WHICH OF COURSE JUST MADE IT MORE ANGRY, PLUS I THINK IT WAS AN EAGLE
WHAT IS THAT SOUND?
PLIP PLIP PLIP PLIP PLIP PLIP
PLIP PLIP PLIP PLIP PLIP PLIP PLIP
PLIP PLIP PLIP
HAH!
WINTER'S TEARS!
SAVE IT FOR SOMEONE WHO ISN'T CELEBRATING YOUR DEMISE!

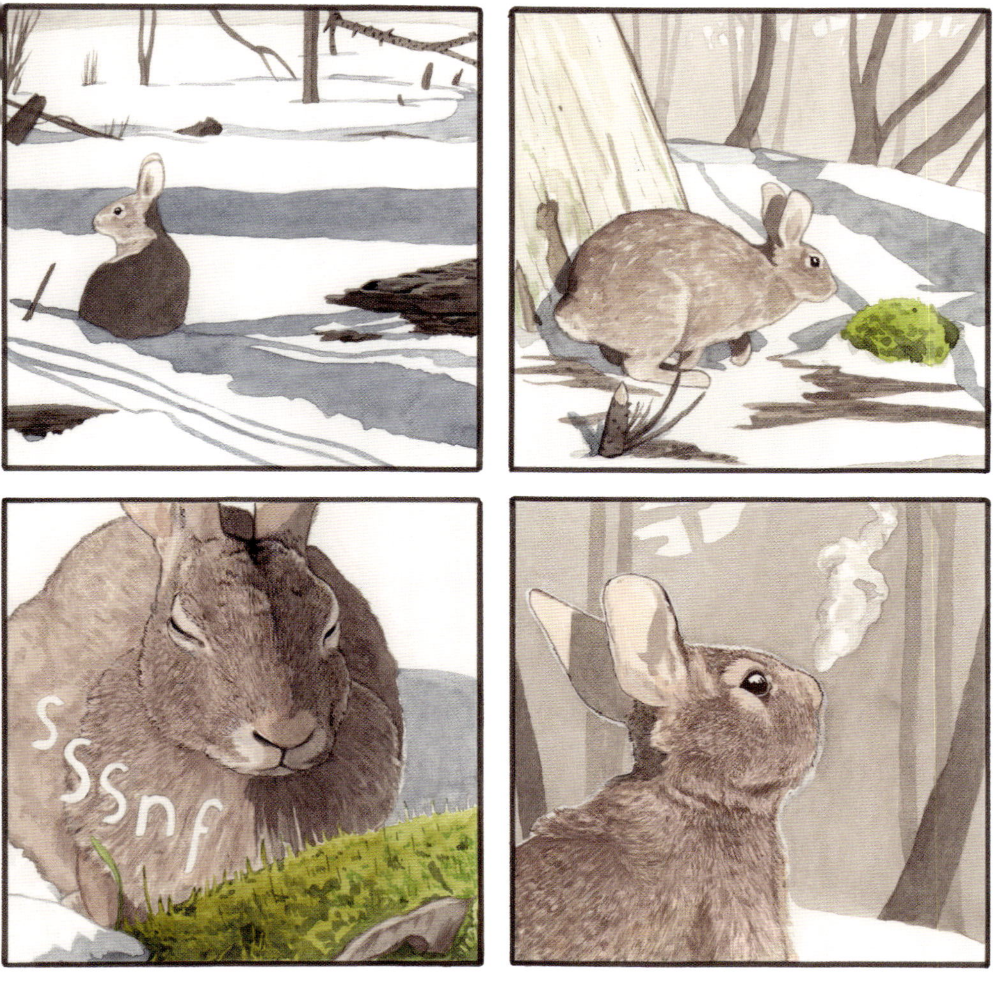
sssnf

Spring

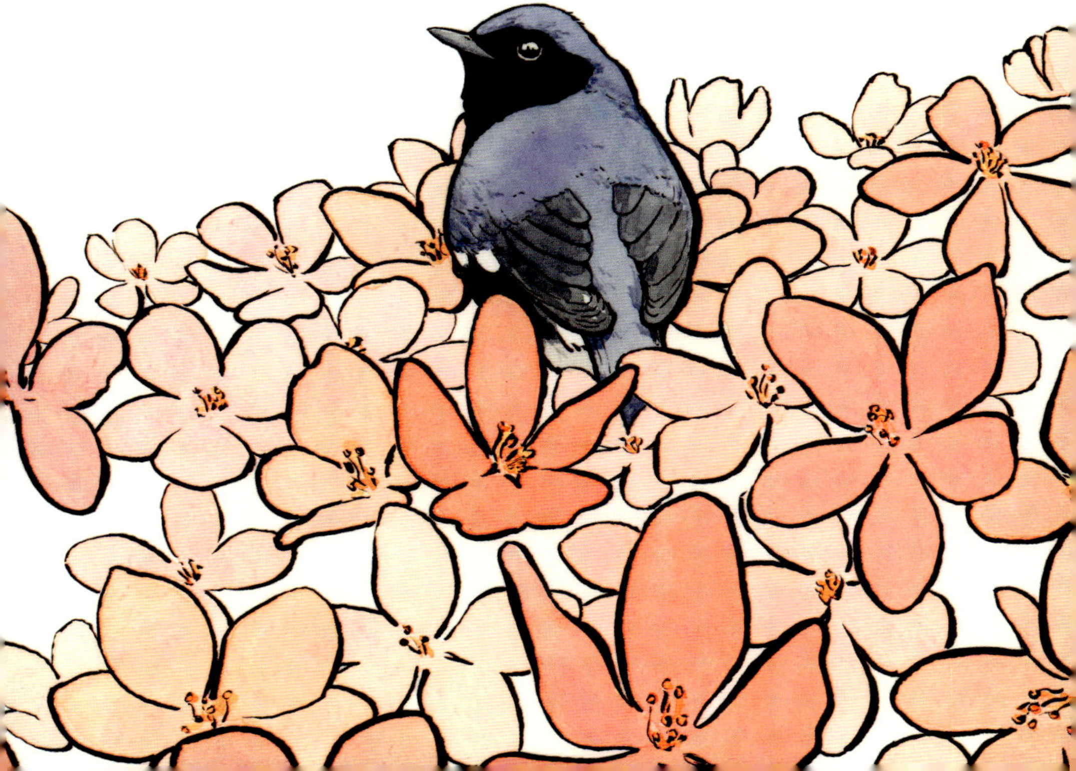

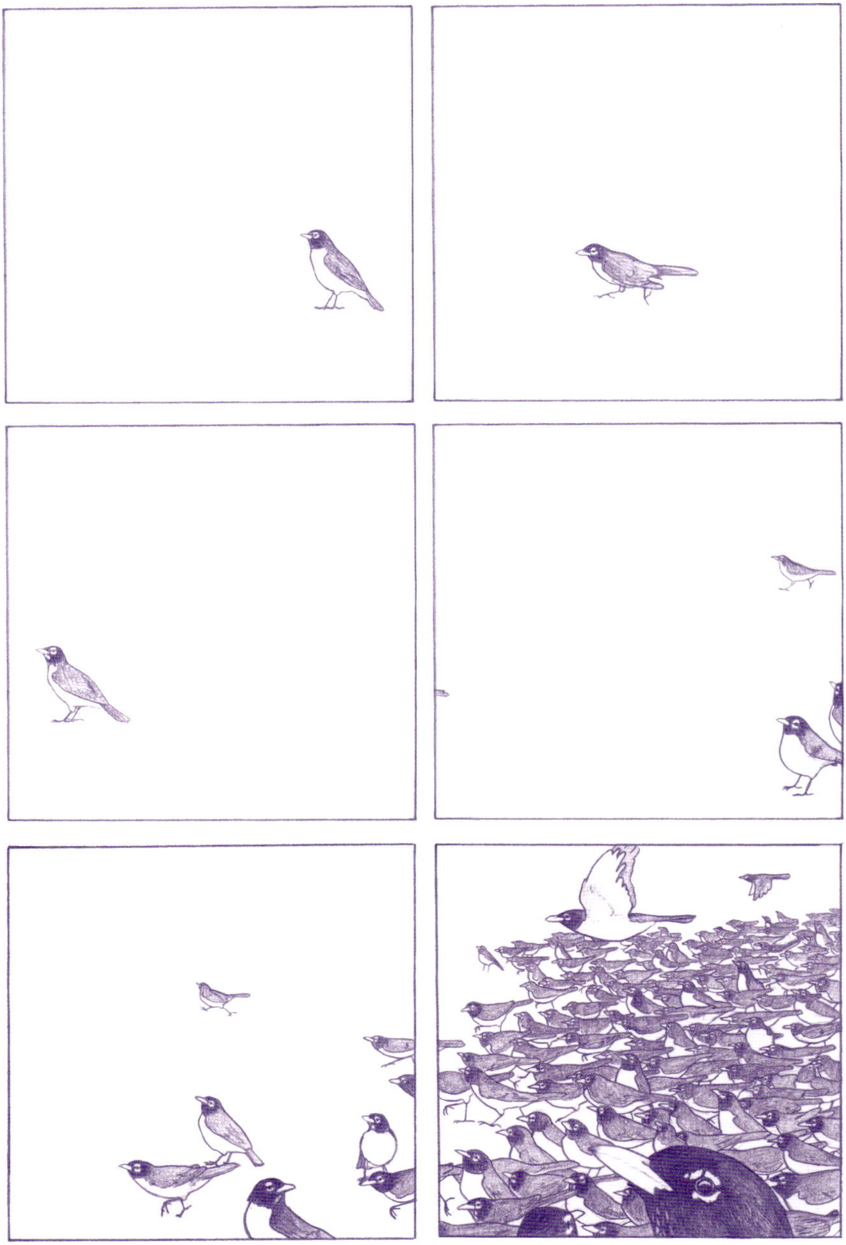

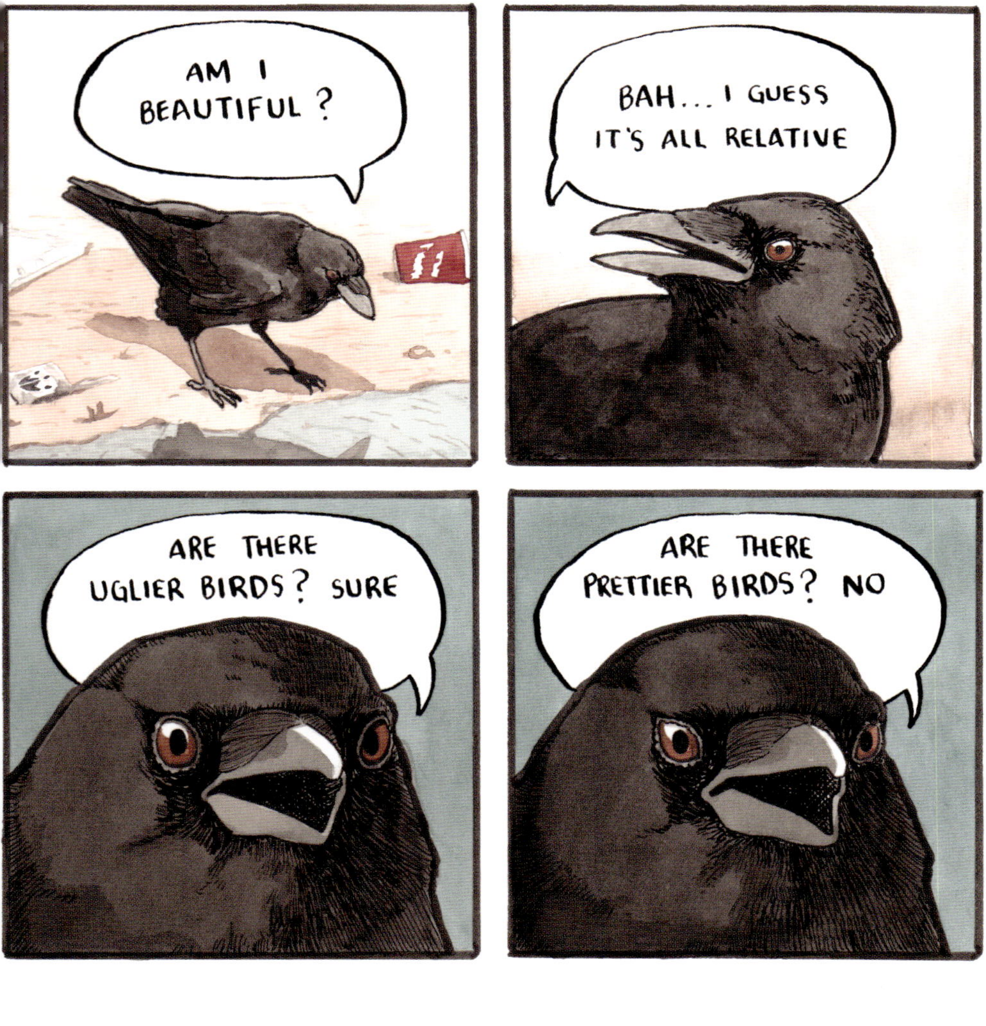
AM I BEAUTIFUL ?
BAH... I GUESS IT'S ALL RELATIVE
ARE THERE UGLIER BIRDS? SURE
ARE THERE PRETTIER BIRDS? NO

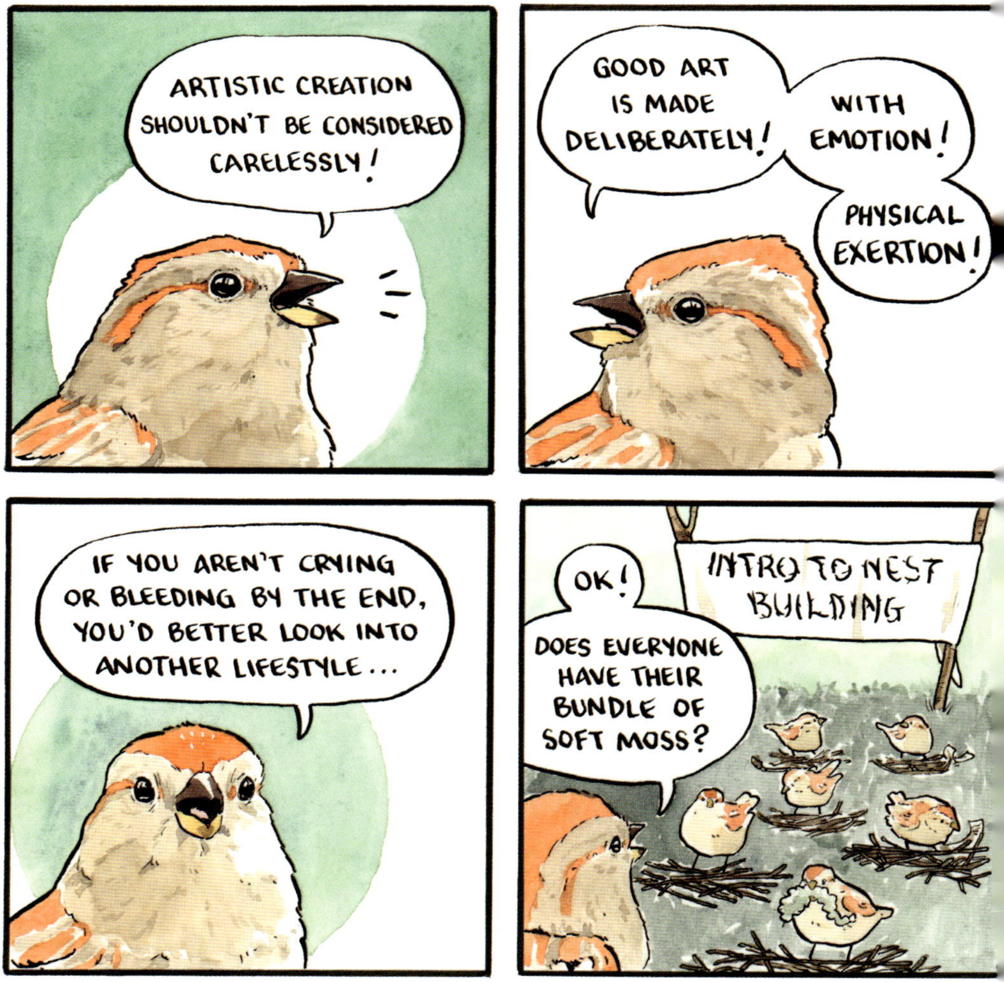
ARTISTIC CREATION SHOULDN'T BE CONSIDERED CARELESSLY!
GOOD ART IS MADE DELIBERATELY!
WITH EMOTION!
PHYSICAL EXERTION!
IF YOU AREN'T CRYING OR BLEEDING BY THE END, YOU'D BETTER LOOK INTO ANOTHER LIFESTYLE...
INTRO TO NEST BUILDING
OK!
DOES EVERYONE HAVE THEIR BUNDLE OF SOFT MOSS?

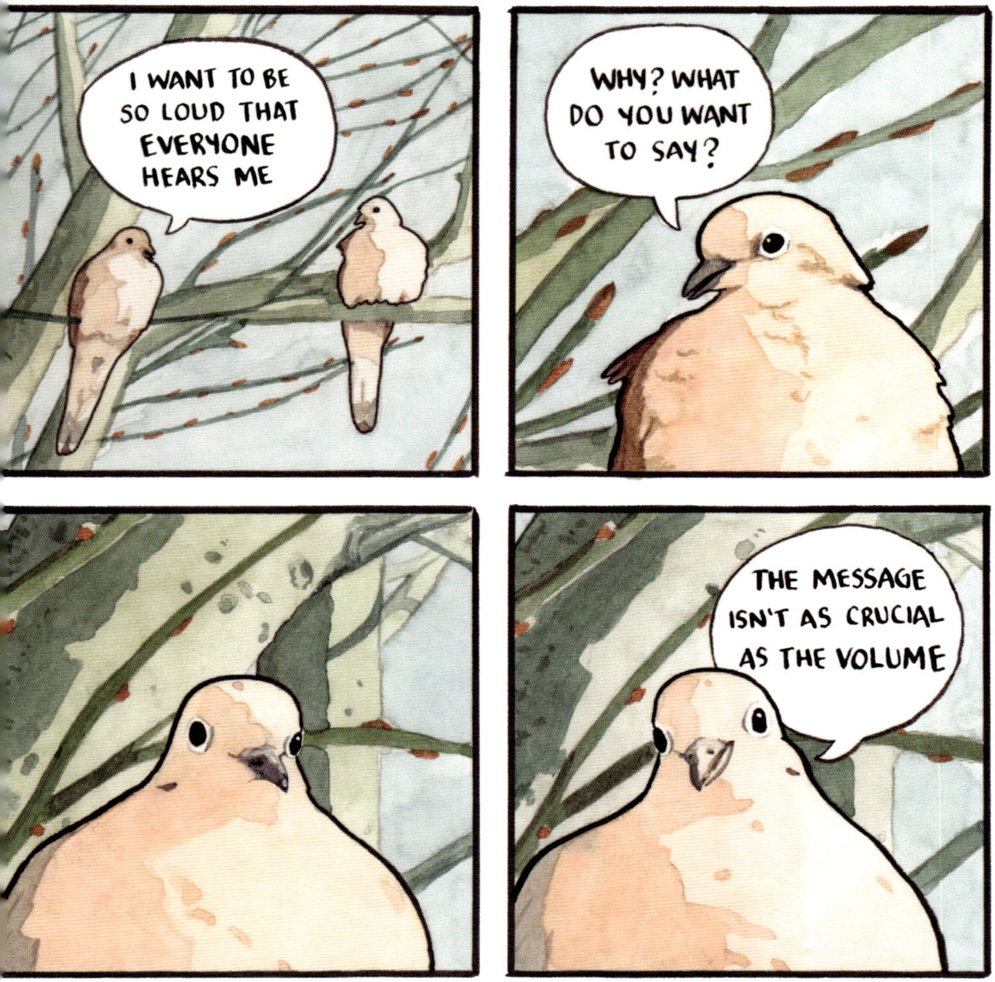
I WANT TO BE SO LOUD THAT EVERYONE HEARS ME
WHY? WHAT DO YOU WANT TO SAY?
THE MESSAGE ISN'T AS CRUCIAL AS THE VOLUME

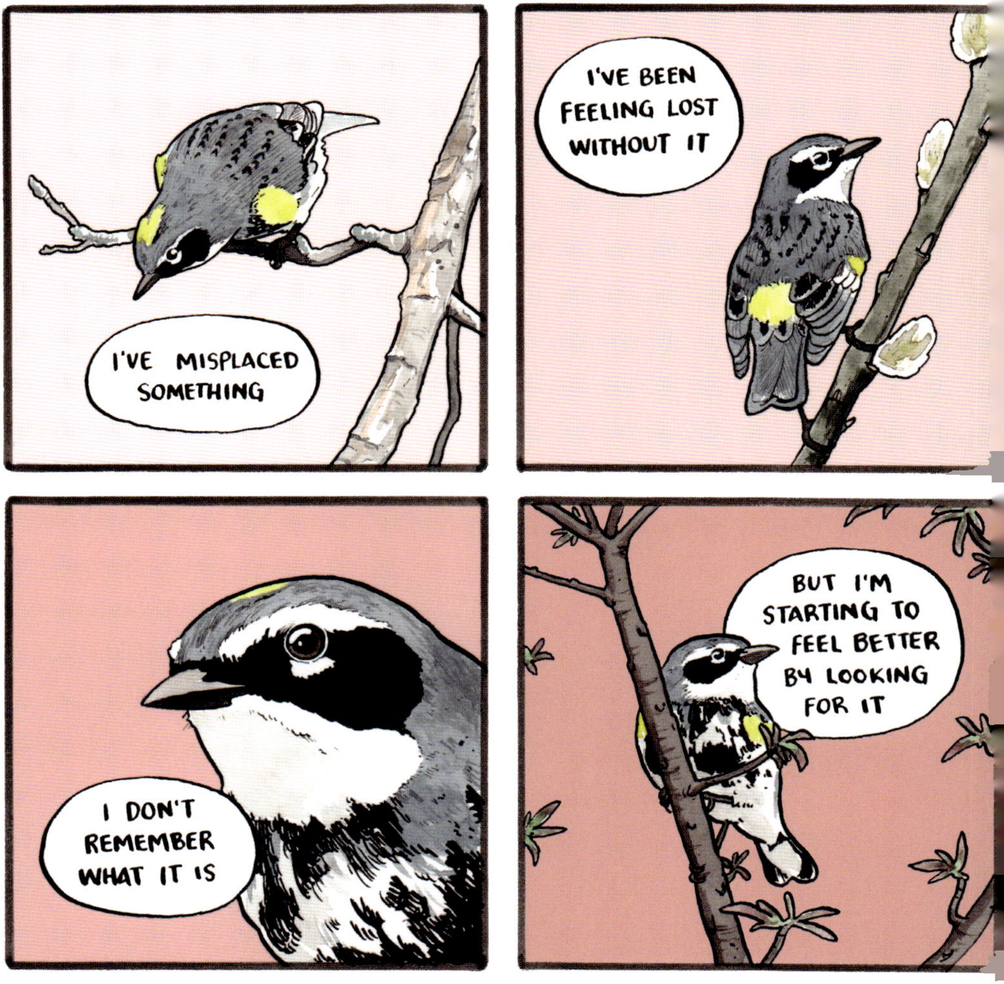

I'VE MISPLACED SOMETHING
I'VE BEEN FEELING LOST WITHOUT IT
I DON'T REMEMBER WHAT IT IS
BUT I'M STARTING TO FEEL BETTER BY LOOKING FOR IT

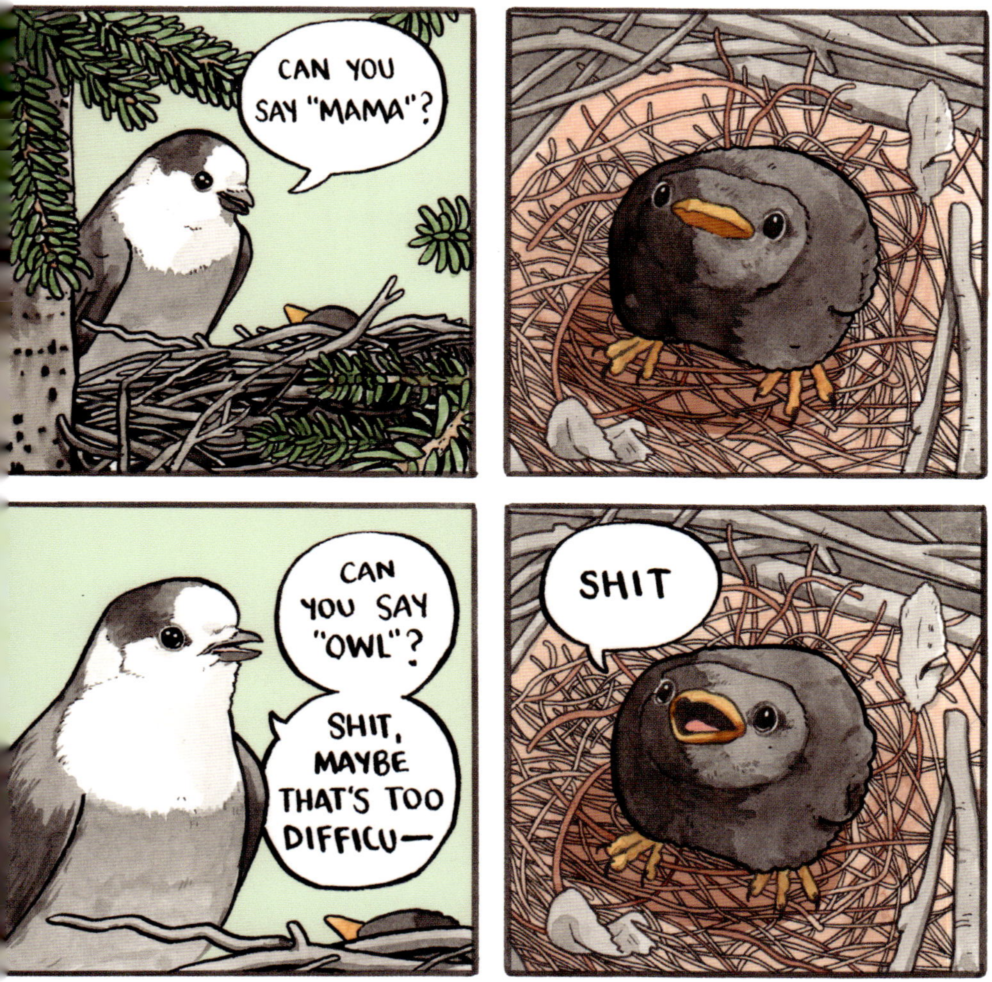
CAN YOU SAY "MAMA"?
CAN YOU SAY "OWL"?
SHIT, MAYBE THAT'S TOO DIFFICU—
SHIT

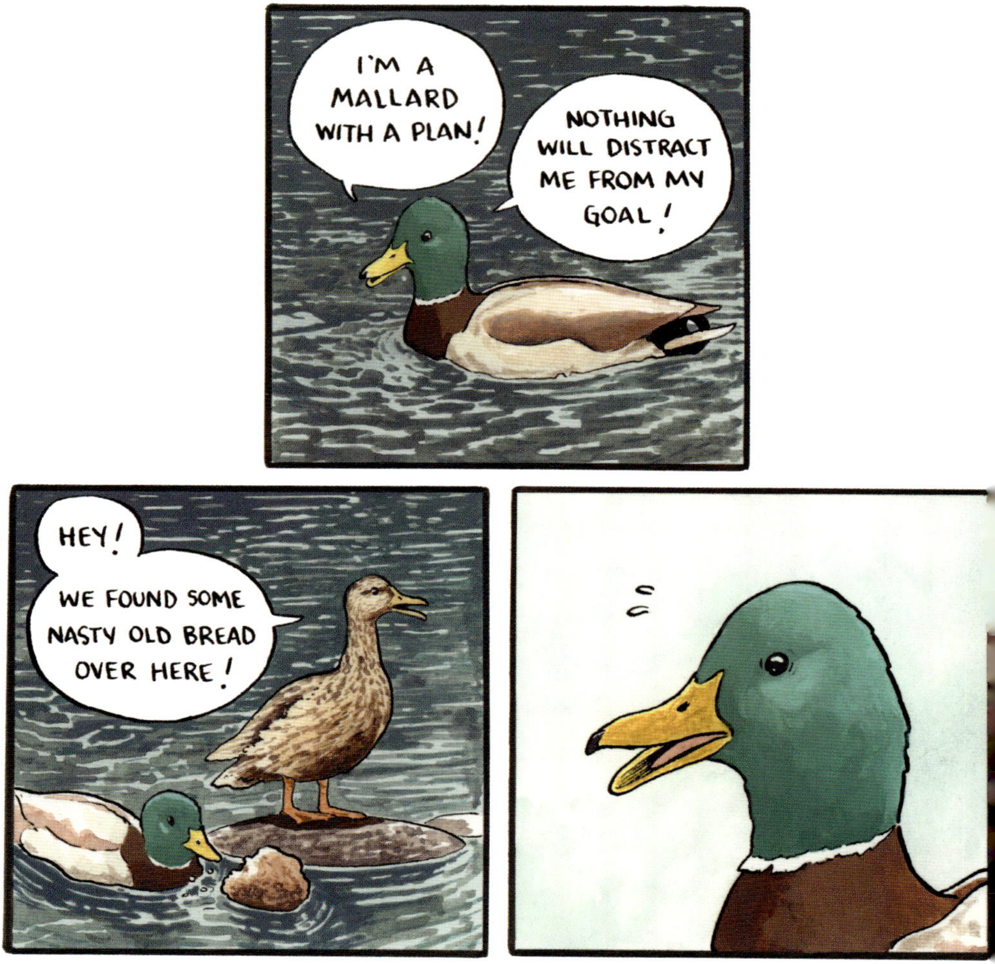
I'M A MALLARD WITH A PLAN!
NOTHING WILL DISTRACT ME FROM MY GOAL!
HEY!
WE FOUND SOME NASTY OLD BREAD OVER HERE!

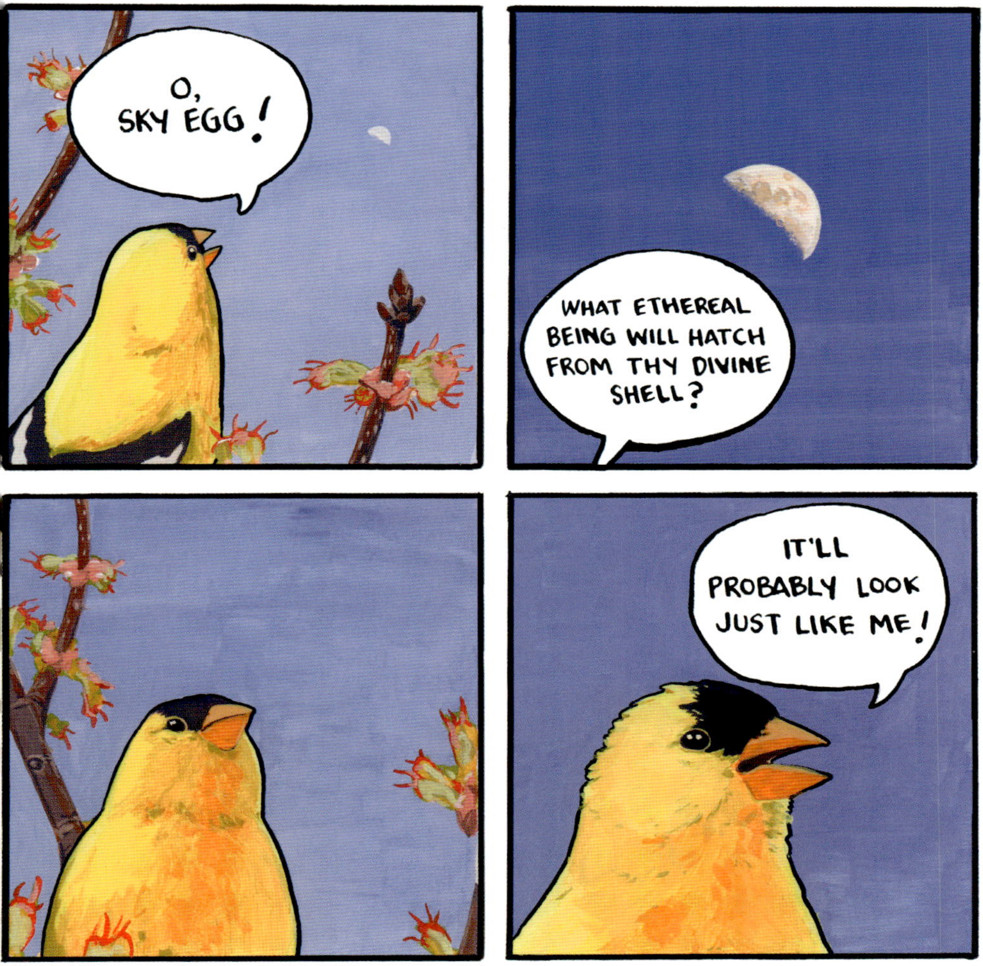
O, SKY EGG!
WHAT ETHEREAL BEING WILL HATCH FROM THY DIVINE SHELL?
IT'LL PROBABLY LOOK JUST LIKE ME!

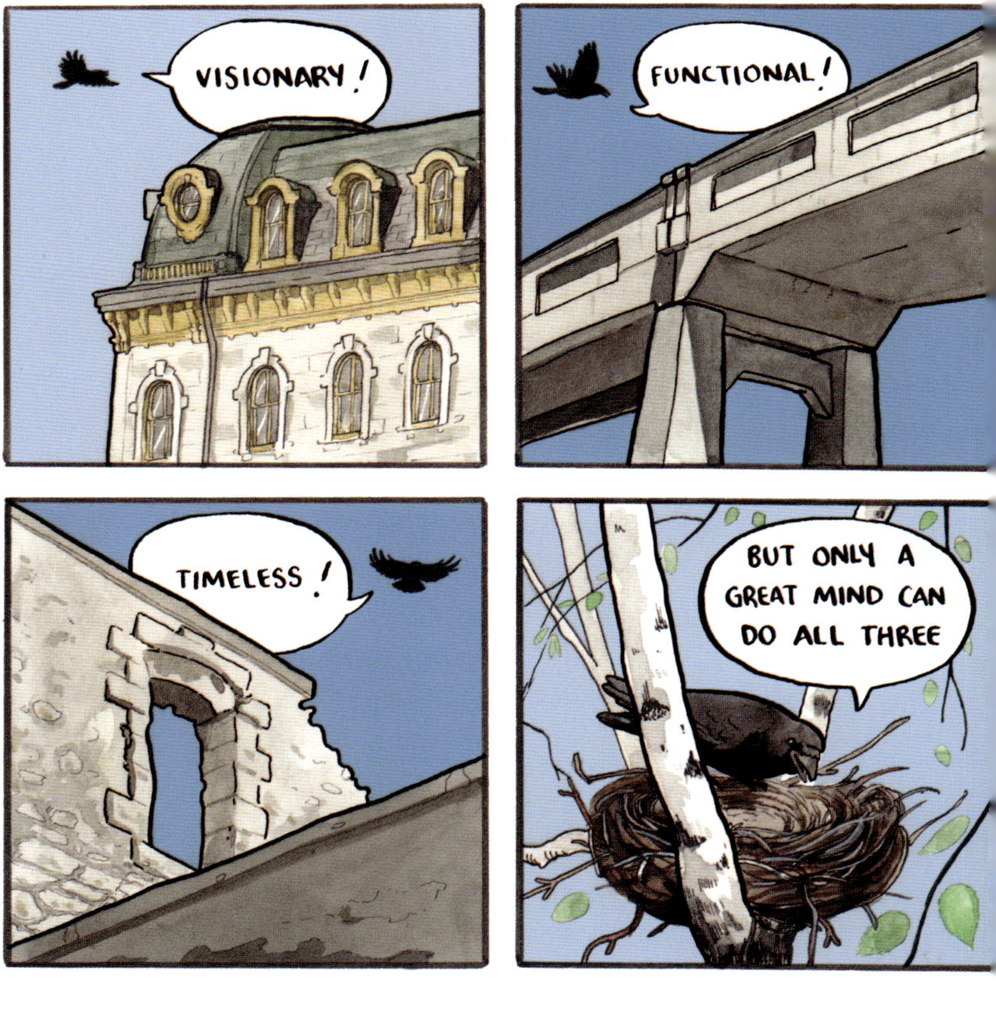
VISIONARY!
FUNCTIONAL!
TIMELESS!
BUT ONLY A GREAT MIND CAN DO ALL THREE

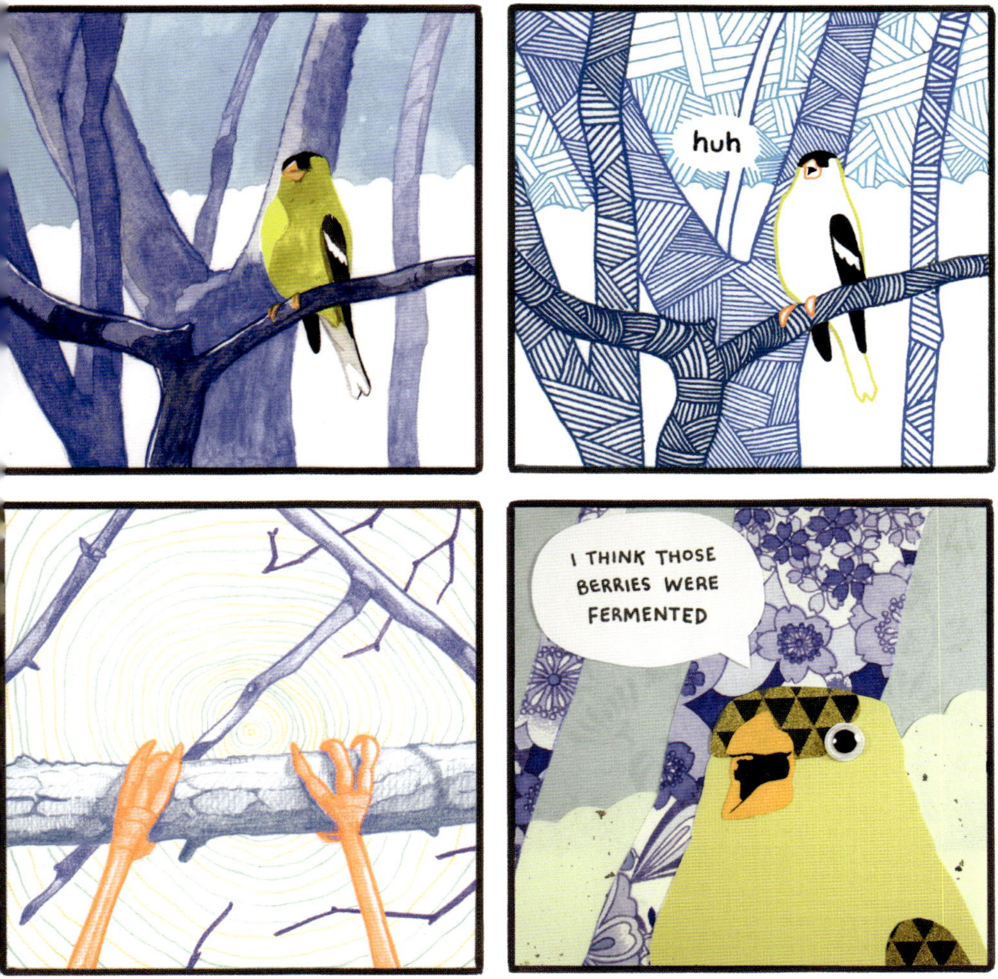
huh
I THINK THOSE BERRIES WERE FERMENTED

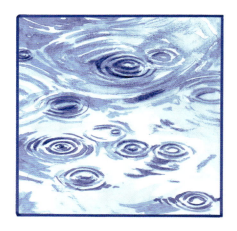

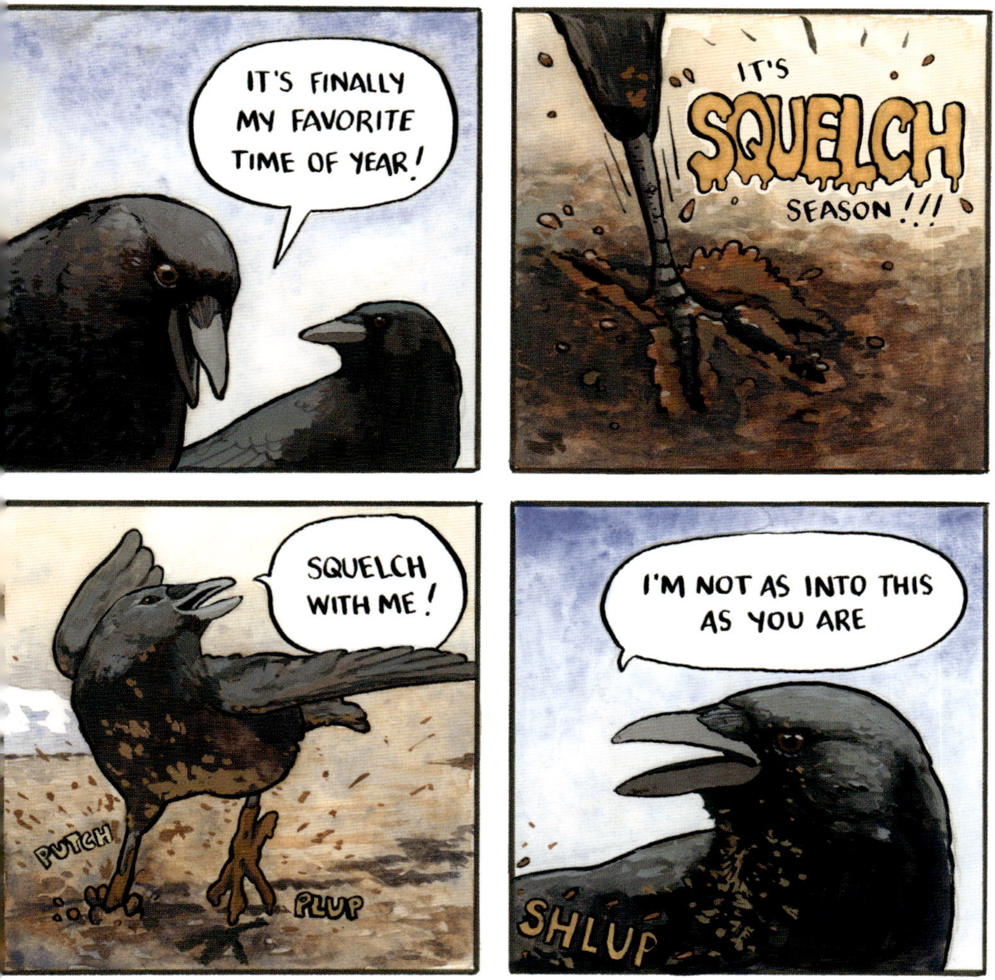
IT'S FINALLY MY FAVORITE TIME OF YEAR!
IT'S
SQUELCH
SEASON!!!
SQUELCH WITH ME!
PUTCH
PLUP
I'M NOT AS INTO THIS AS YOU ARE
SHLUP

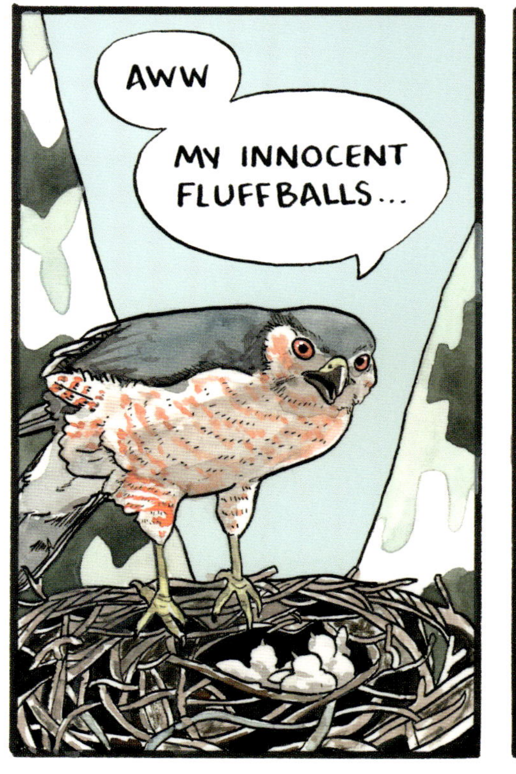
AWW
MY INNOCENT FLUFFBALLS...

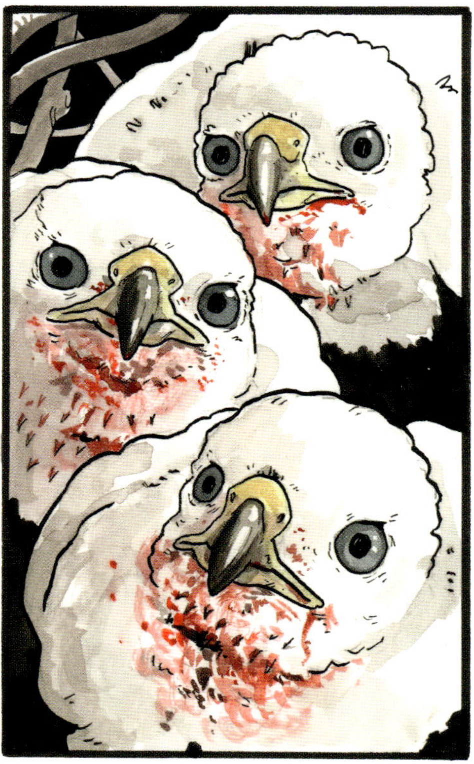

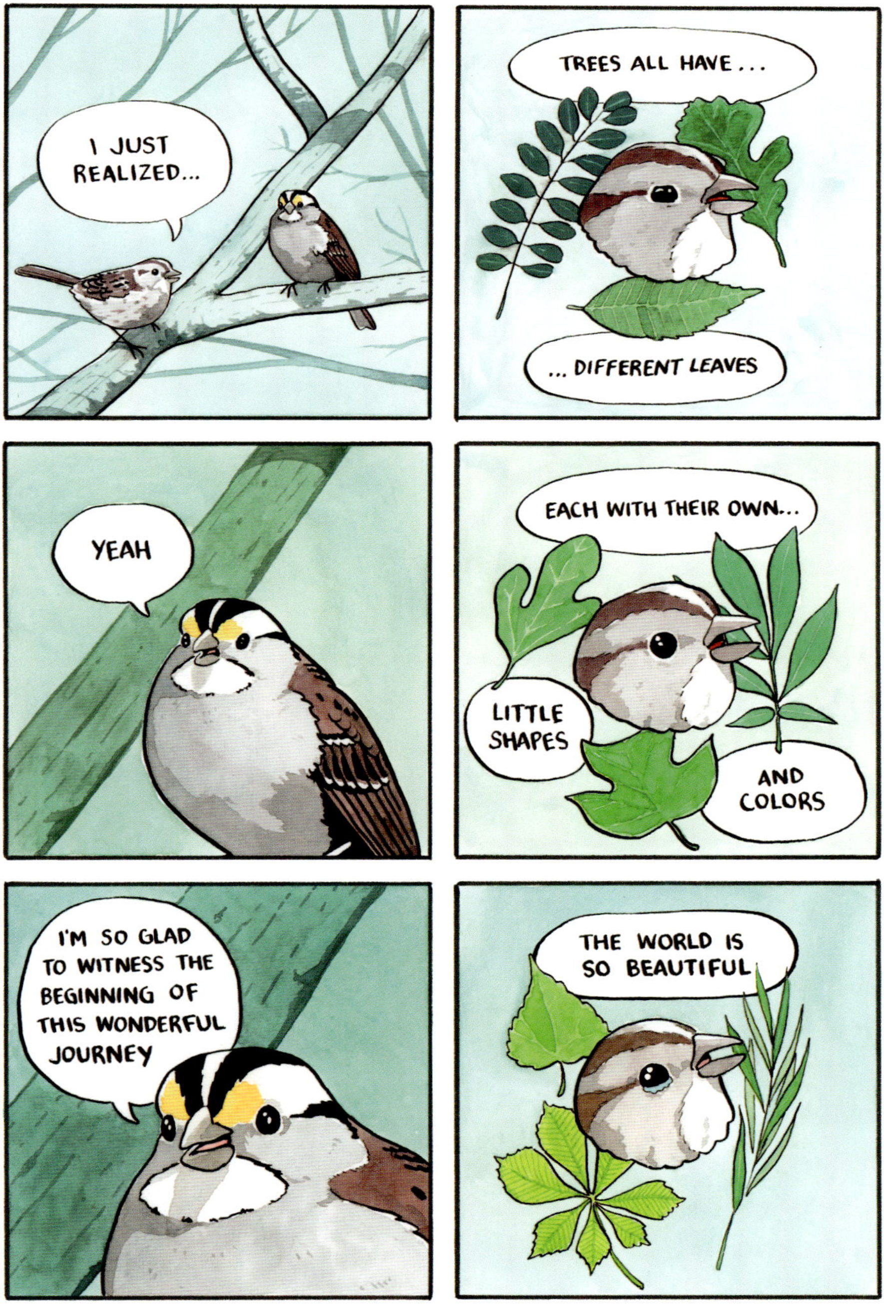
I JUST REALIZED...
TREES ALL HAVE...
... DIFFERENT LEAVES
YEAH
EACH WITH THEIR OWN...
LITTLE SHAPES
AND COLORS
I'M SO GLAD TO WITNESS THE BEGINNING OF THIS WONDERFUL JOURNEY
THE WORLD IS SO BEAUTIFUL

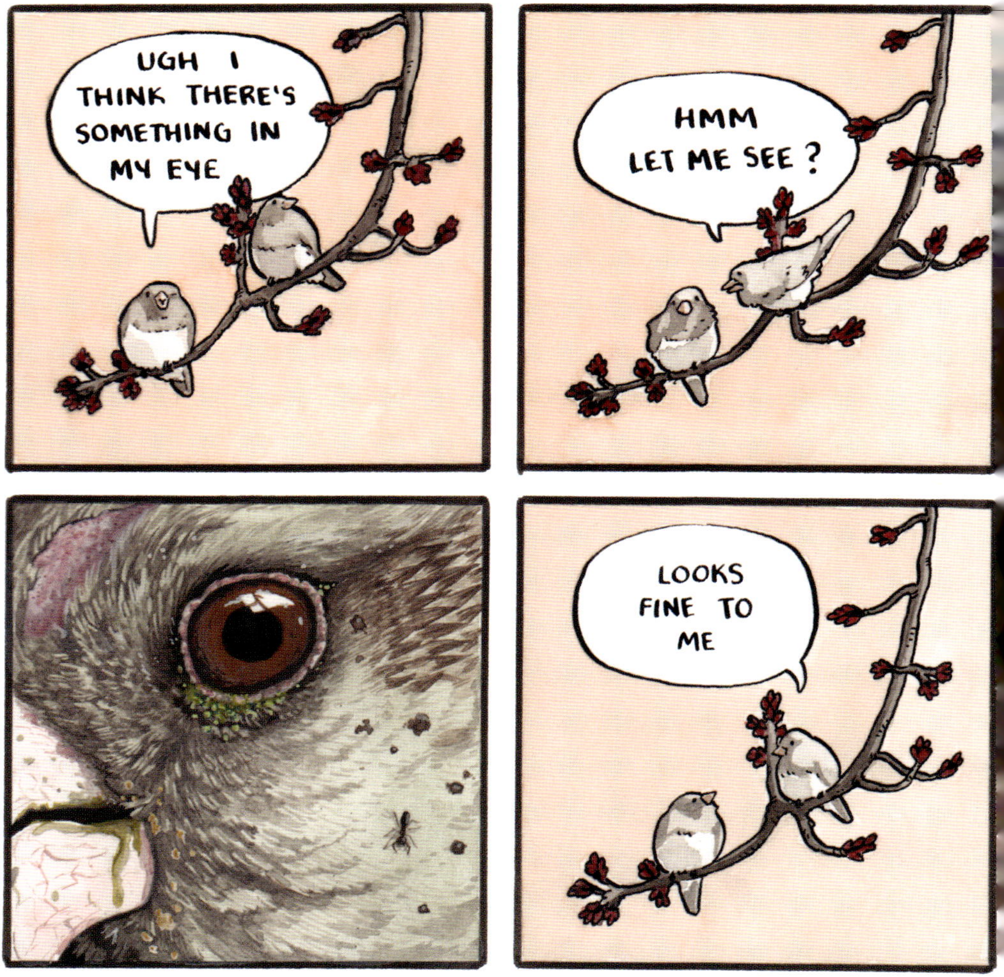
UGH I THINK THERE'S SOMETHING IN MY EYE
HMM LET ME SEE ?
LOOKS FINE TO ME

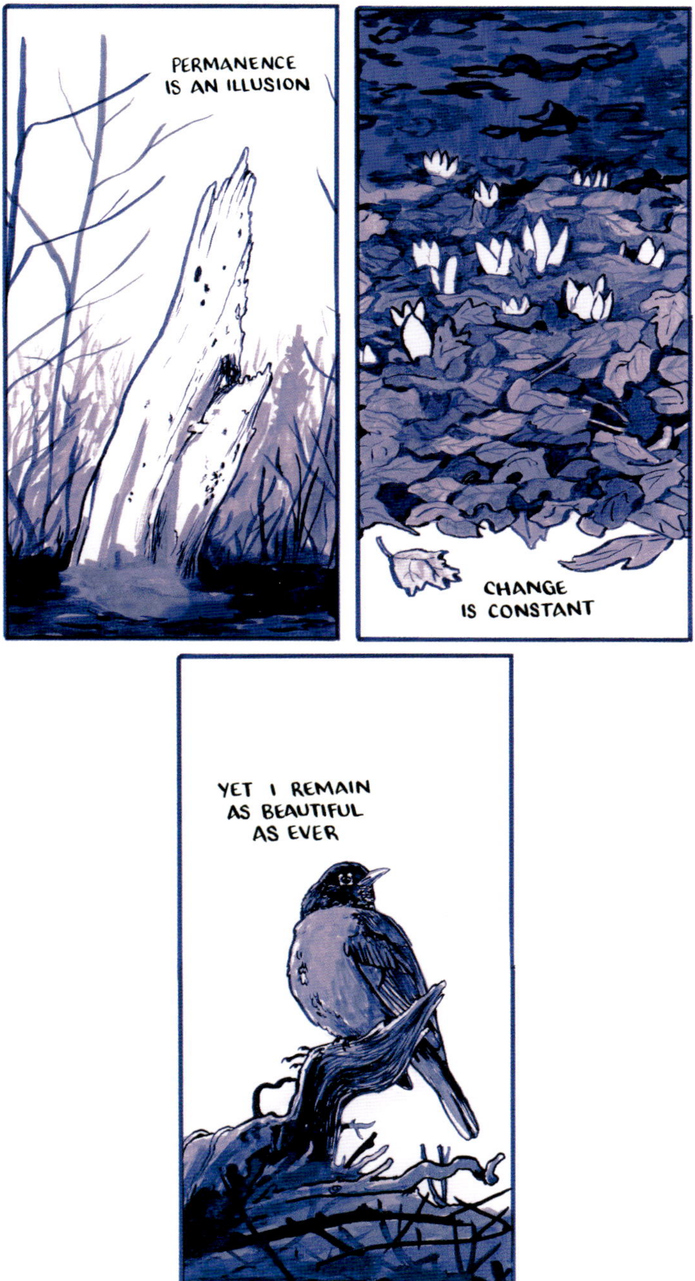
PERMANENCE IS AN ILLUSION
CHANGE IS CONSTANT
YET I REMAIN AS BEAUTIFUL AS EVER

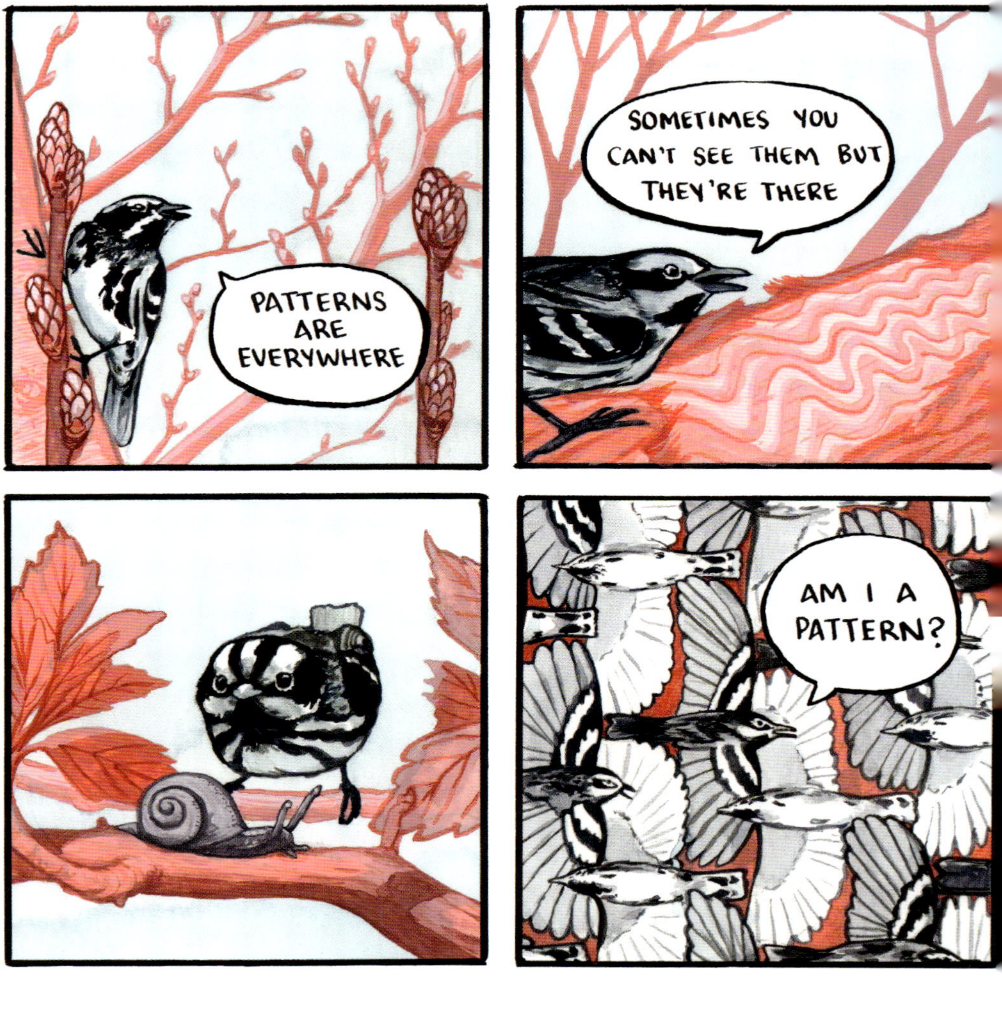
PATTERNS ARE EVERYWHERE
SOMETIMES YOU CAN'T SEE THEM BUT THEY'RE THERE
AM I A PATTERN?

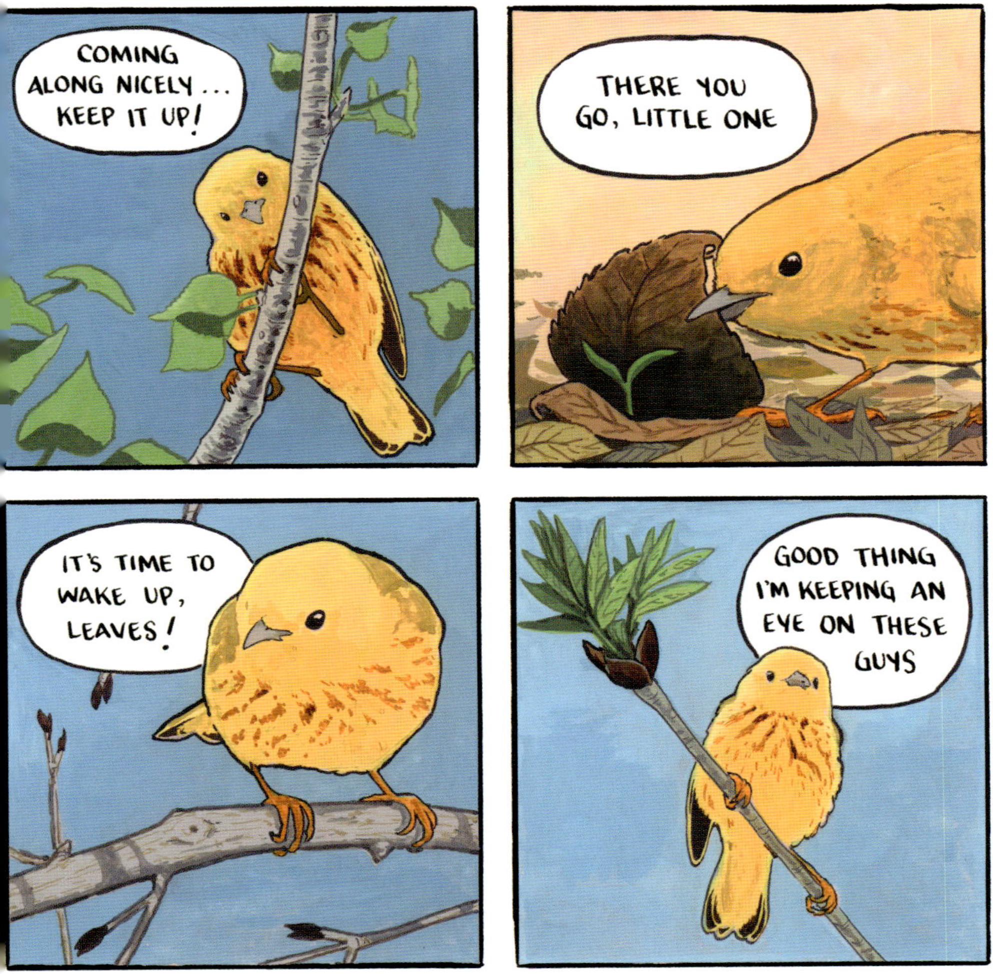
COMING ALONG NICELY... KEEP IT UP!
THERE YOU GO, LITTLE ONE
IT'S TIME TO WAKE UP, LEAVES!
GOOD THING I'M KEEPING AN EYE ON THESE GUYS

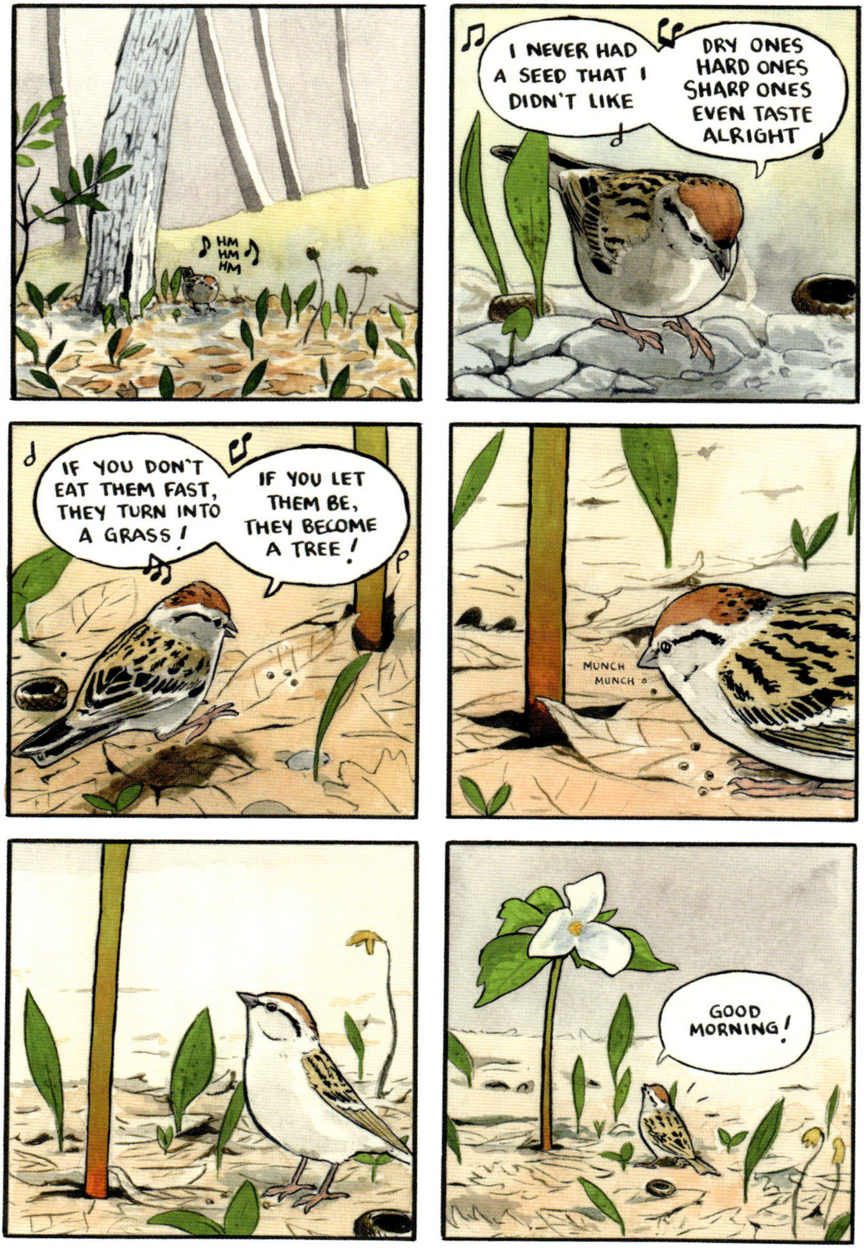
HM HM HM
I NEVER HAD A SEED THAT I DIDN'T LIKE
DRY ONES HARD ONES SHARP ONES EVEN TASTE ALRIGHT
IF YOU DON'T EAT THEM FAST, THEY TURN INTO A GRASS!
IF YOU LET THEM BE, THEY BECOME A TREE!
MUNCH MUNCH
GOOD MORNING!

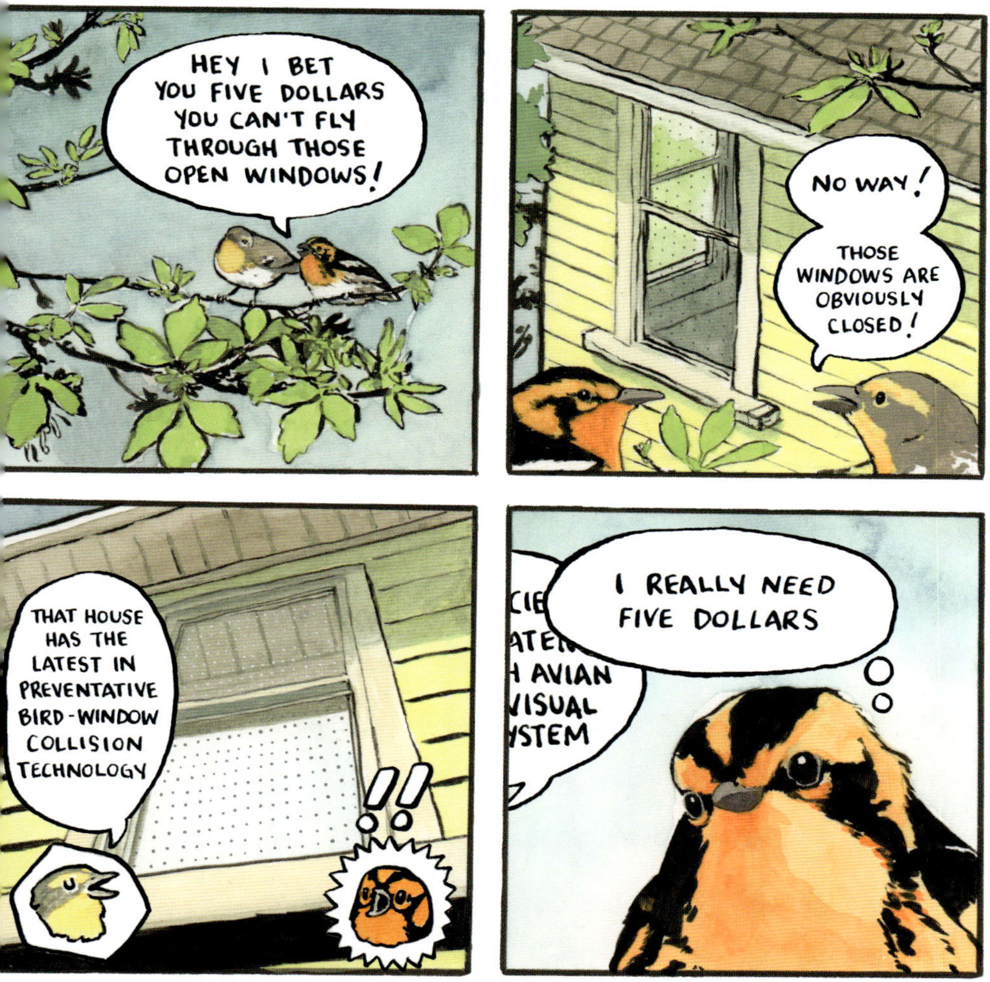

HEY I BET YOU FIVE DOLLARS YOU CAN'T FLY THROUGH THOSE OPEN WINDOWS!
NO WAY!
THOSE WINDOWS ARE OBVIOUSLY CLOSED!
THAT HOUSE HAS THE LATEST IN PREVENTATIVE BIRD-WINDOW COLLISION TECHNOLOGY
!!
I REALLY NEED FIVE DOLLARS

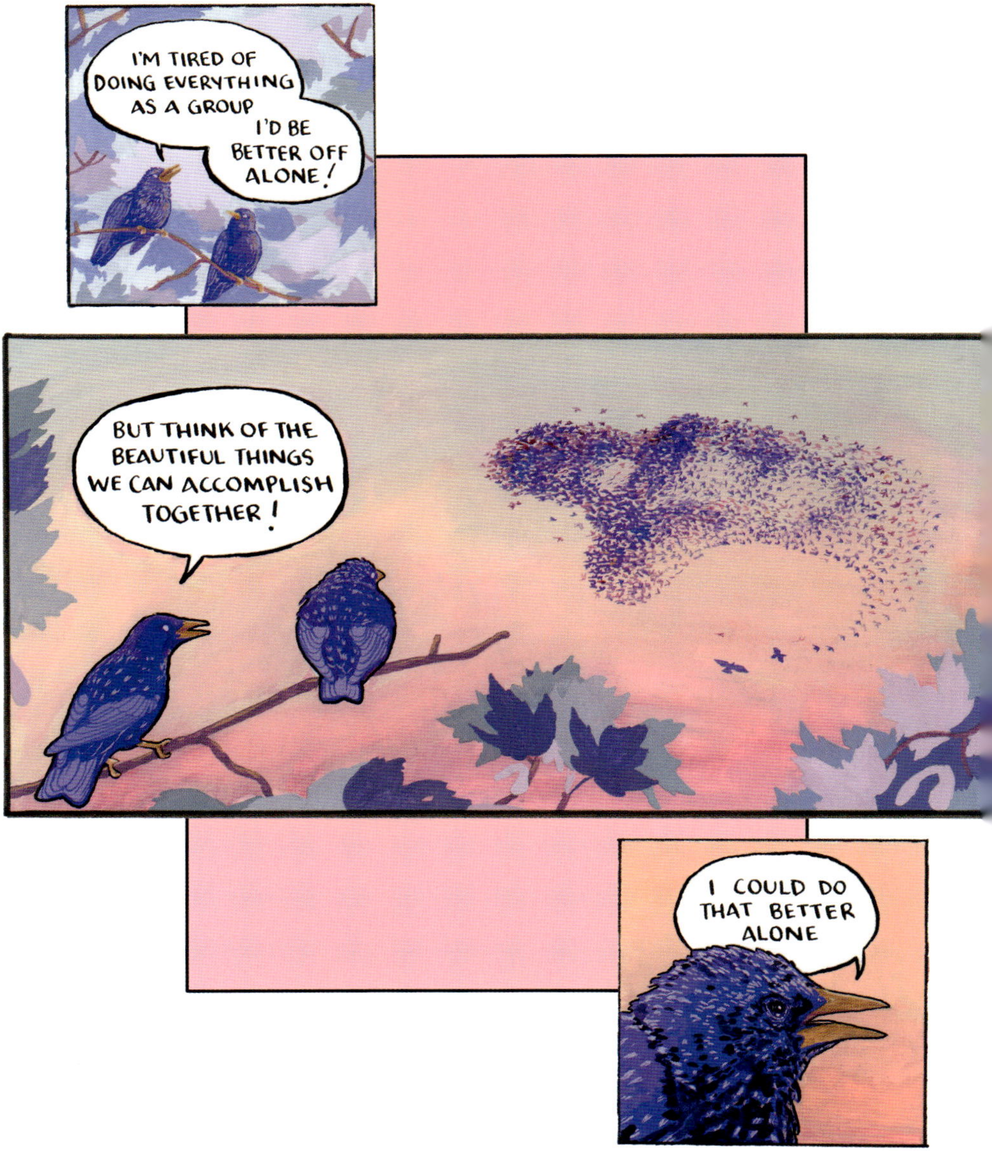
I'M TIRED OF DOING EVERYTHING AS A GROUP
I'D BE BETTER OFF ALONE!
BUT THINK OF THE BEAUTIFUL THINGS WE CAN ACCOMPLISH TOGETHER!
I COULD DO THAT BETTER ALONE

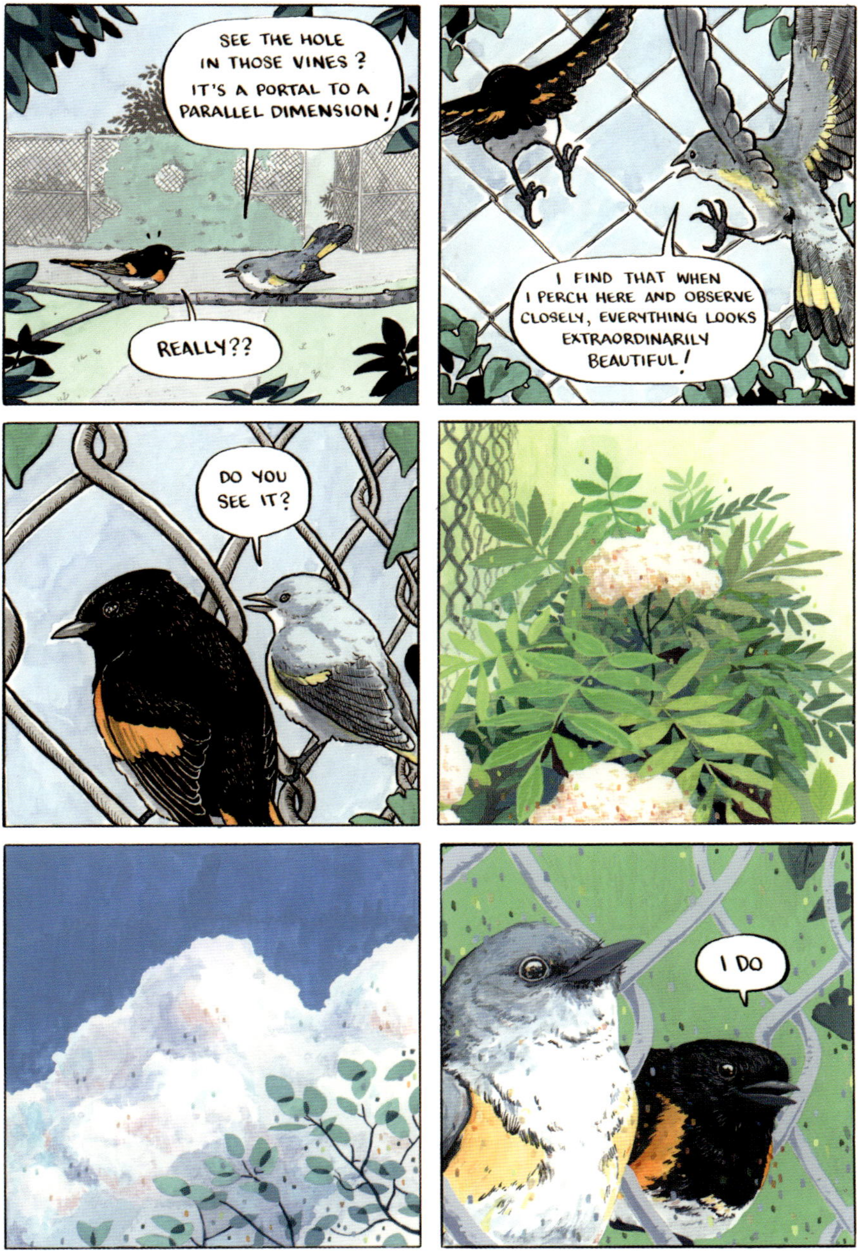
SEE THE HOLE IN THOSE VINES ? IT'S A PORTAL TO A PARALLEL DIMENSION !
REALLY??
I FIND THAT WHEN I PERCH HERE AND OBSERVE CLOSELY, EVERYTHING LOOKS EXTRAORDINARILY BEAUTIFUL !
DO YOU SEE IT?
I DO

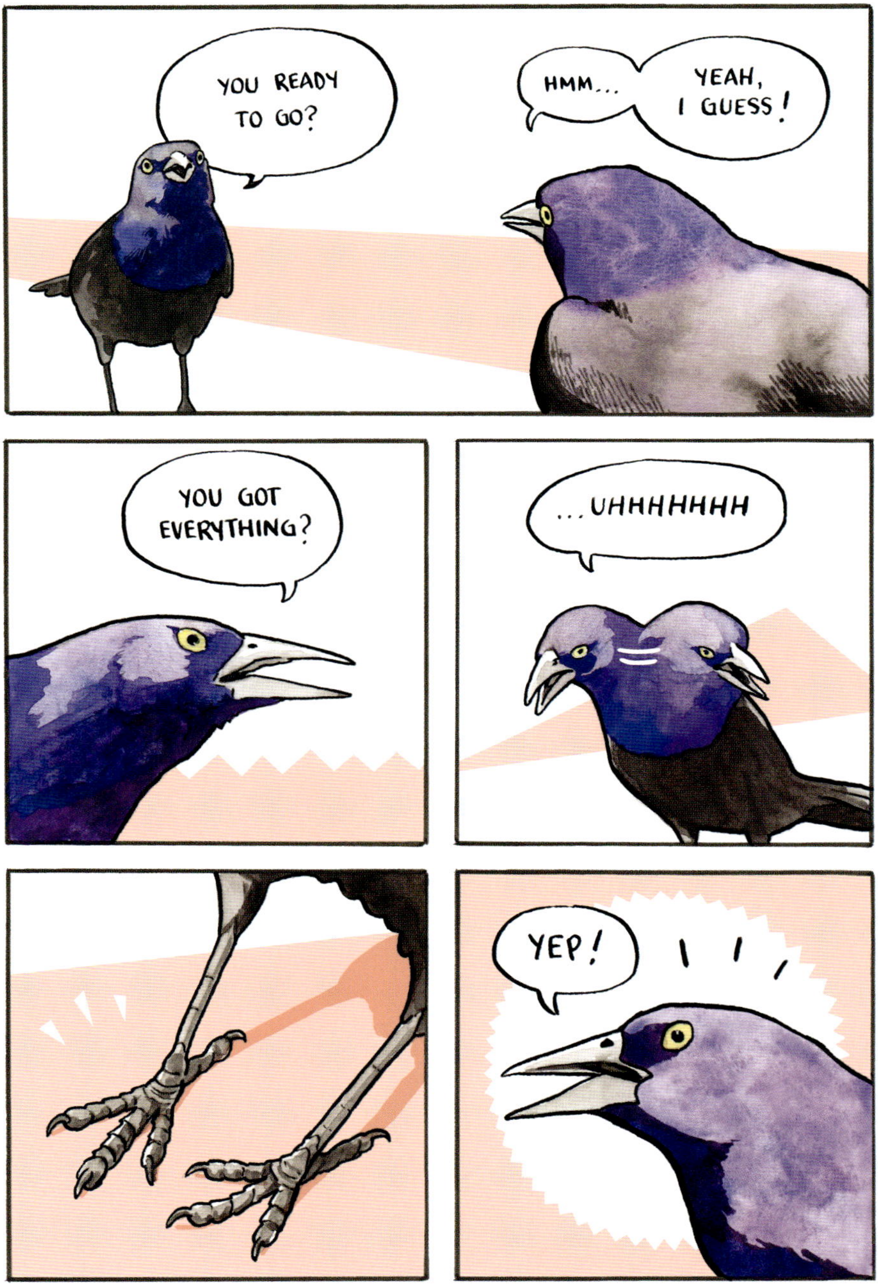
YOU READY TO GO?
HMM...
YEAH, I GUESS!
YOU GOT EVERYTHING?
...UHHHHHHH
YEP!

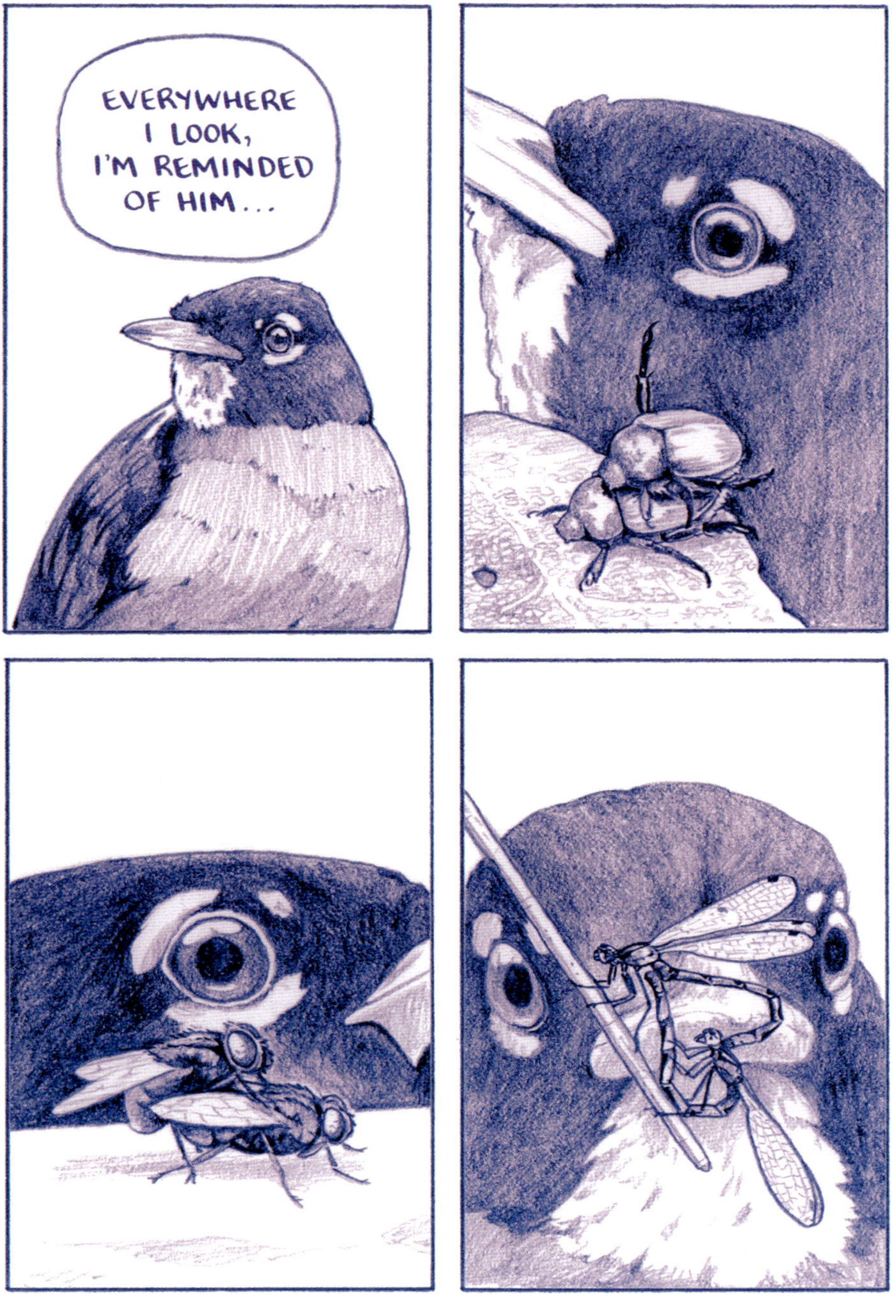
EVERYWHERE I LOOK, I'M REMINDED OF HIM...

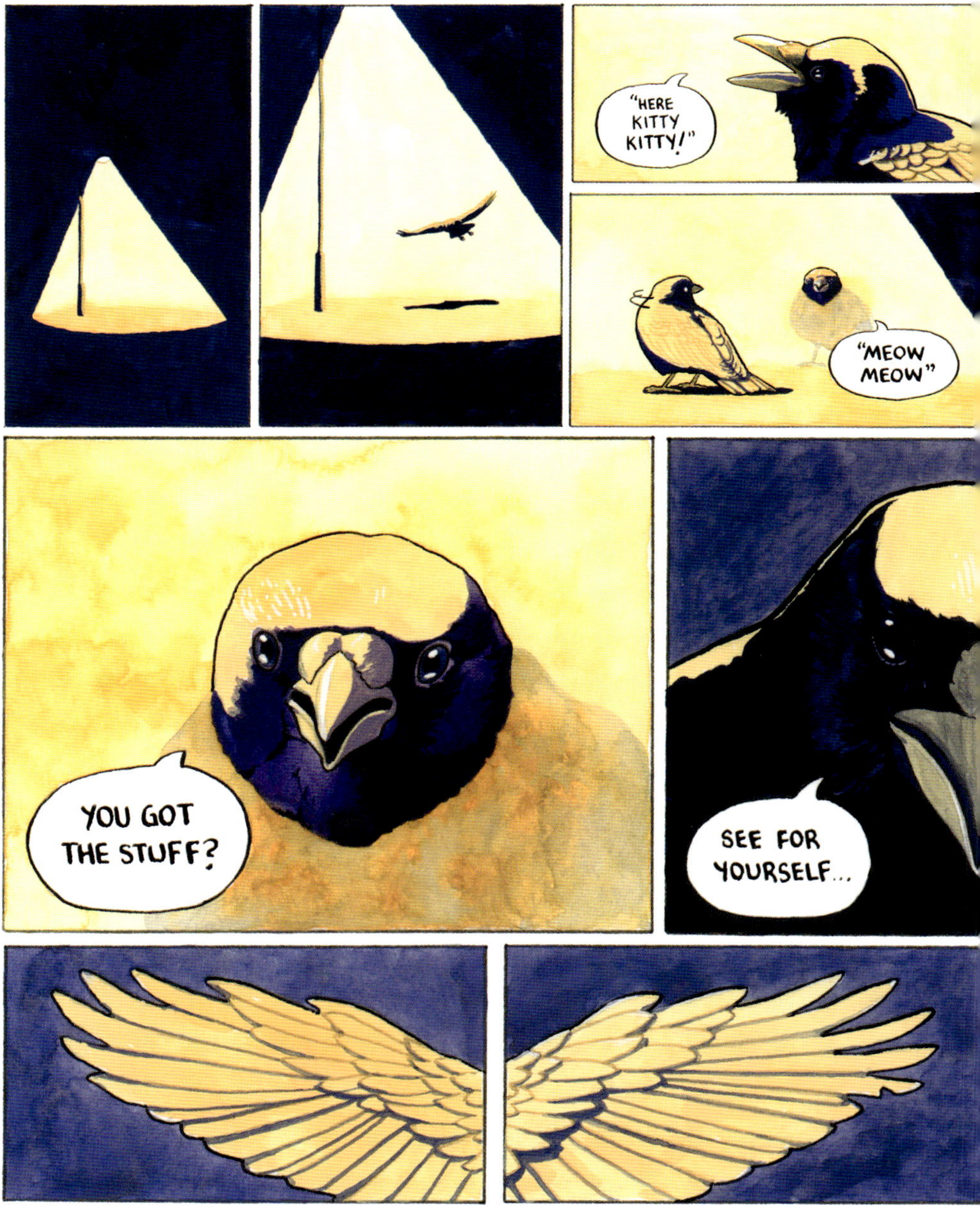
"HERE KITTY KITTY!"
"MEOW MEOW"
YOU GOT THE STUFF?
SEE FOR YOURSELF...

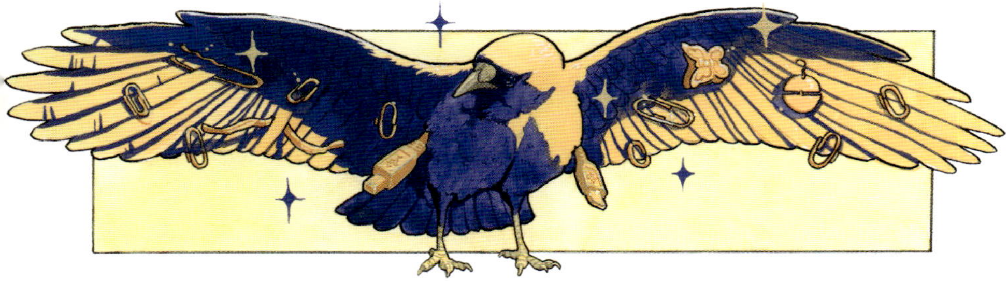

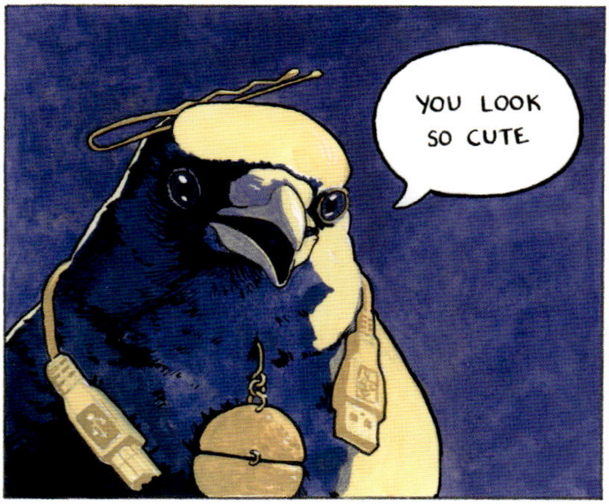
YOU LOOK SO CUTE

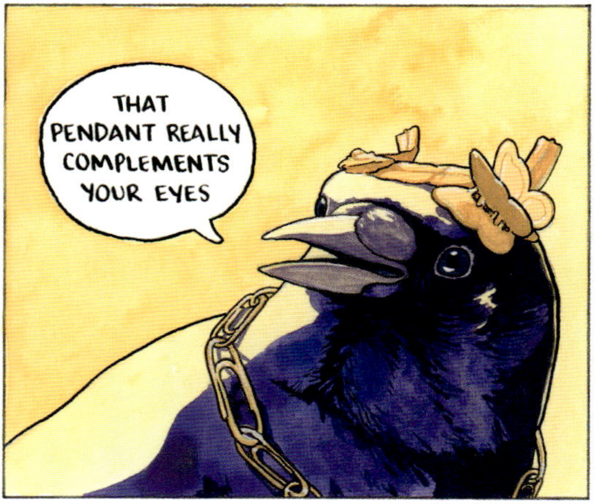
THAT PENDANT REALLY COMPLEMENTS YOUR EYES

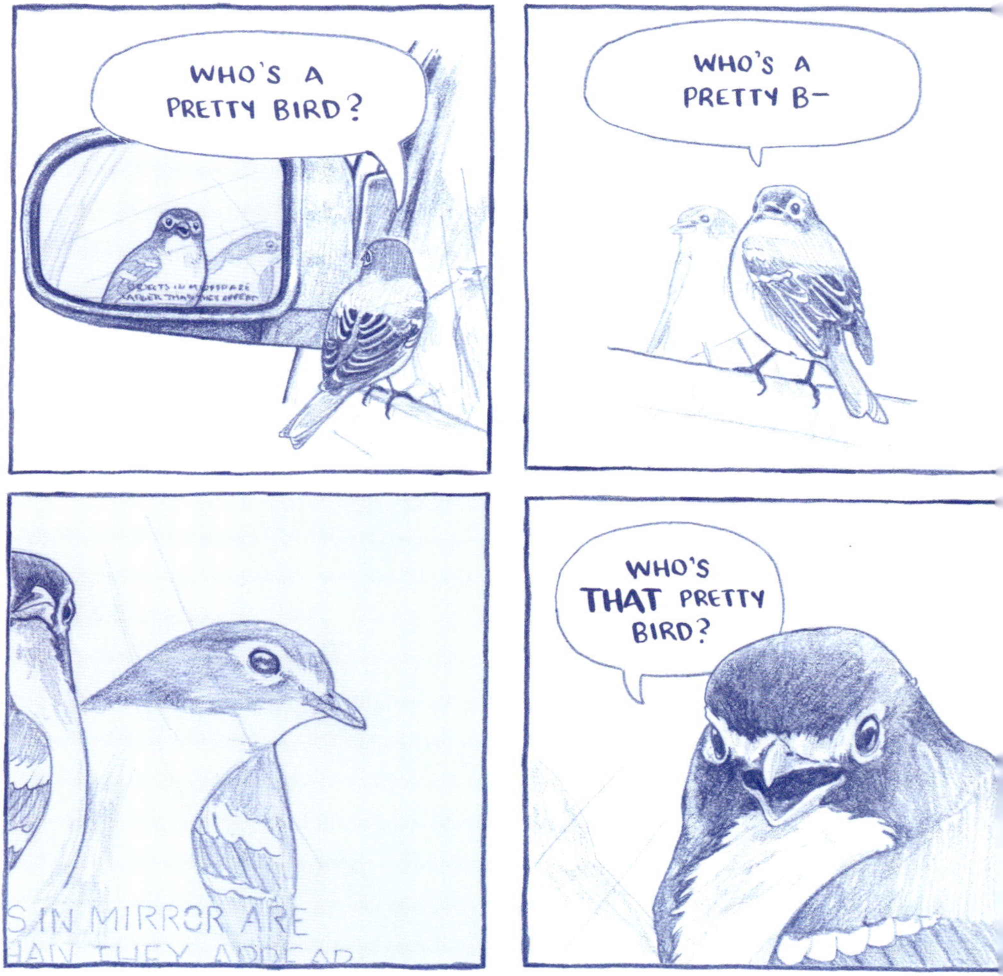
WHO'S A PRETTY BIRD?
WHO'S A PRETTY B—
S IN MIRROR ARE
WHO'S THAT PRETTY BIRD?

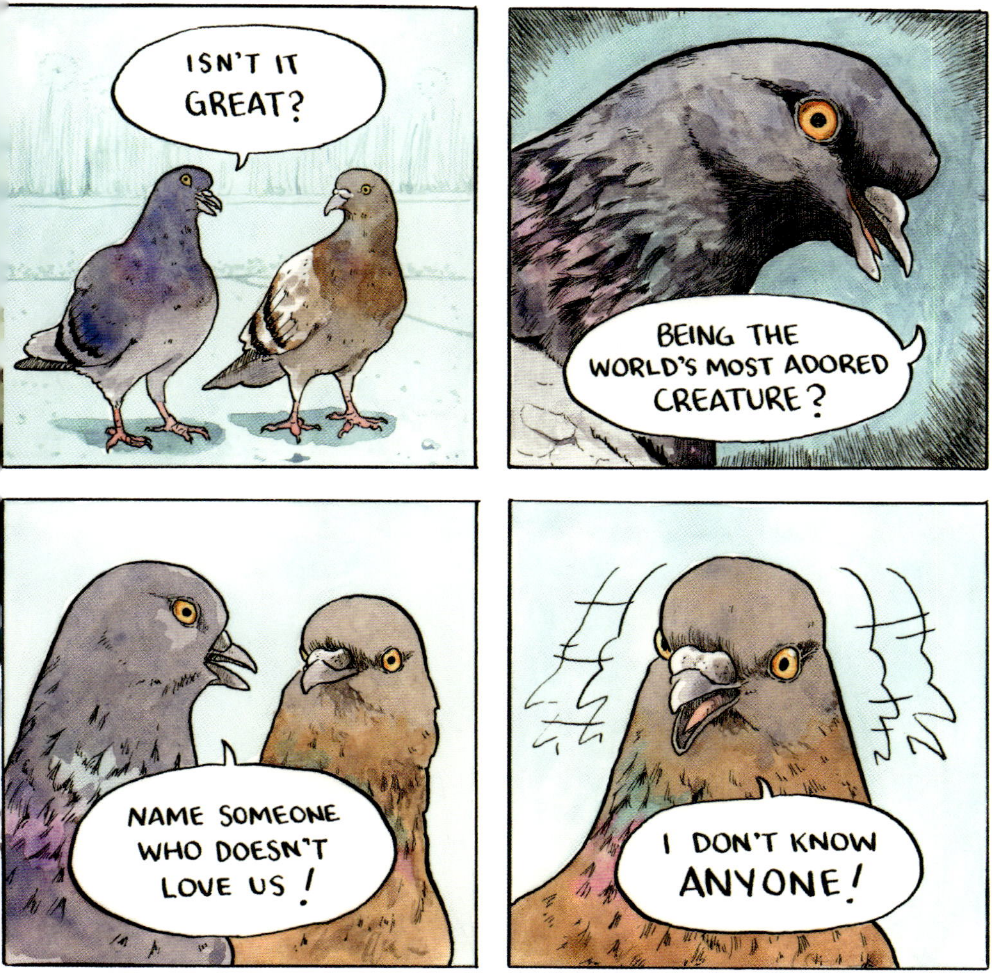
ISN'T IT GREAT?
BEING THE WORLD'S MOST ADORED CREATURE?
NAME SOMEONE WHO DOESN'T LOVE US!
I DON'T KNOW ANYONE!

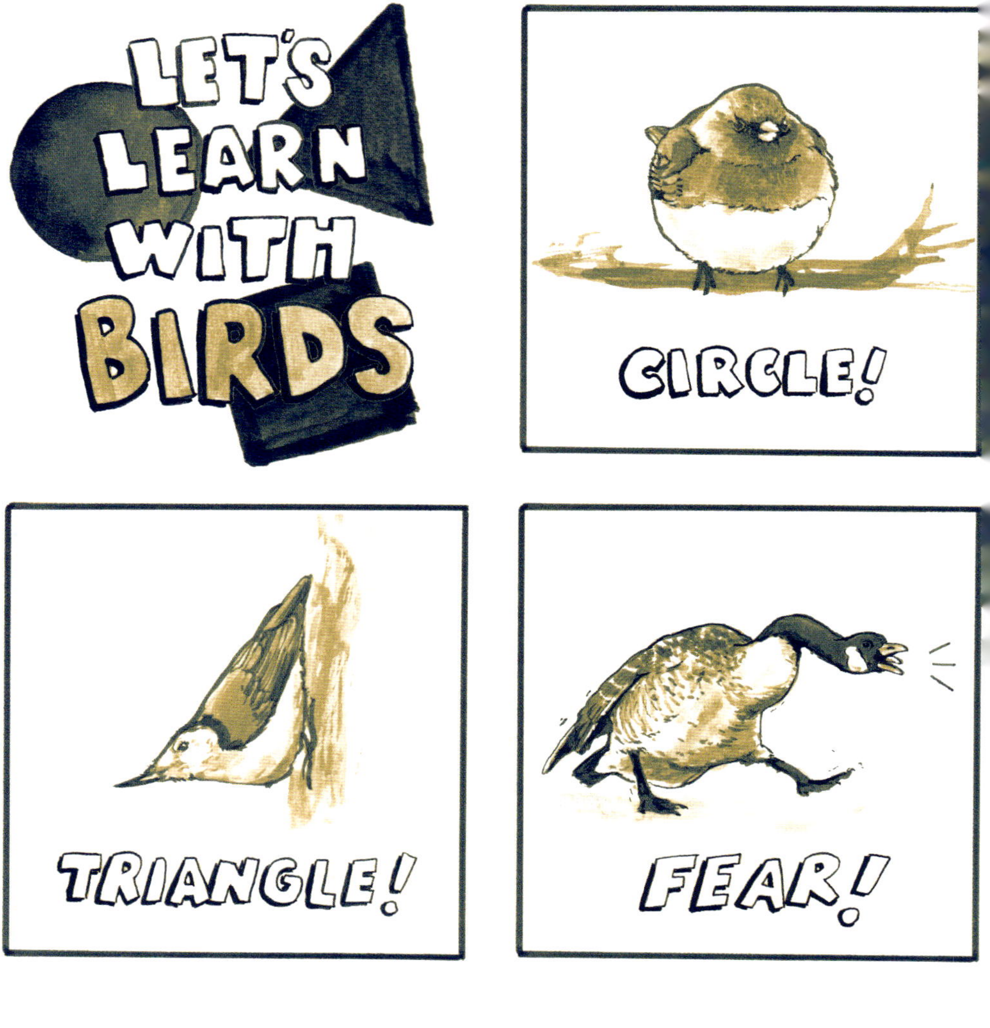
LET'S LEARN WITH BIRDS
CIRCLE!
TRIANGLE!
FEAR!

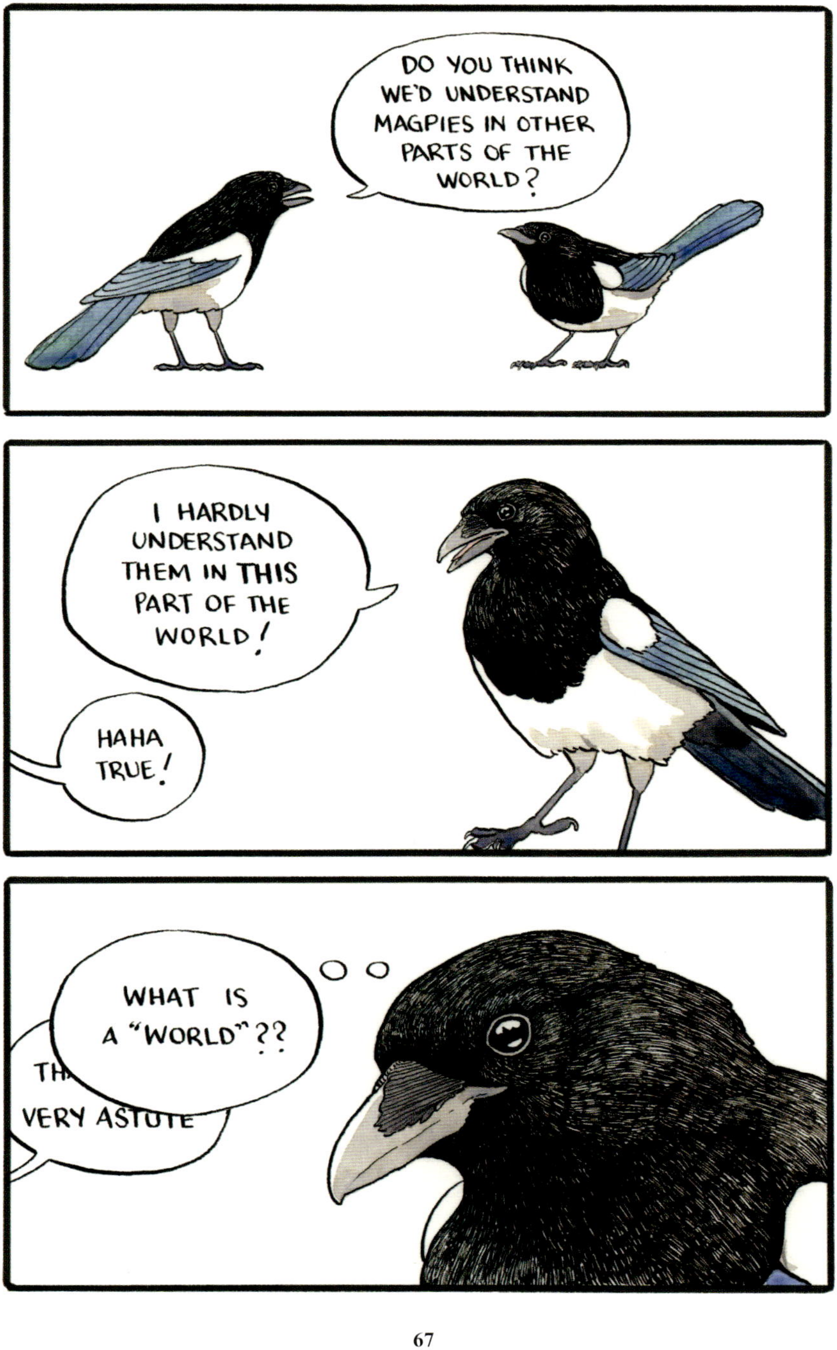
DO YOU THINK WE'D UNDERSTAND MAGPIES IN OTHER PARTS OF THE WORLD?
I HARDLY UNDERSTAND THEM IN THIS PART OF THE WORLD!
HAHA TRUE!
WHAT IS A "WORLD"??
VERY ASTUTE

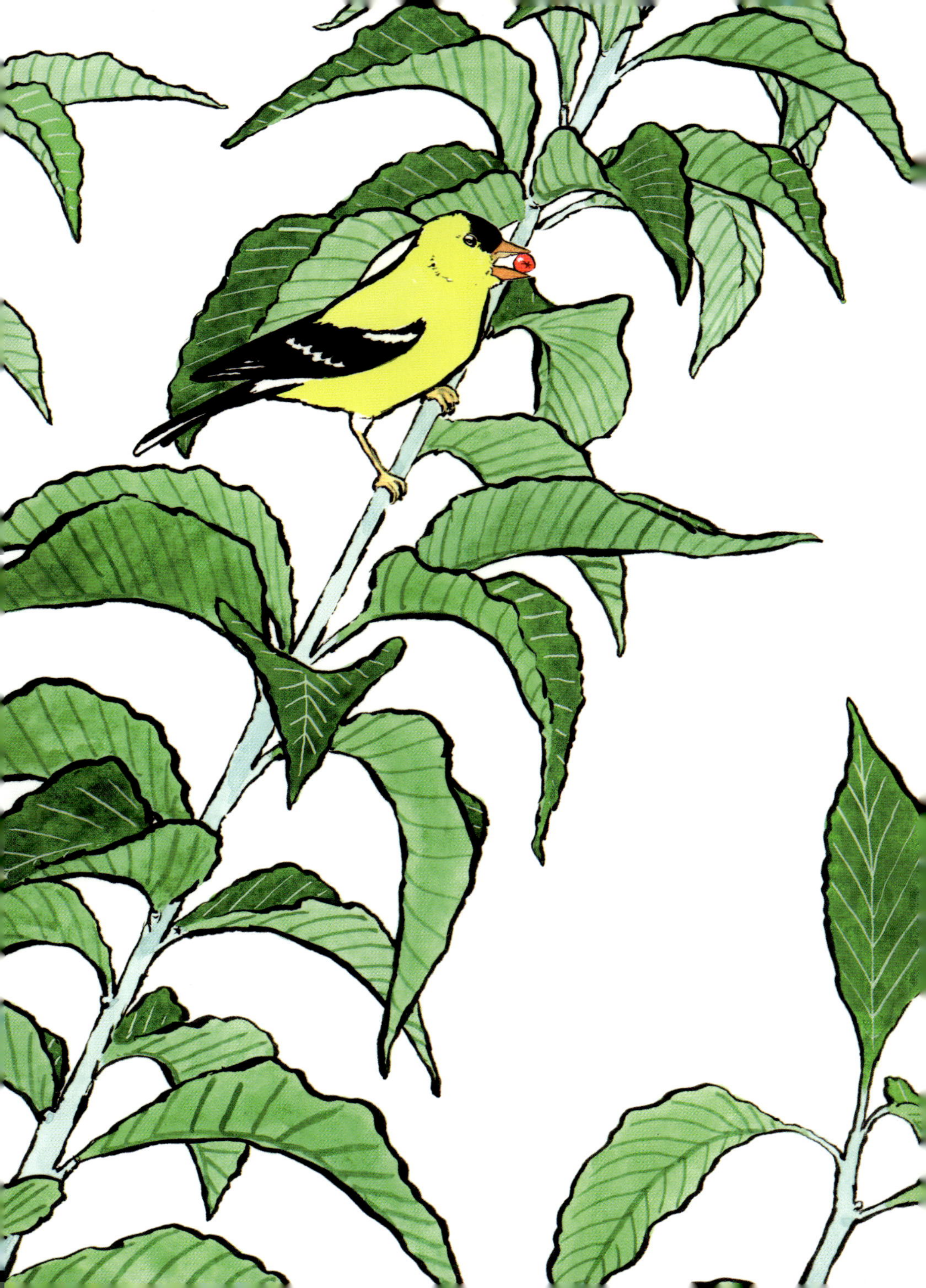

Summer

RUSTLE RUSTLE
THIS IS IT. IT'S MY TIME.
I'M NOT READY!
BUT I GUESS I NEVER WOULD'VE BEEN.
IT FEELS SO BRIEF NOW...
MY BIGGEST REGRET WAS HAVING CHI—
OH IT'S JUST A BEETLE
zzzzz
...
SLIGHT BREEZE
THIS IS IT. IT'S MY TIME.

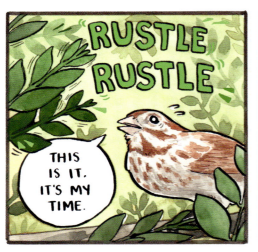

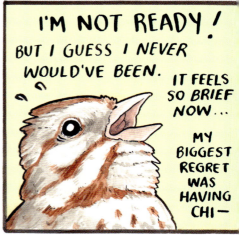

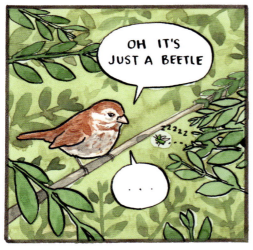

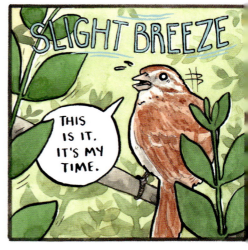

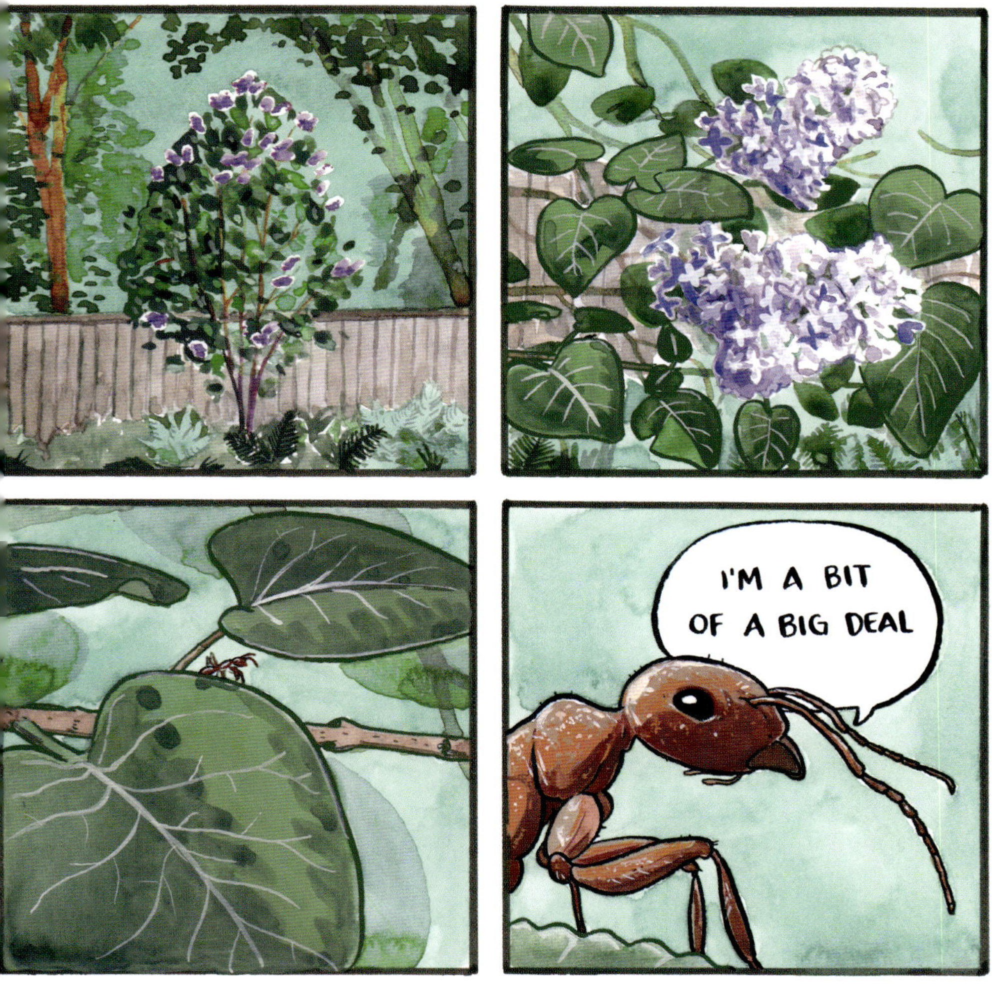
I'M A BIT OF A BIG DEAL

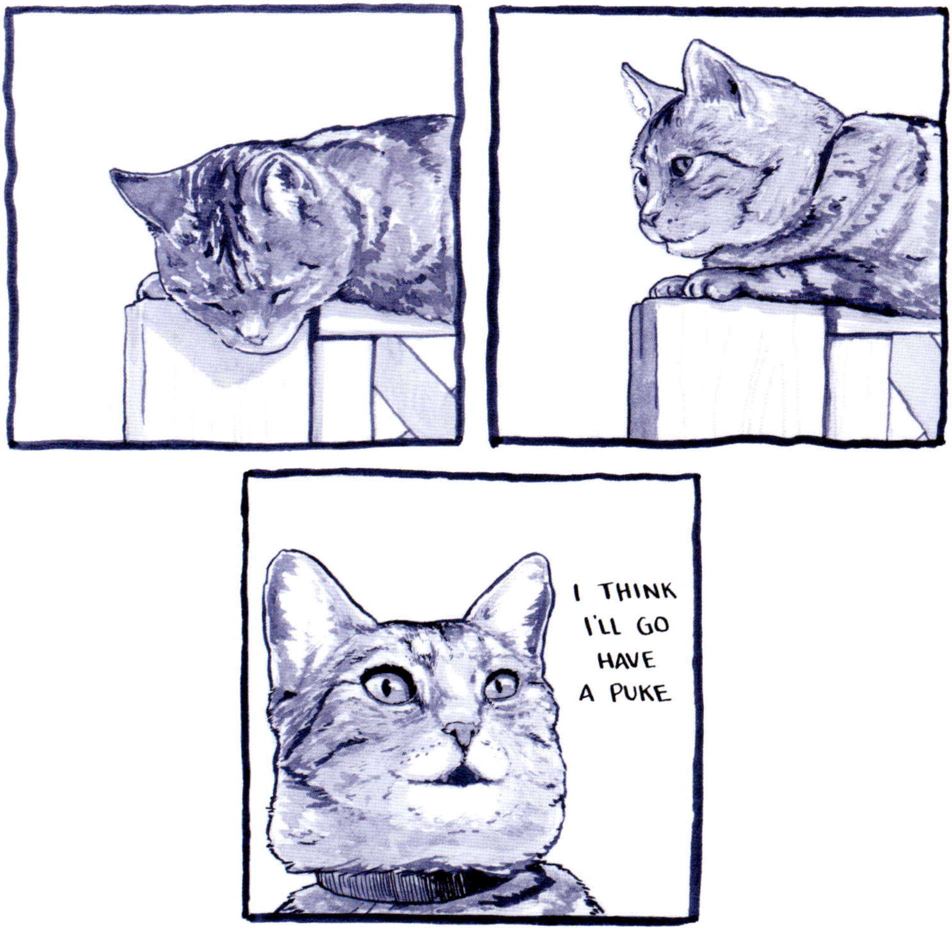
I THINK I'LL GO HAVE A PUKE

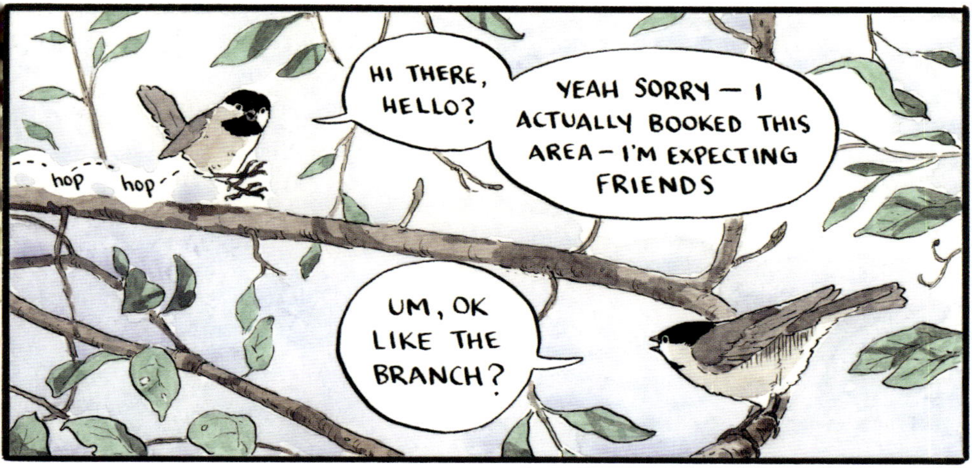
hop hop
HI THERE, HELLO?
YEAH SORRY — I ACTUALLY BOOKED THIS AREA — I'M EXPECTING FRIENDS
UM, OK LIKE THE BRANCH?

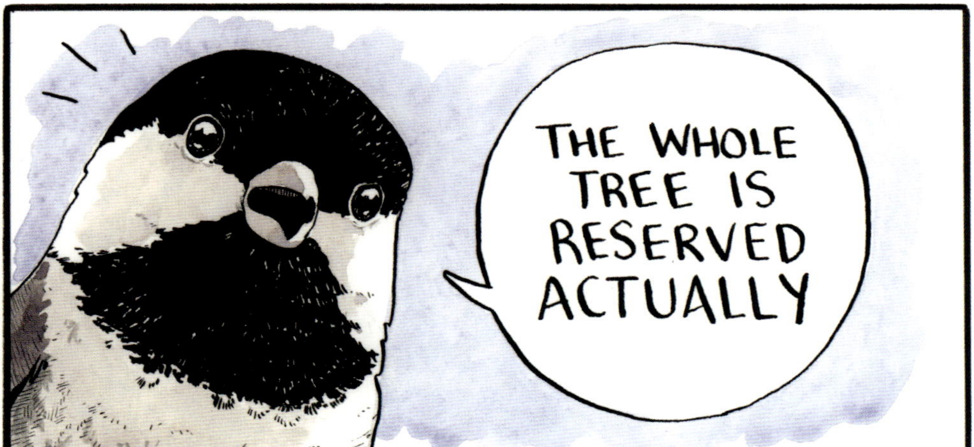
THE WHOLE TREE IS RESERVED ACTUALLY

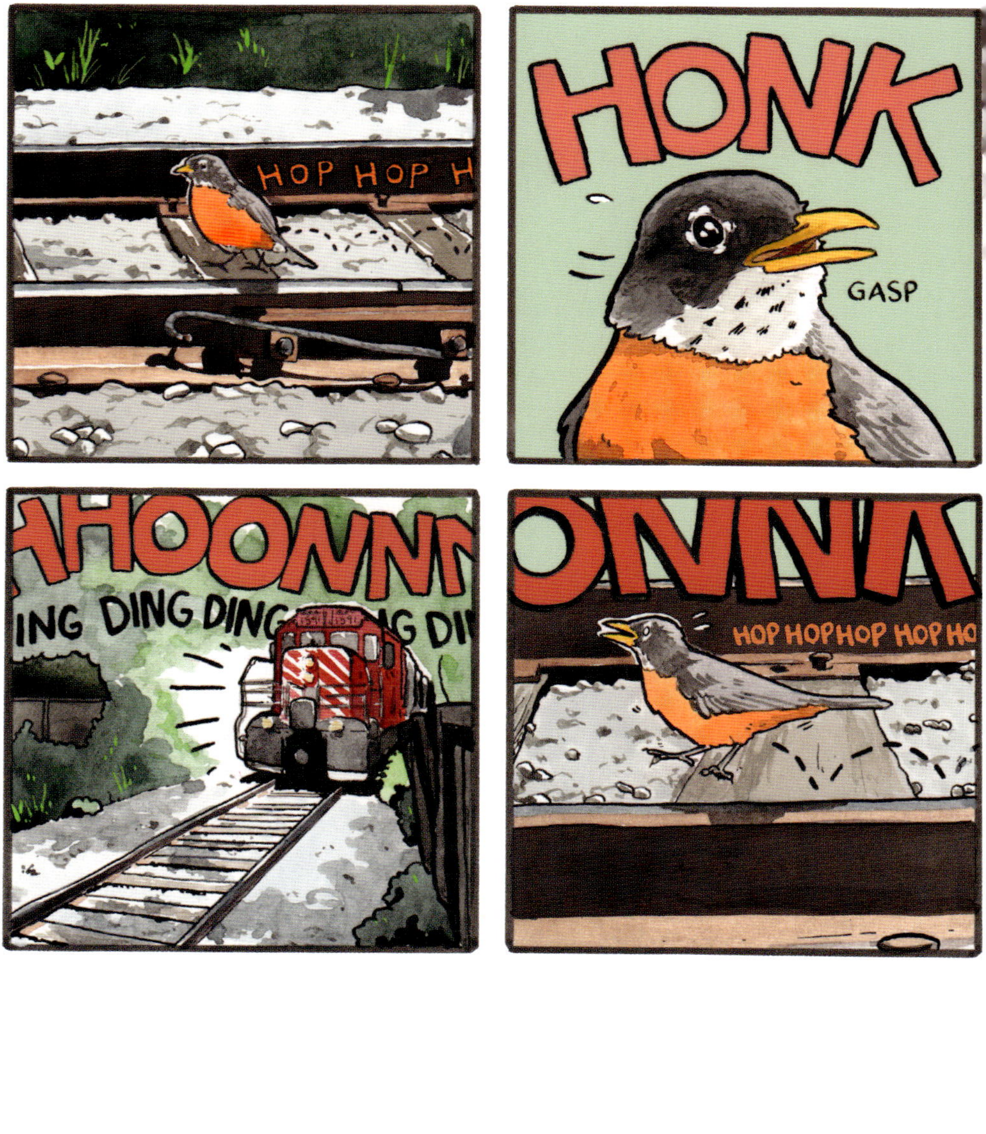
HOP HOP H
HONK
GASP
HOONNN
ING DING DING
DI
ONNN
HOP HOP HOP HOP HO

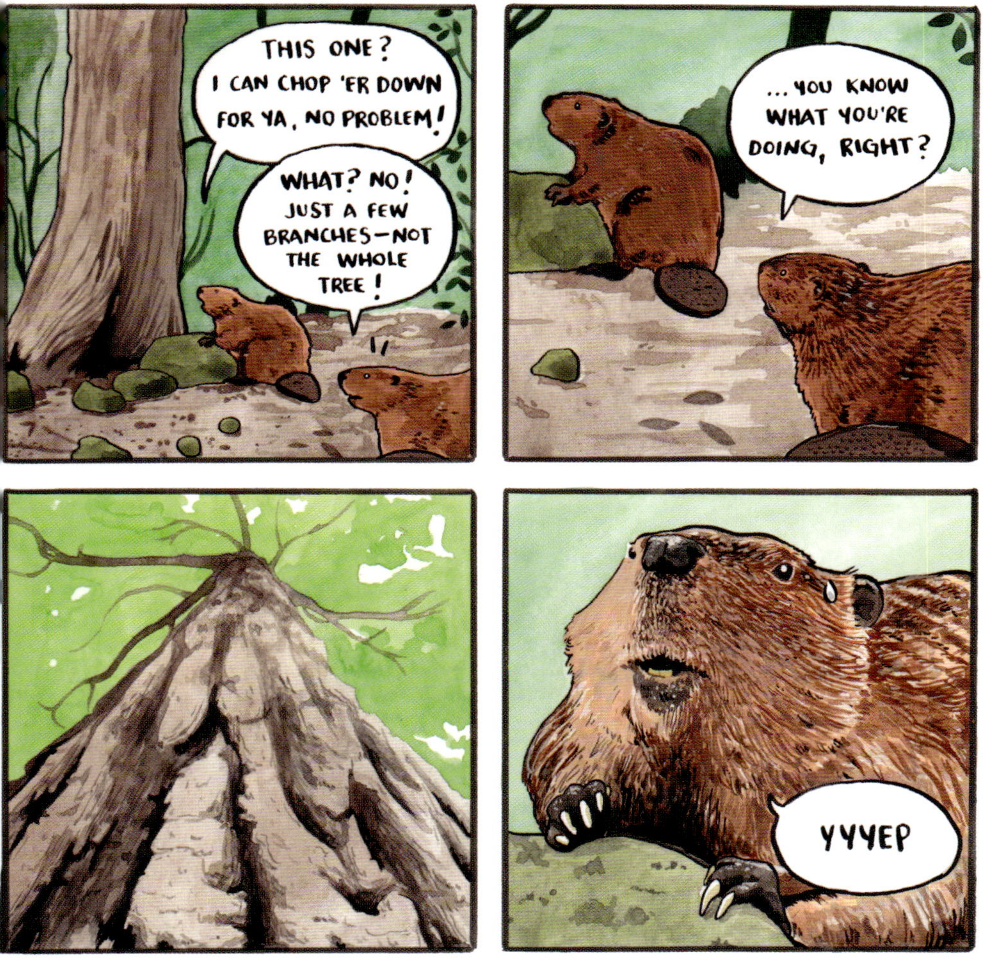
THIS ONE? I CAN CHOP 'ER DOWN FOR YA, NO PROBLEM!
WHAT? NO! JUST A FEW BRANCHES—NOT THE WHOLE TREE!
...YOU KNOW WHAT YOU'RE DOING, RIGHT?
YYYEP

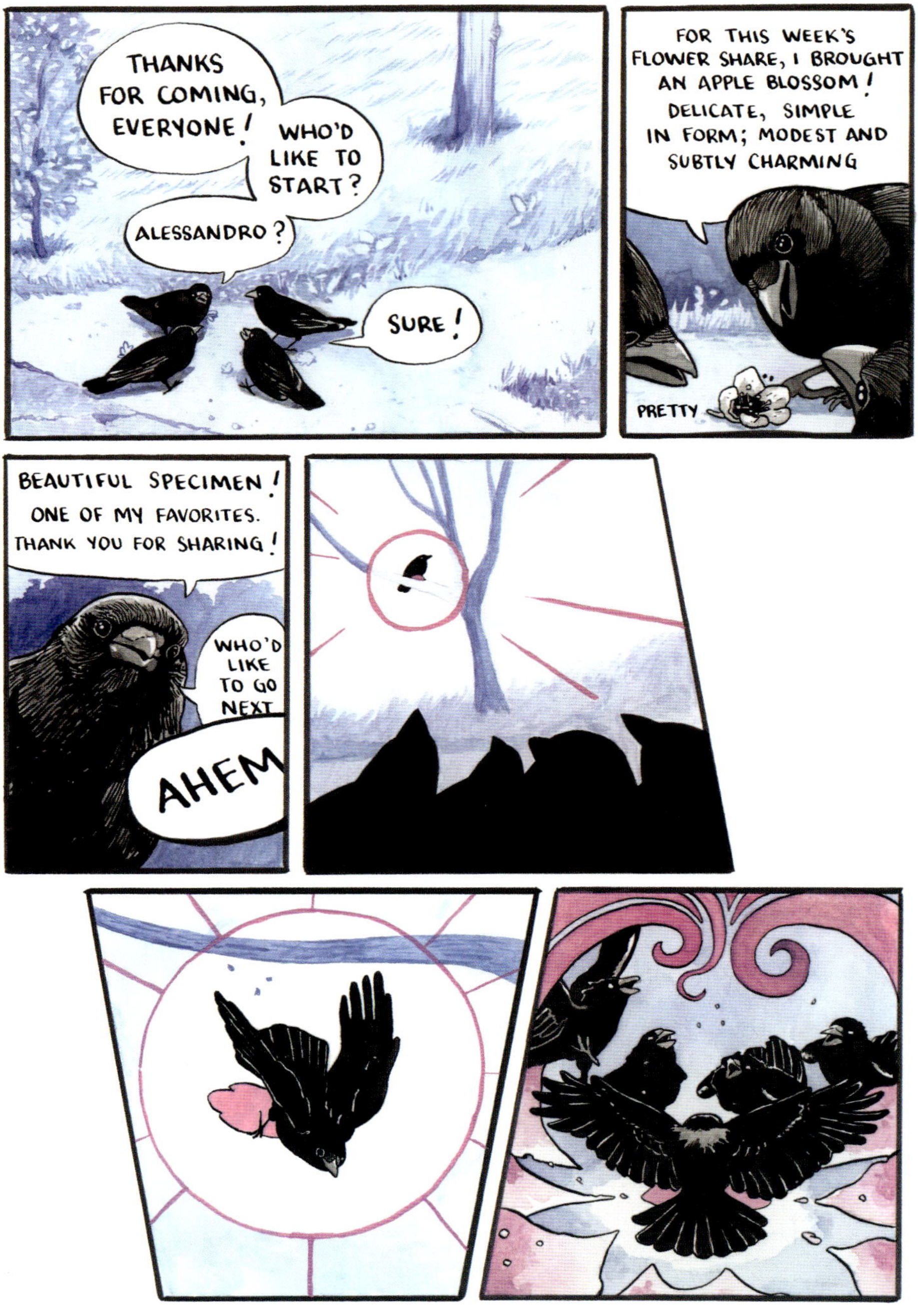
THANKS FOR COMING, EVERYONE!
WHO'D LIKE TO START?
ALESSANDRO?
SURE!
FOR THIS WEEK'S FLOWER SHARE, I BROUGHT AN APPLE BLOSSOM! DELICATE, SIMPLE IN FORM; MODEST AND SUBTLY CHARMING
PRETTY
BEAUTIFUL SPECIMEN! ONE OF MY FAVORITES. THANK YOU FOR SHARING!
WHO'D LIKE TO GO NEXT
AHEM

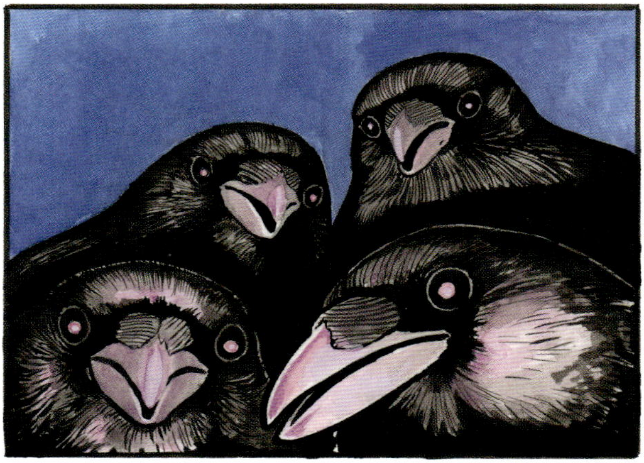

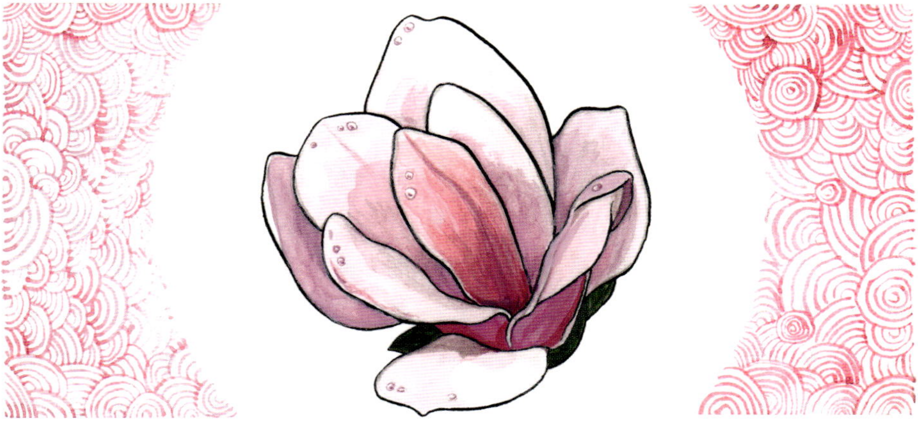

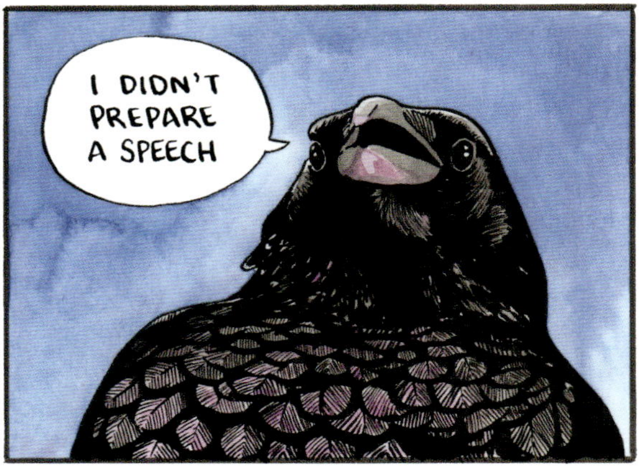
I DIDN'T PREPARE A SPEECH

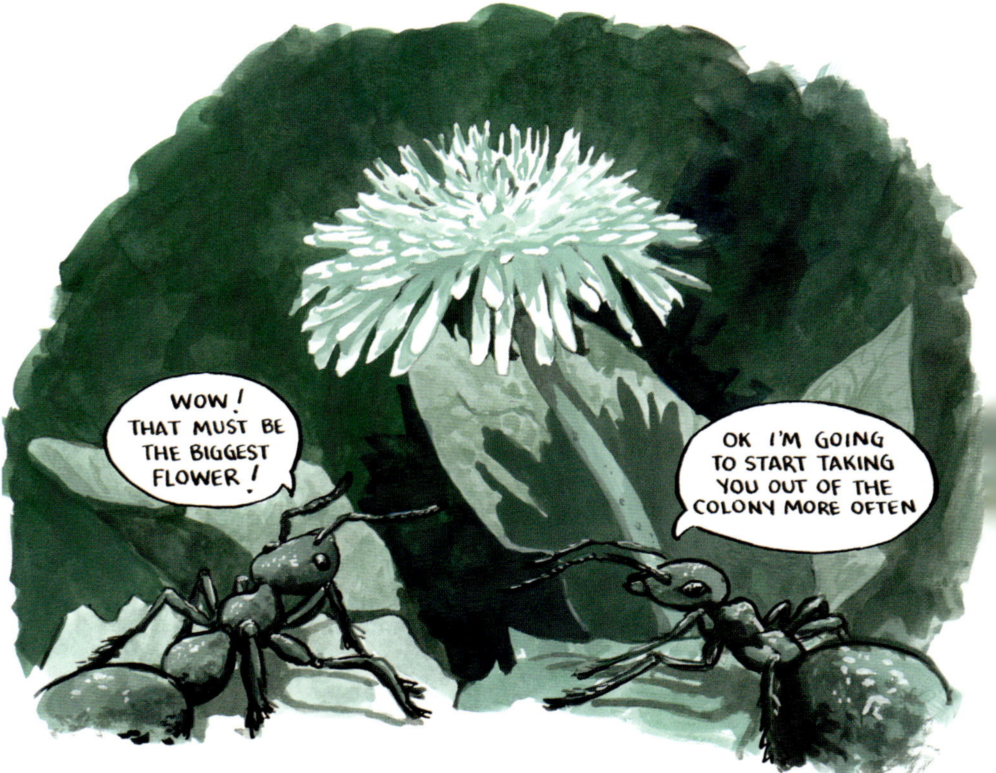
WOW! THAT MUST BE THE BIGGEST FLOWER!
OK I'M GOING TO START TAKING YOU OUT OF THE COLONY MORE OFTEN

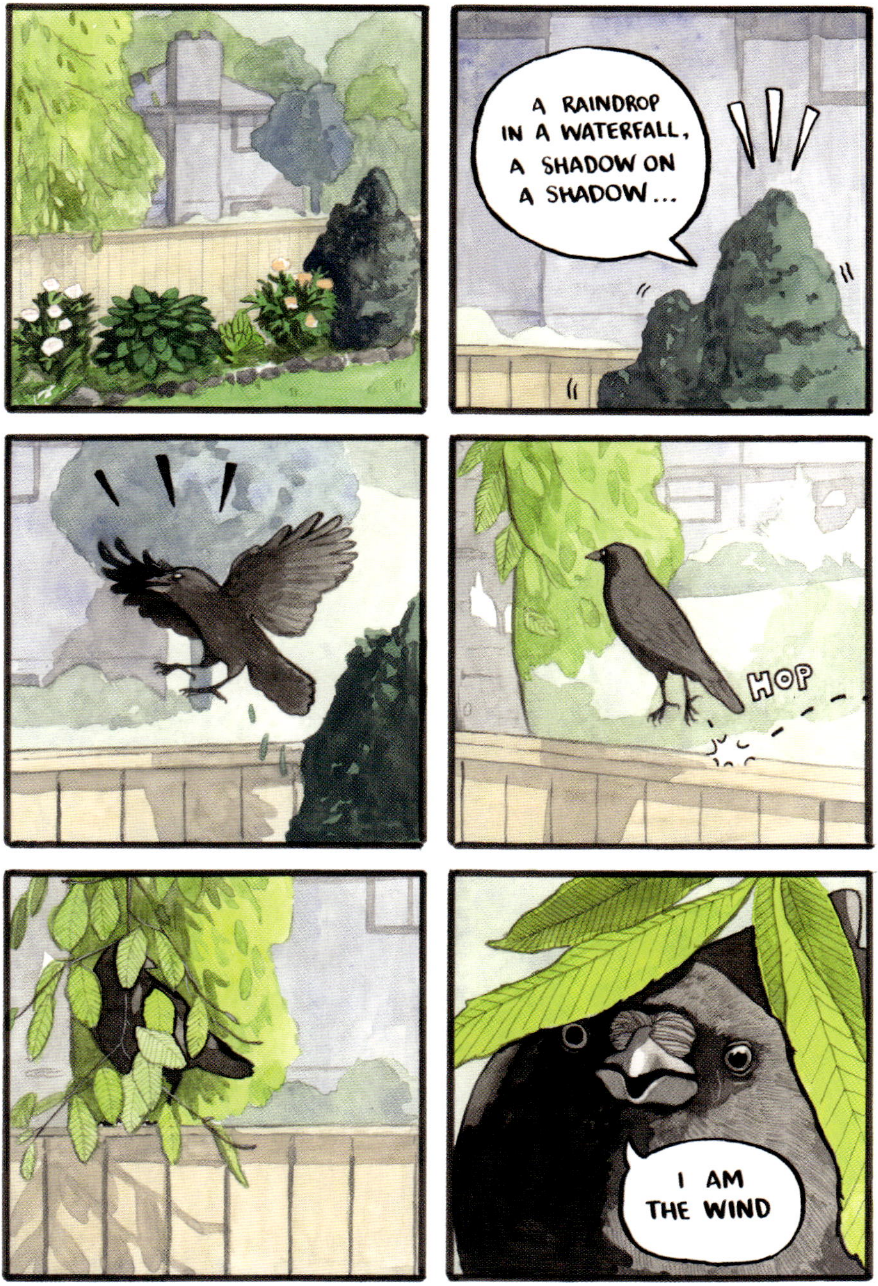
A RAINDROP IN A WATERFALL, A SHADOW ON A SHADOW...
HOP
I AM THE WIND

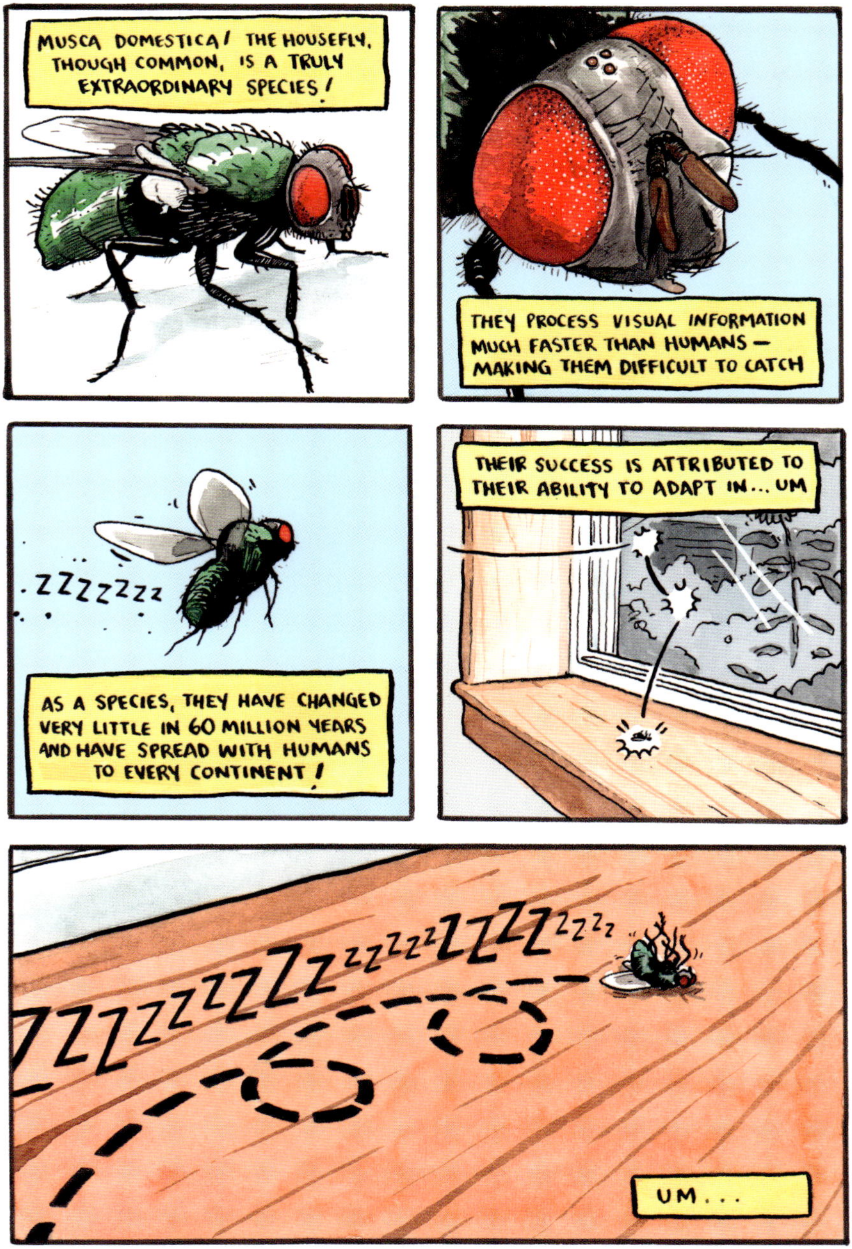
MUSCA DOMESTICA! THE HOUSEFLY. THOUGH COMMON, IS A TRULY EXTRAORDINARY SPECIES!
THEY PROCESS VISUAL INFORMATION MUCH FASTER THAN HUMANS — MAKING THEM DIFFICULT TO CATCH
ZZZZZZZ
AS A SPECIES, THEY HAVE CHANGED VERY LITTLE IN 60 MILLION YEARS AND HAVE SPREAD WITH HUMANS TO EVERY CONTINENT!
THEIR SUCCESS IS ATTRIBUTED TO THEIR ABILITY TO ADAPT IN... UM
ZZZZZZZZZZzzzzzzzZZZZzzzz
UM...

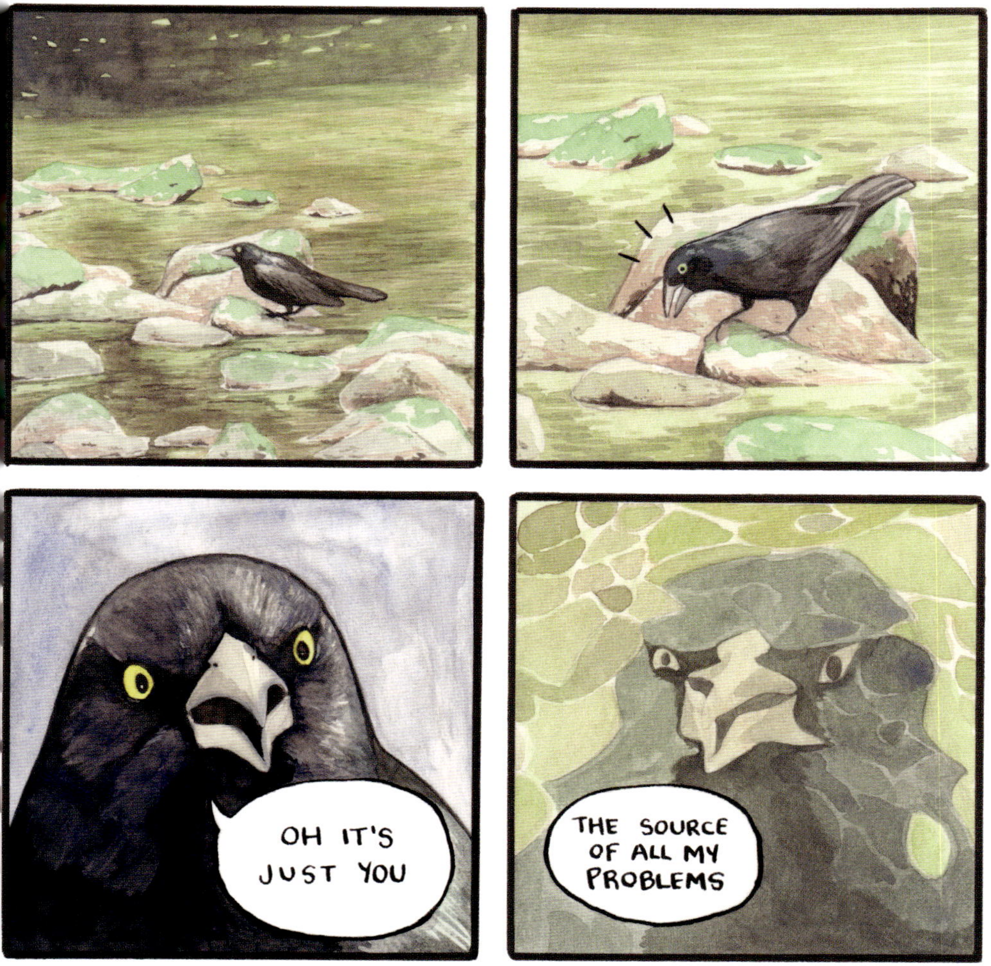
OH IT'S JUST YOU
THE SOURCE OF ALL MY PROBLEMS

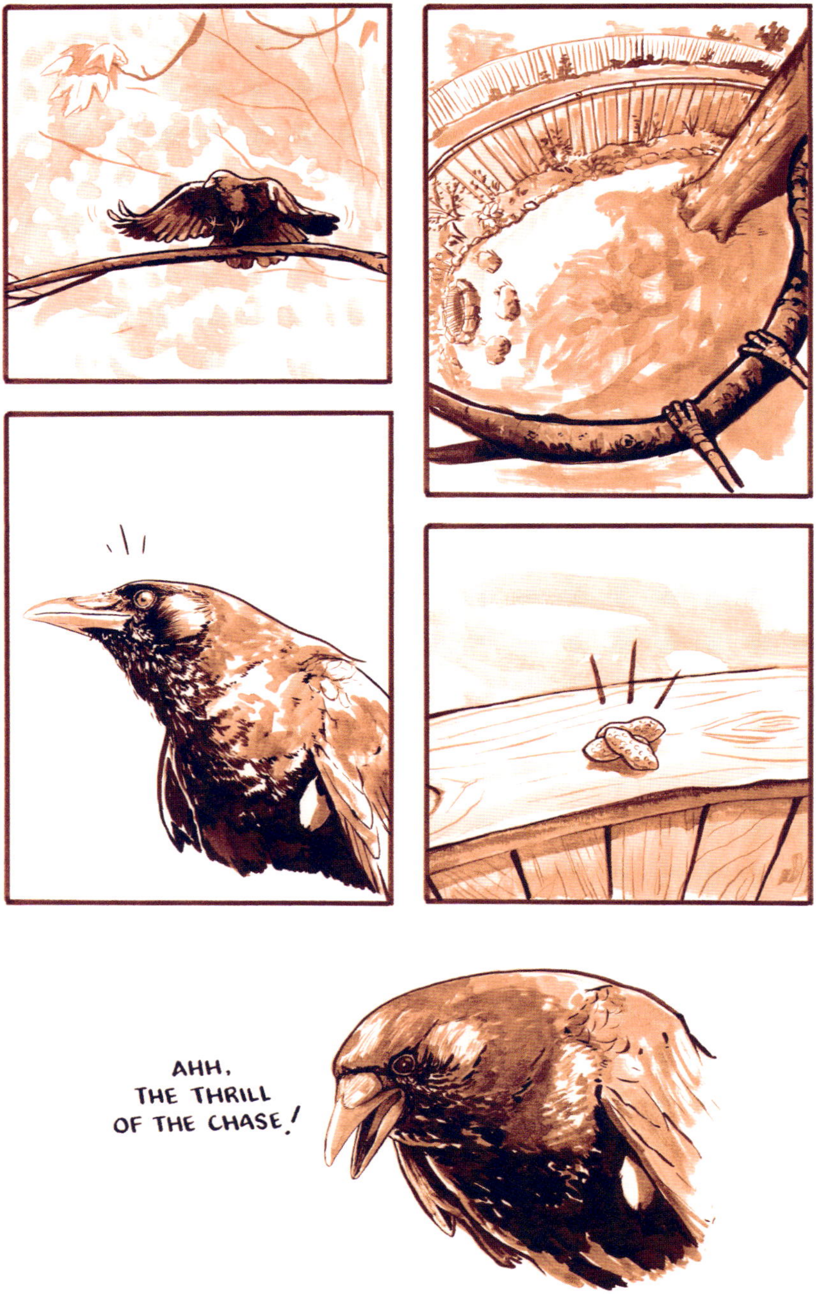
AHH,
THE THRILL
OF THE CHASE!

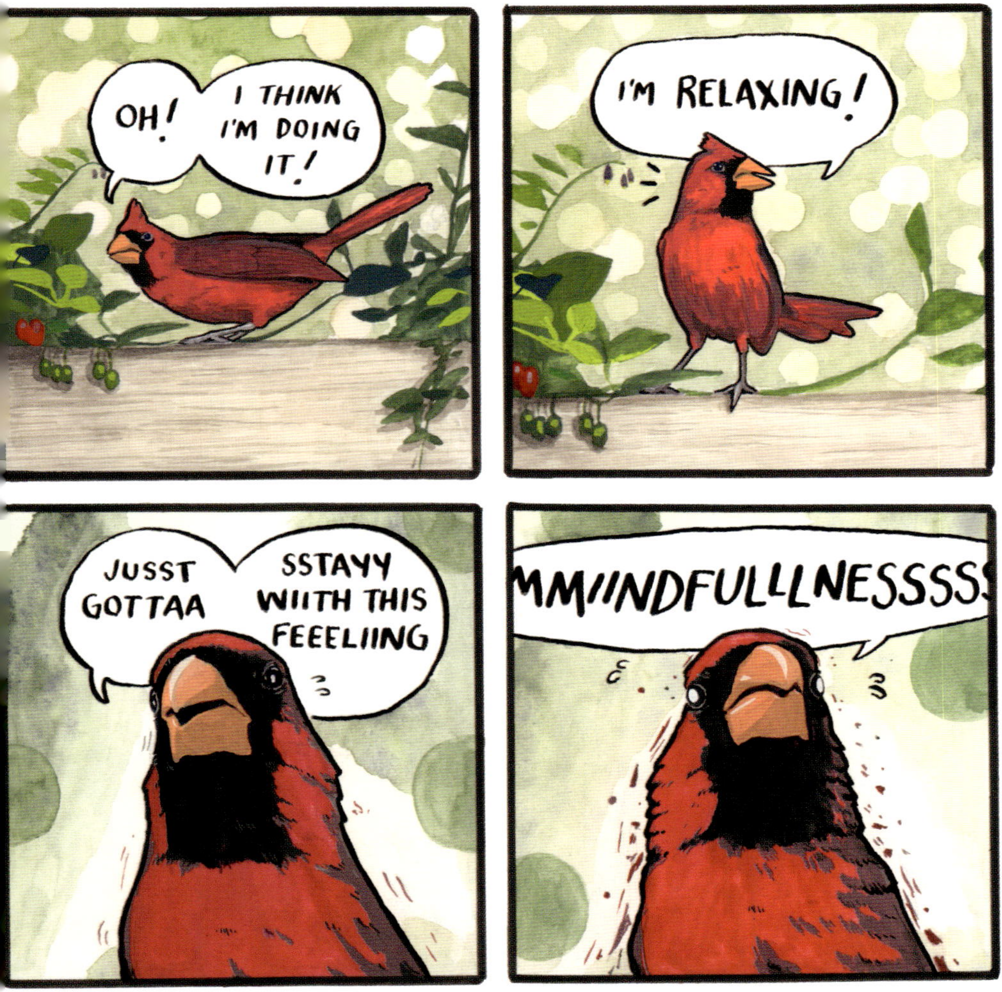
OH!
I THINK I'M DOING IT!
I'M RELAXING!
JUSST GOTTAA
SSTAYY WIITH THIS FEEELIING
MM//NDFULLLNESSSS

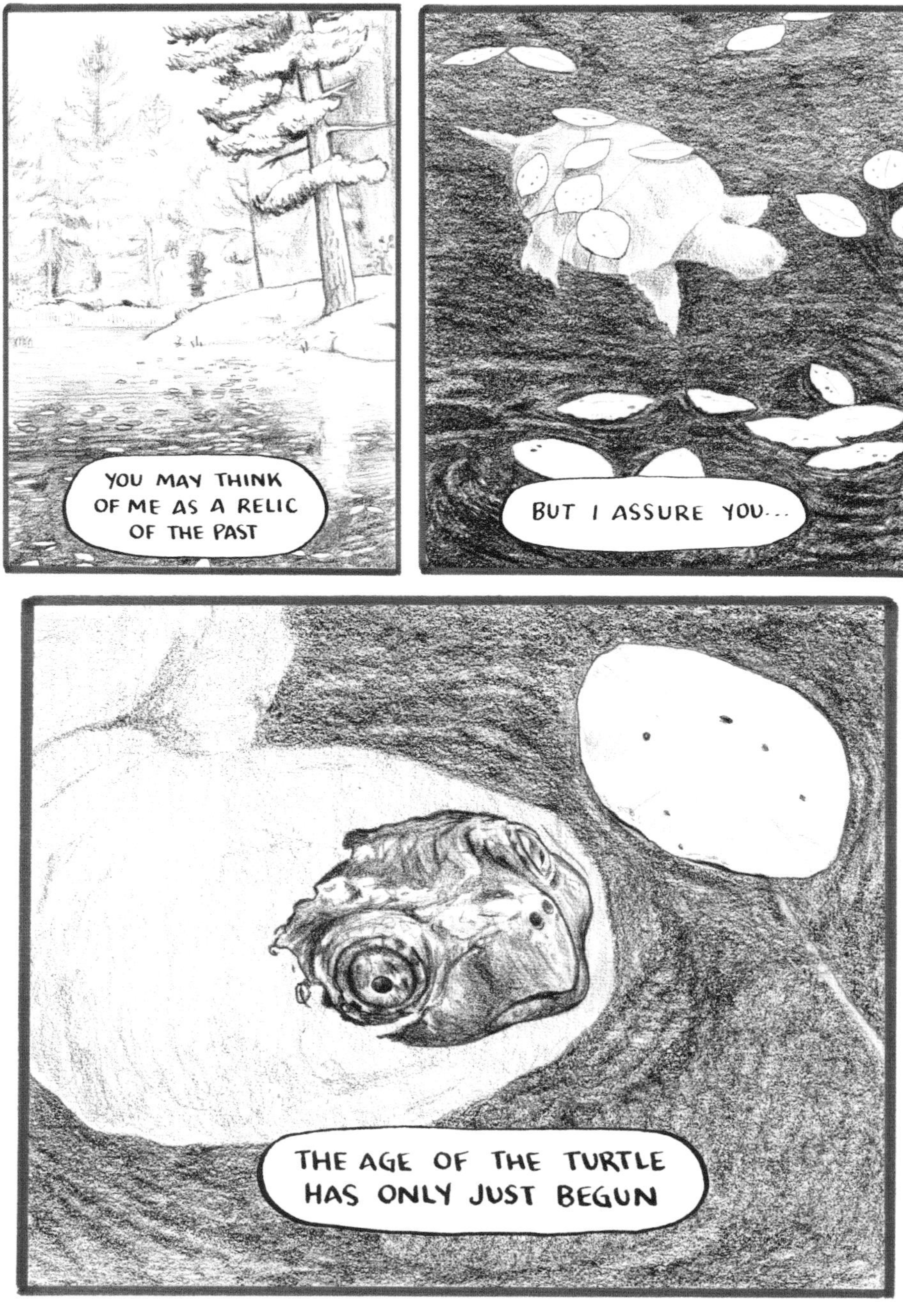
YOU MAY THINK OF ME AS A RELIC OF THE PAST
BUT I ASSURE YOU...
THE AGE OF THE TURTLE HAS ONLY JUST BEGUN

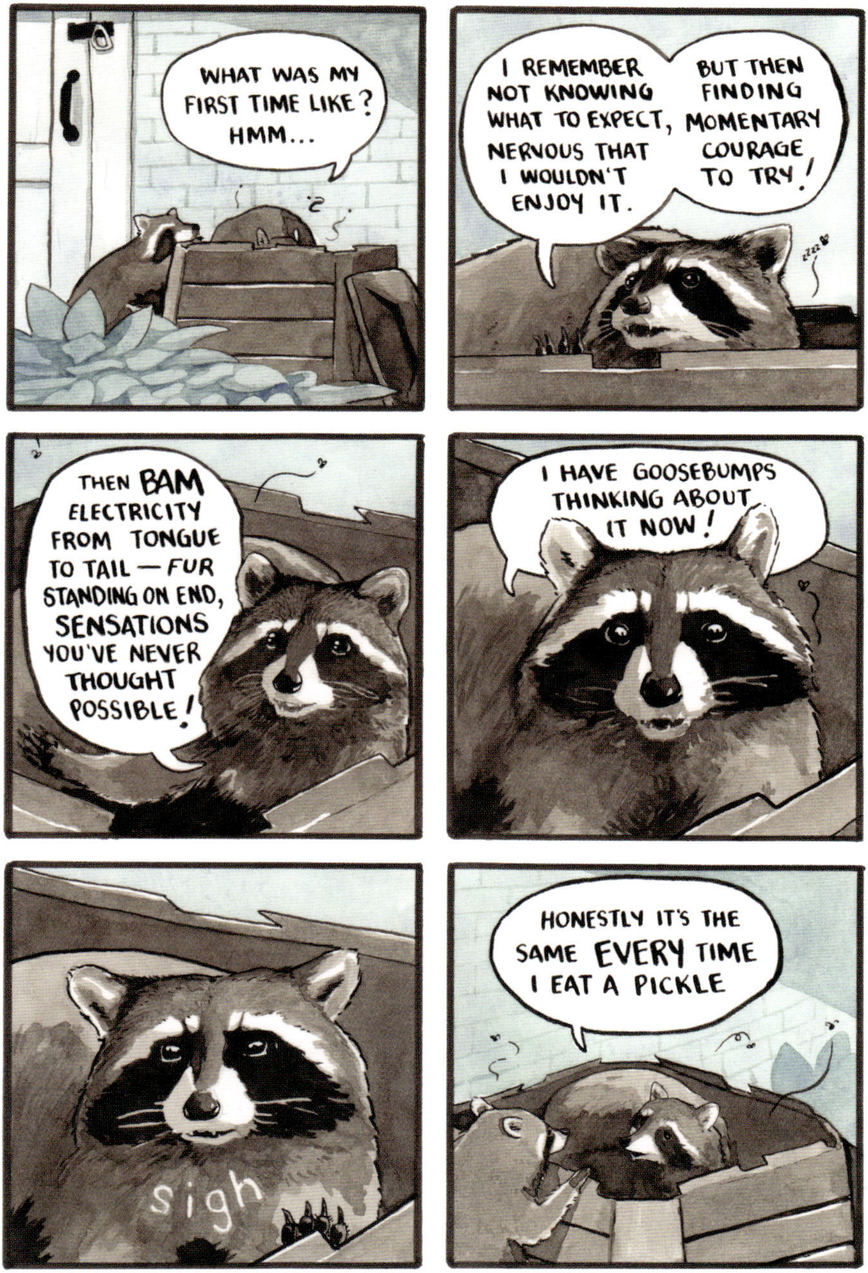
WHAT WAS MY FIRST TIME LIKE? HMM...
I REMEMBER NOT KNOWING WHAT TO EXPECT, NERVOUS THAT I WOULDN'T ENJOY IT.
BUT THEN FINDING MOMENTARY COURAGE TO TRY!
THEN BAM ELECTRICITY FROM TONGUE TO TAIL — FUR STANDING ON END, SENSATIONS YOU'VE NEVER THOUGHT POSSIBLE!
I HAVE GOOSEBUMPS THINKING ABOUT IT NOW!
sigh
HONESTLY IT'S THE SAME EVERY TIME I EAT A PICKLE

IN HOMAGE TO CHARLES SCHULZ

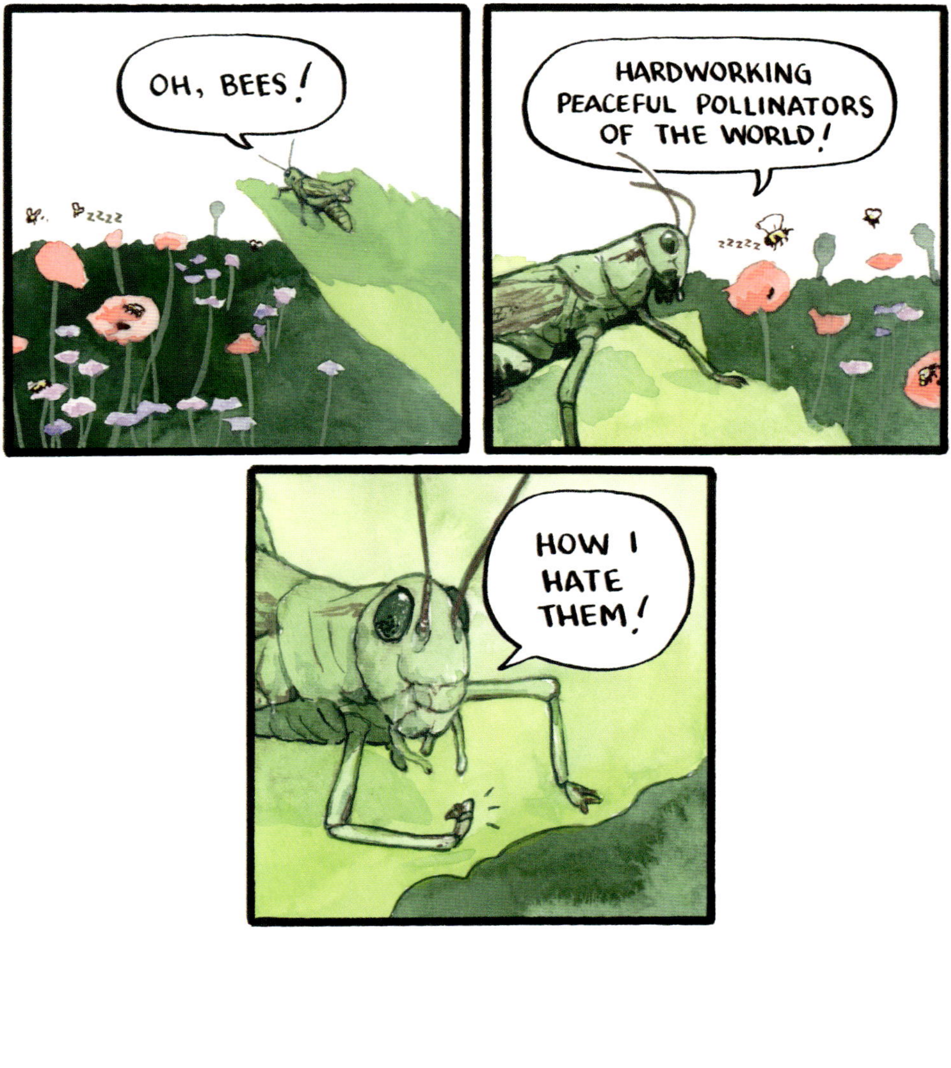
OH, BEES!
HARDWORKING PEACEFUL POLLINATORS OF THE WORLD!
HOW I HATE THEM!

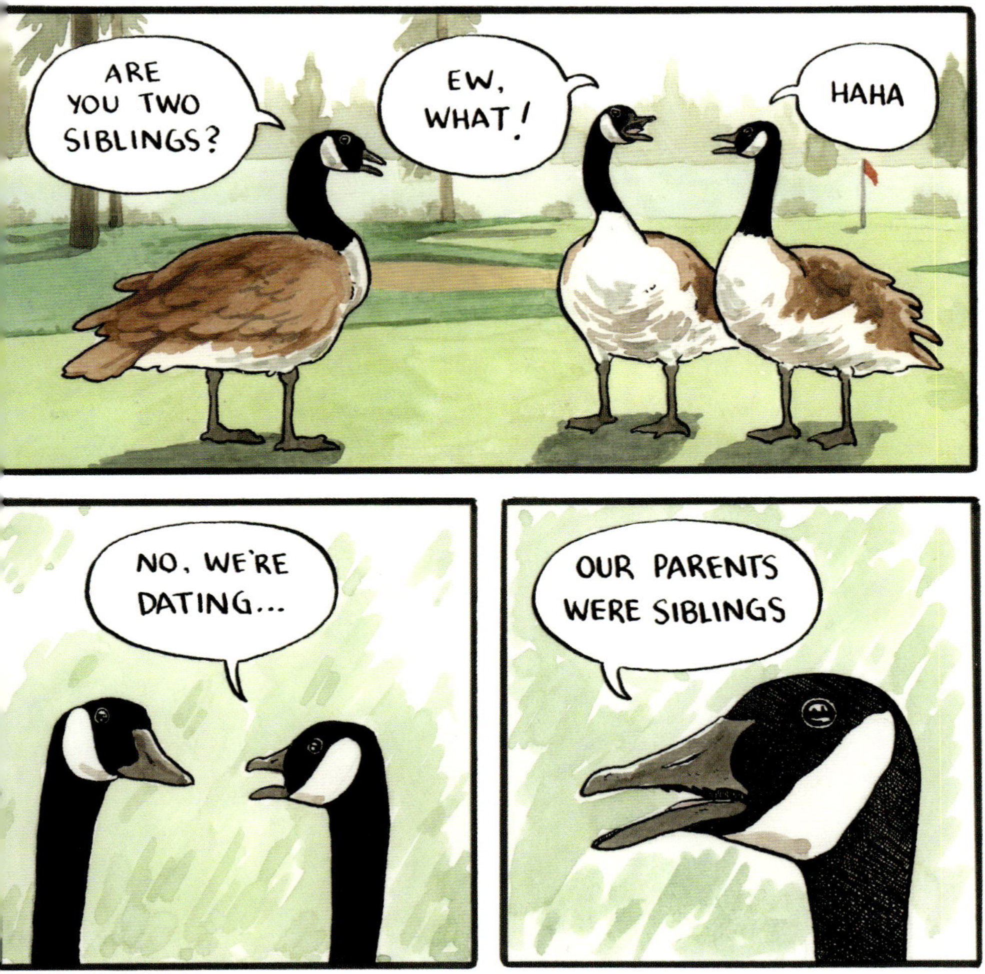
ARE YOU TWO SIBLINGS?
EW, WHAT!
HAHA
NO, WE'RE DATING...
OUR PARENTS WERE SIBLINGS

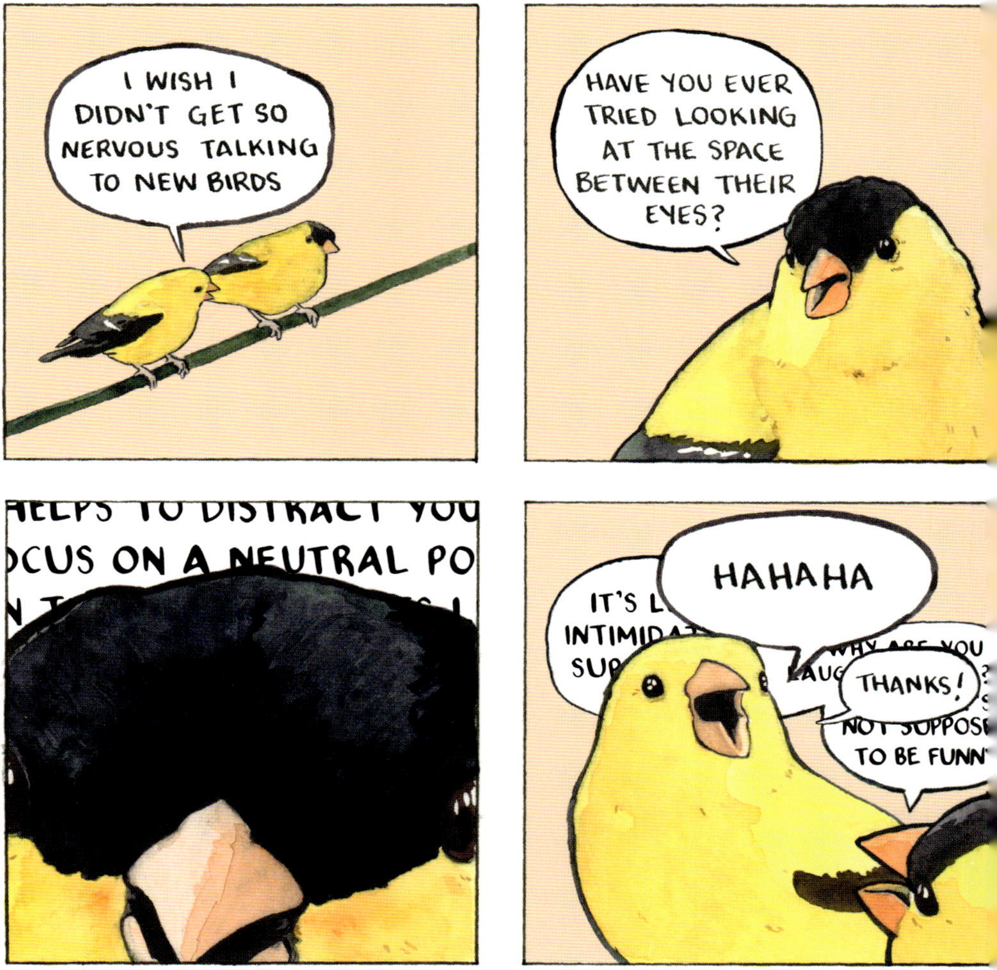
I WISH I DIDN'T GET SO NERVOUS TALKING TO NEW BIRDS
HAVE YOU EVER TRIED LOOKING AT THE SPACE BETWEEN THEIR EYES?
OCUS ON A NEUTRAL PO
IT'S L
INTIMIDA
SUP
HAHAHA
LAUG
THANKS!
NOT SUPPOSE
TO BE FUNN

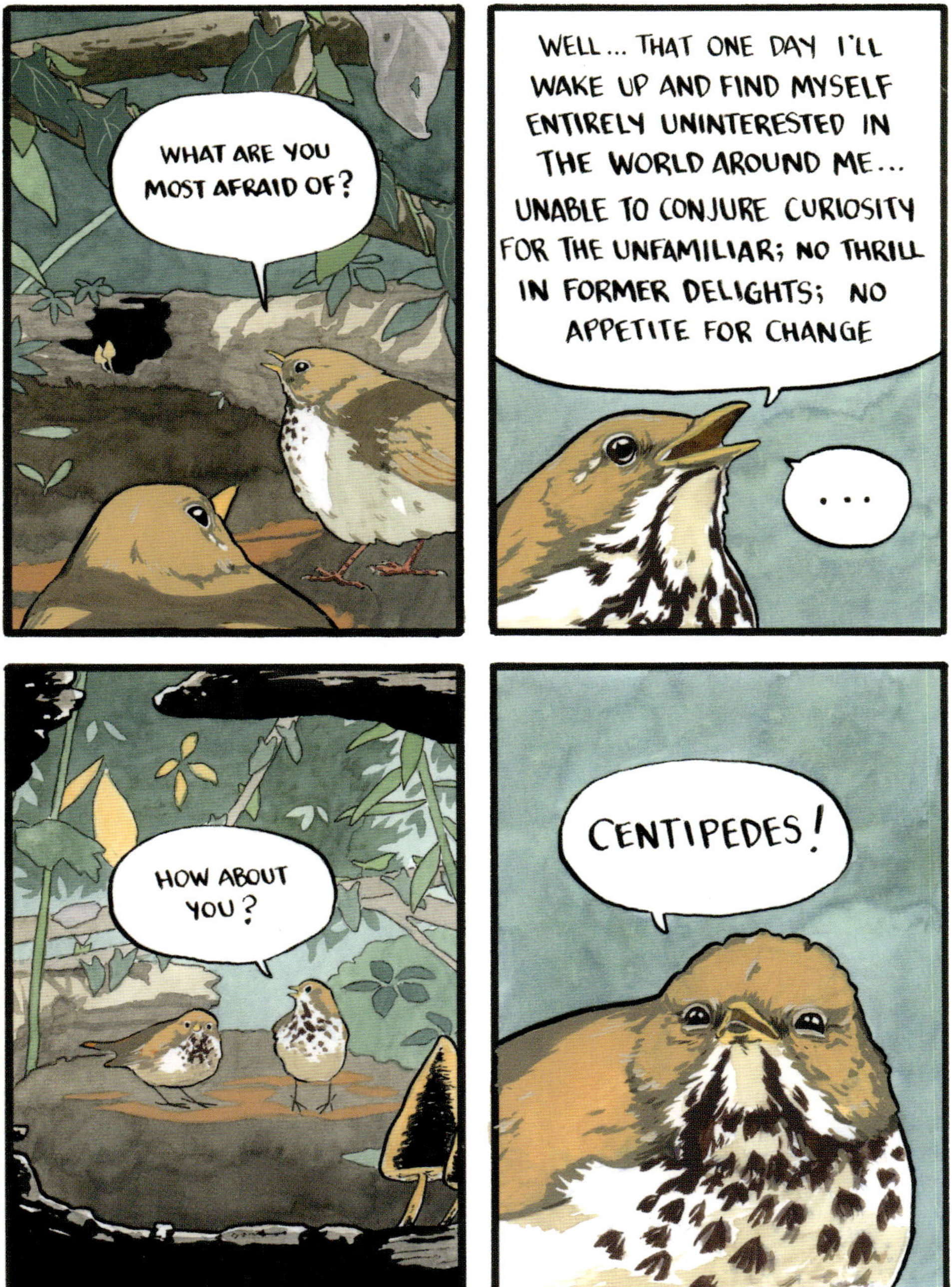
WHAT ARE YOU MOST AFRAID OF?
WELL... THAT ONE DAY I'LL WAKE UP AND FIND MYSELF ENTIRELY UNINTERESTED IN THE WORLD AROUND ME... UNABLE TO CONJURE CURIOSITY FOR THE UNFAMILIAR; NO THRILL IN FORMER DELIGHTS; NO APPETITE FOR CHANGE
...
HOW ABOUT YOU?
CENTIPEDES!

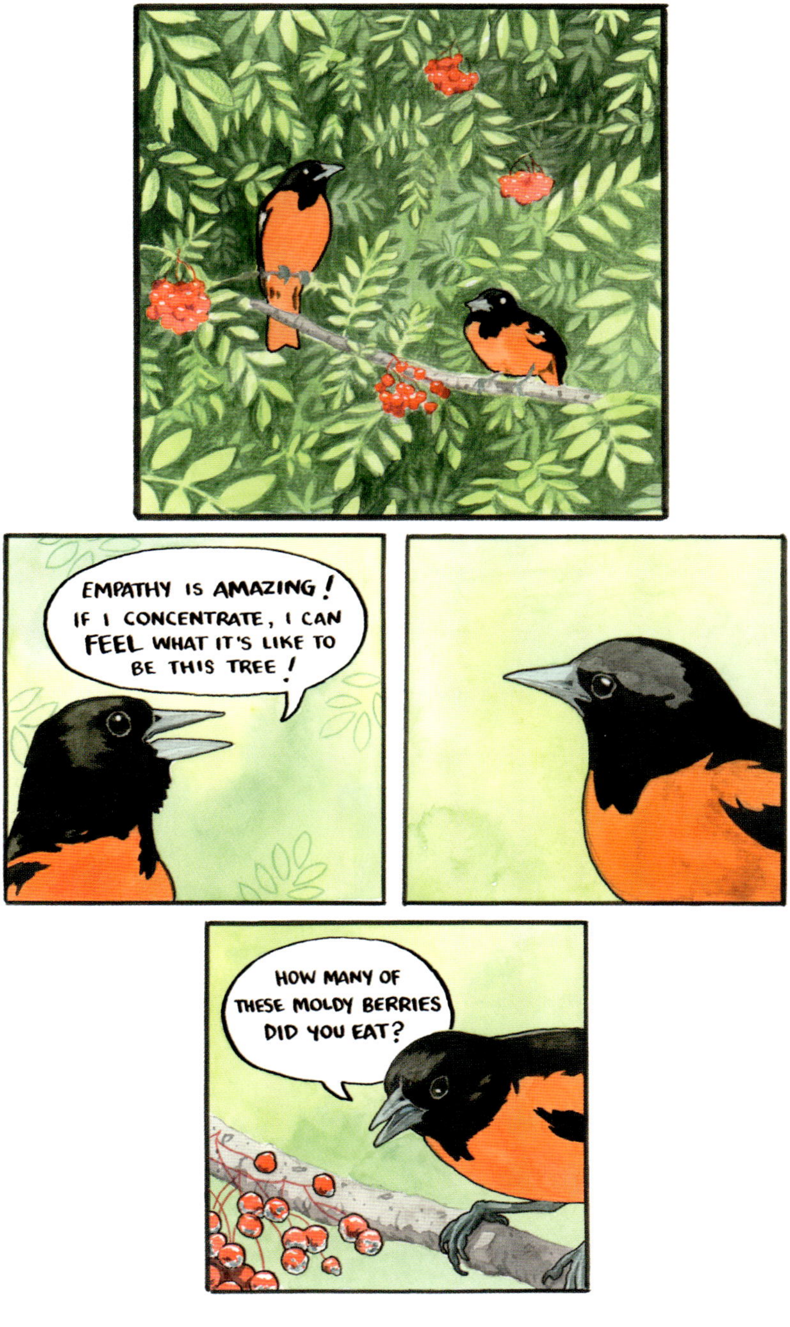
EMPATHY IS AMAZING! IF I CONCENTRATE, I CAN FEEL WHAT IT'S LIKE TO BE THIS TREE!
HOW MANY OF THESE MOLDY BERRIES DID YOU EAT?

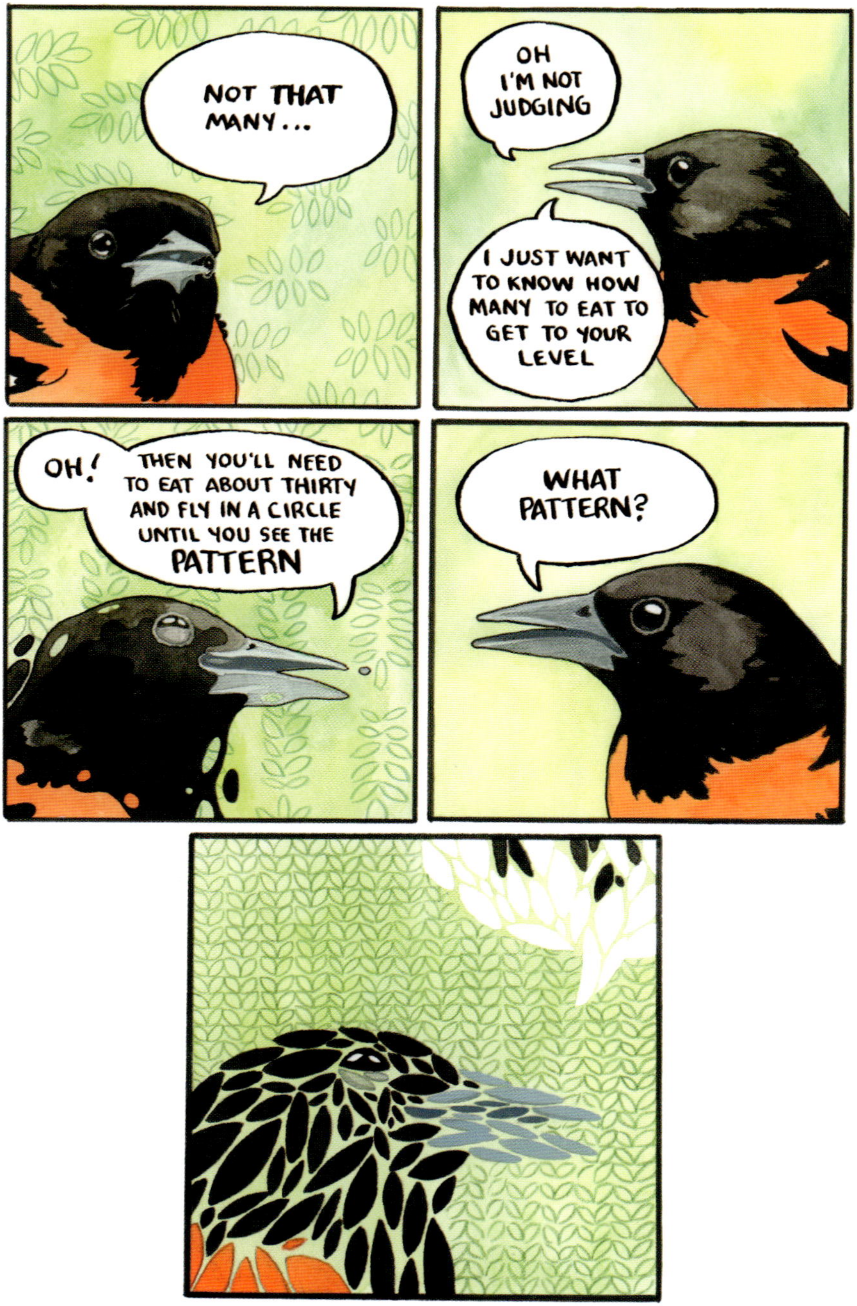
NOT THAT MANY...
OH I'M NOT JUDGING
I JUST WANT TO KNOW HOW MANY TO EAT TO GET TO YOUR LEVEL
OH! THEN YOU'LL NEED TO EAT ABOUT THIRTY AND FLY IN A CIRCLE UNTIL YOU SEE THE PATTERN
WHAT PATTERN?

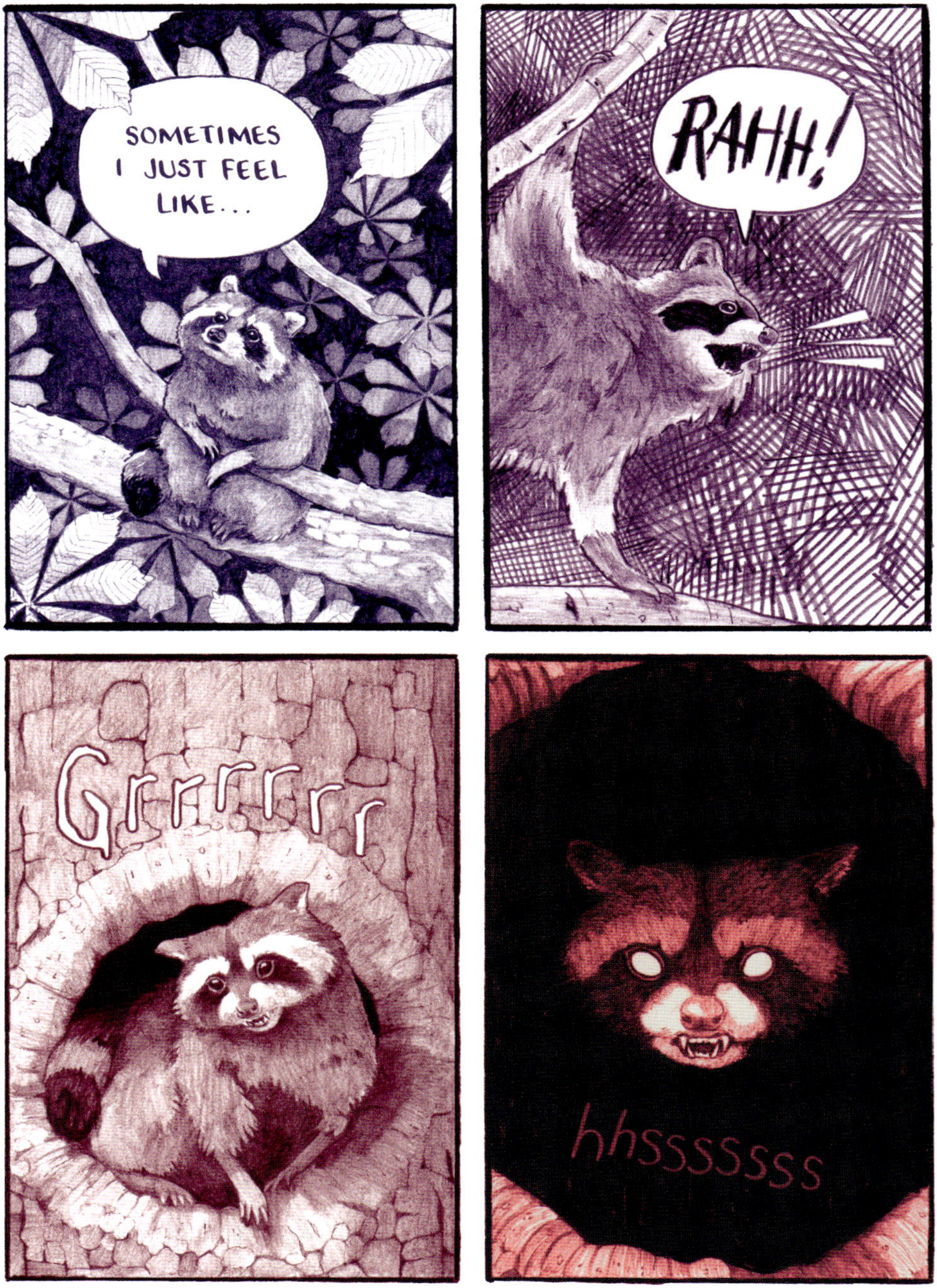
SOMETIMES I JUST FEEL LIKE...
RAHH!
Grrrrrr
hhsssssss

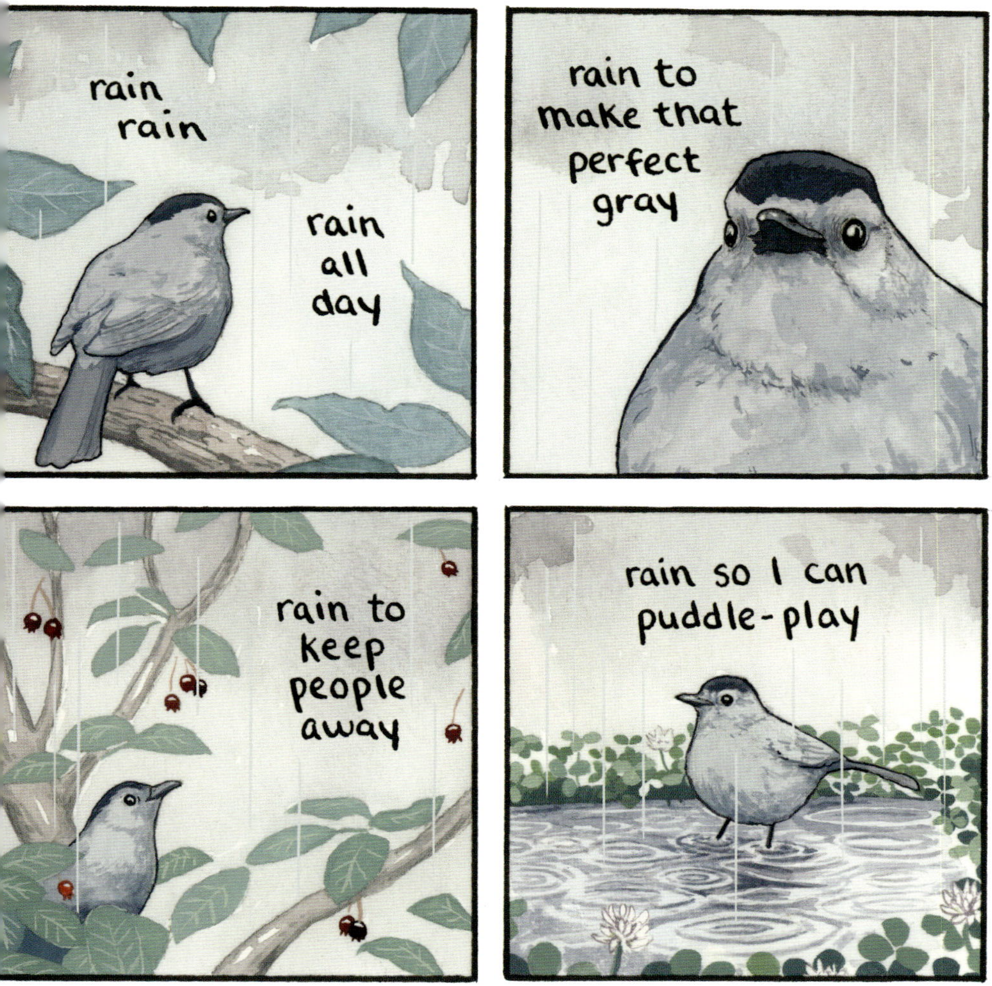
rain
rain
rain
all
day
rain to
make that
perfect
gray
rain to
keep
people
away
rain so I can
puddle-play

you'll regret 100% of the

fries you don't take

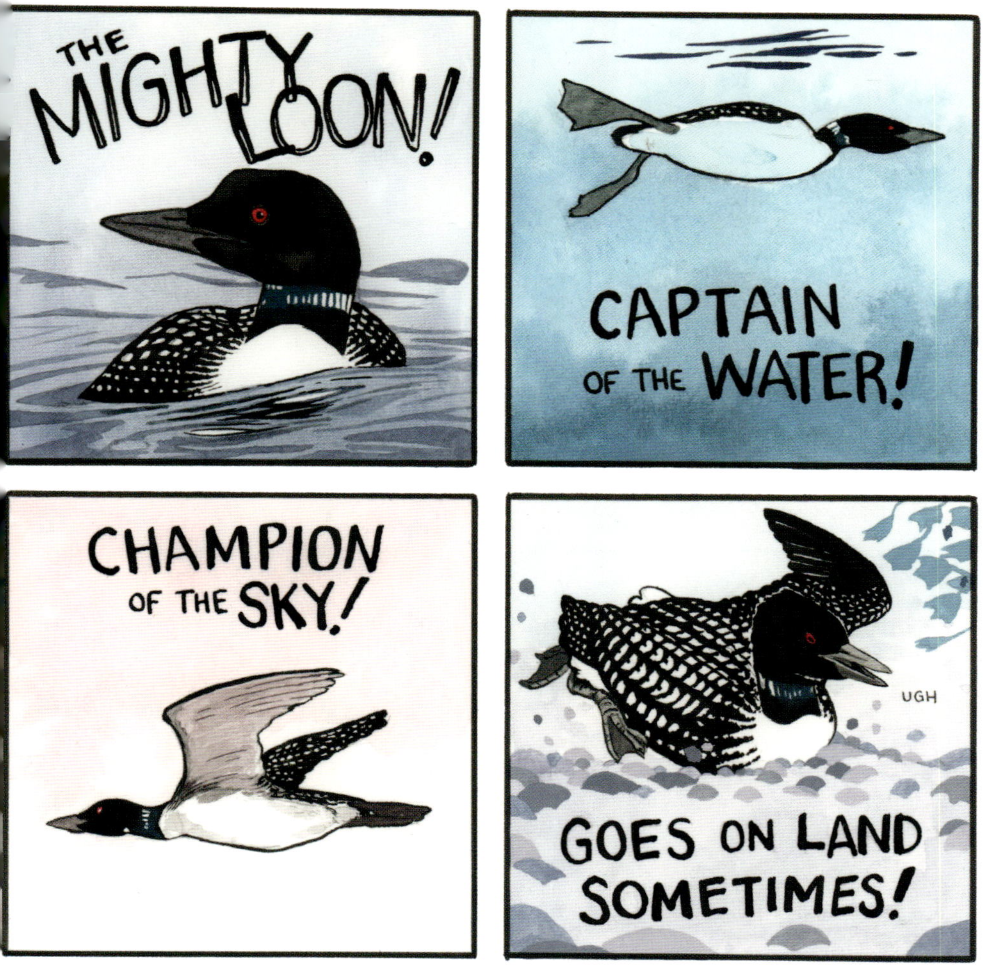
THE MIGHTY LOON!
CAPTAIN OF THE WATER!
CHAMPION OF THE SKY!
GOES ON LAND SOMETIMES!
UGH

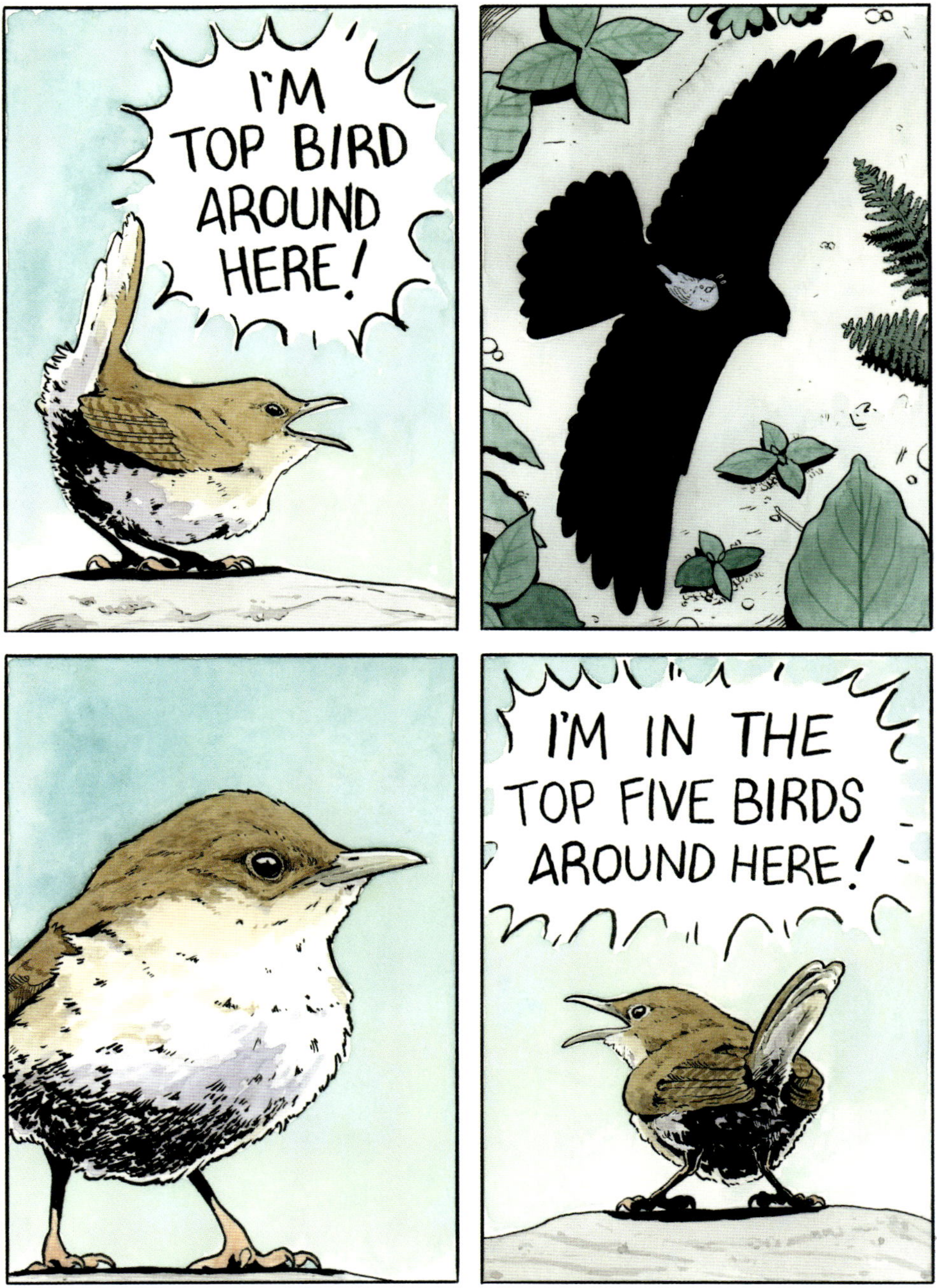
I'M TOP BIRD AROUND HERE!
I'M IN THE TOP FIVE BIRDS AROUND HERE!

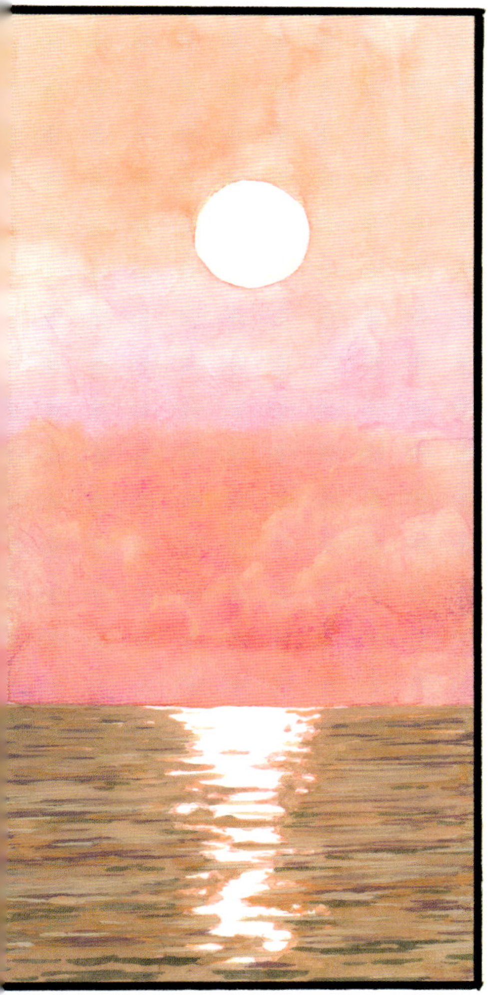
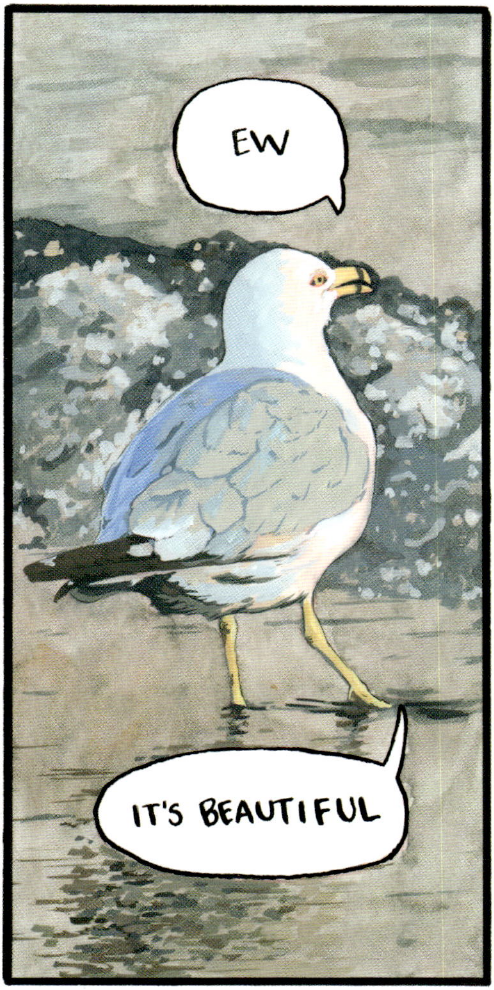
EW
IT'S BEAUTIFUL

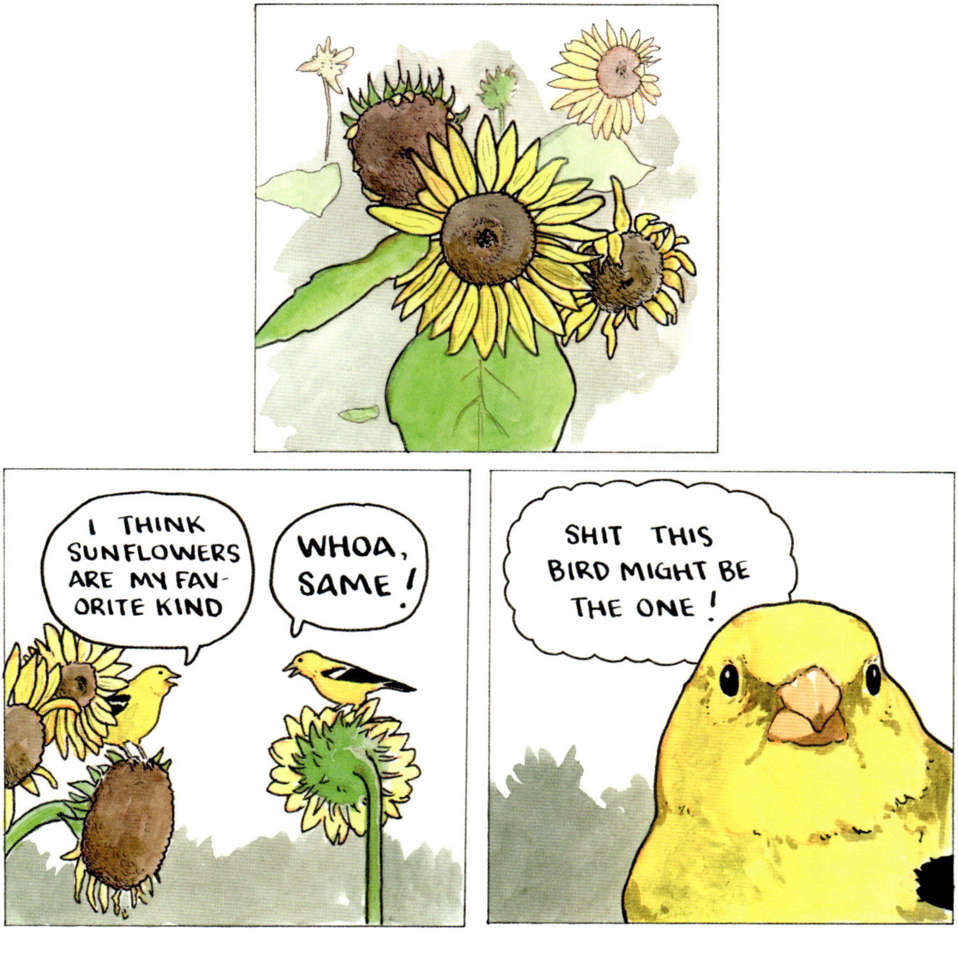
I THINK SUNFLOWERS ARE MY FAV-ORITE KIND
WHOA, SAME!
SHIT THIS BIRD MIGHT BE THE ONE!

BELLY FLOP!!!
HYUH!
GUH!
SPLAT!
DID THAT LOOK COOL?
IT LOOKED LIKE IT HURT...
YEAH
COOL

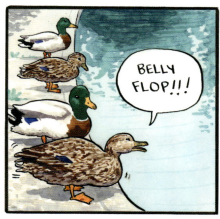

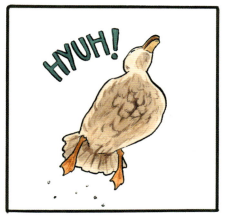

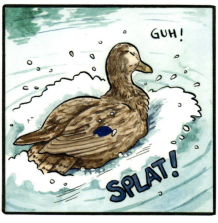

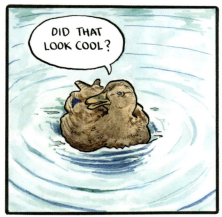

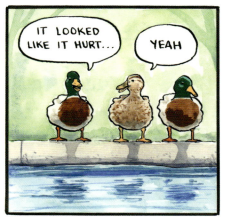

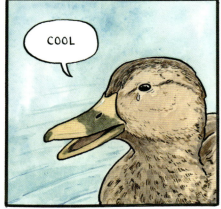

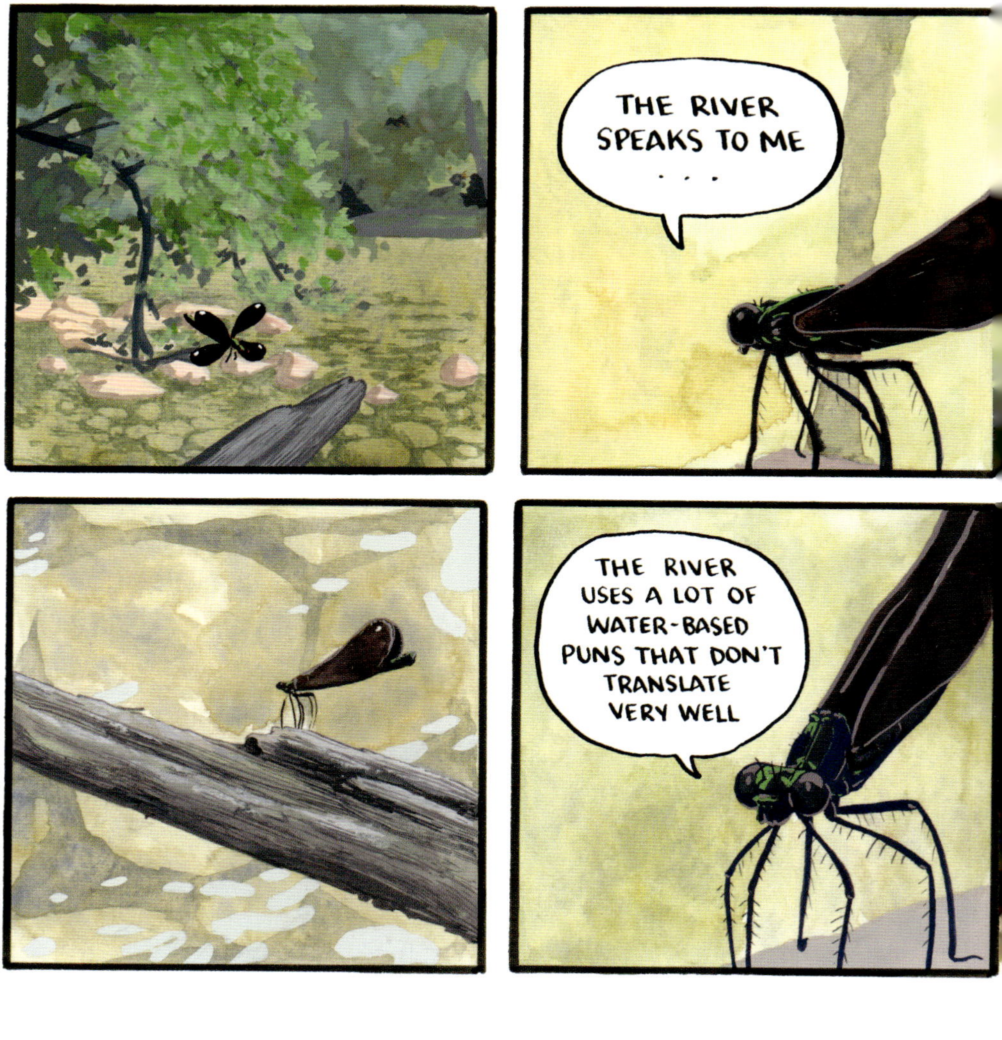
THE RIVER SPEAKS TO ME . . .
THE RIVER USES A LOT OF WATER-BASED PUNS THAT DON'T TRANSLATE VERY WELL

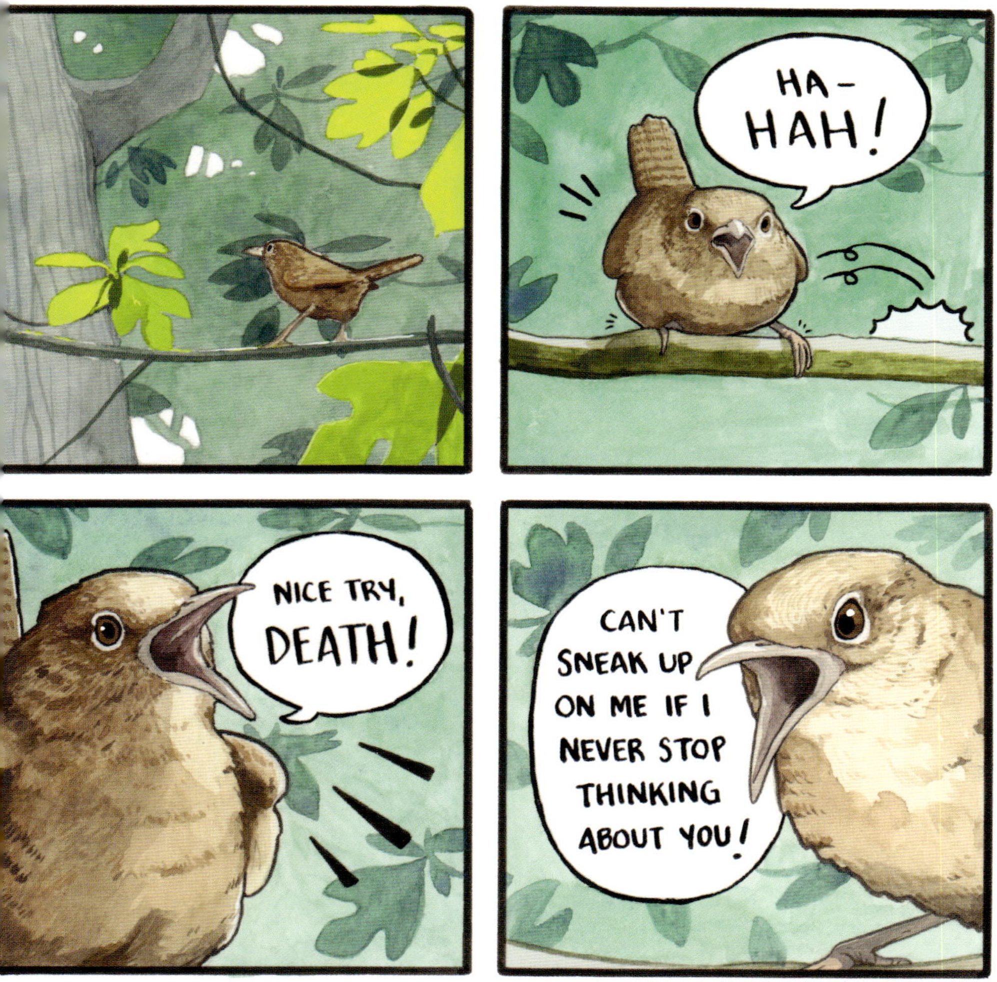
HA-HAH!
NICE TRY, DEATH!
CAN'T SNEAK UP ON ME IF I NEVER STOP THINKING ABOUT YOU!

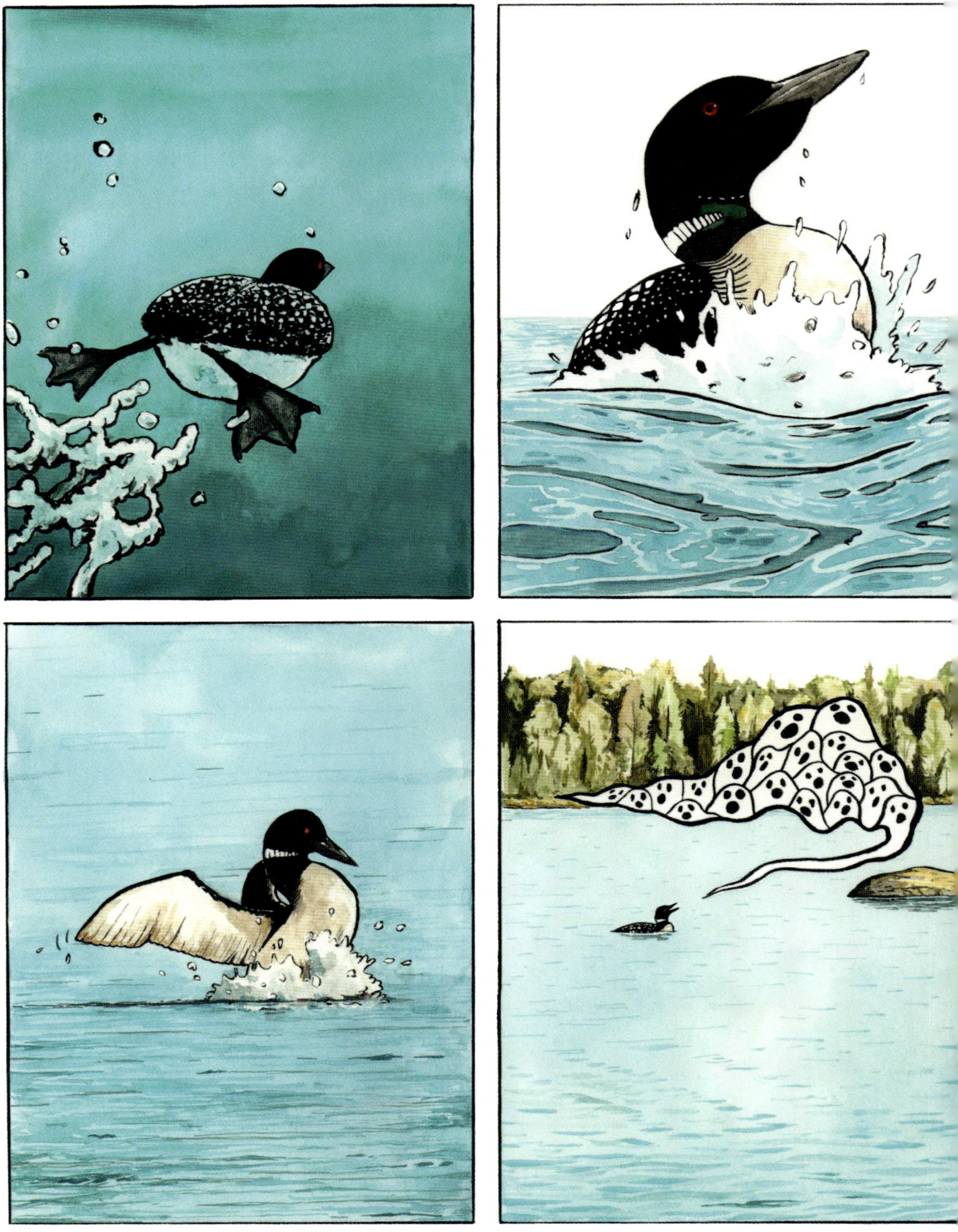

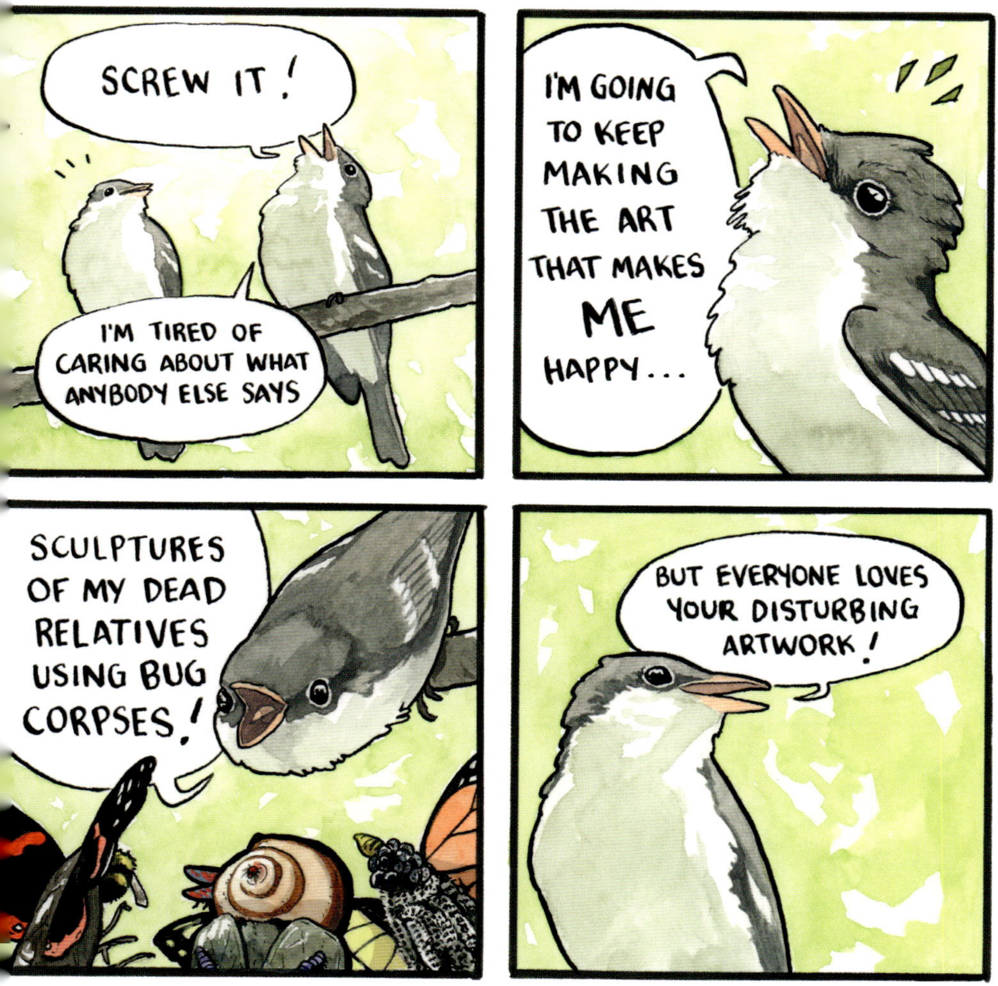
SCREW IT!
I'M TIRED OF CARING ABOUT WHAT ANYBODY ELSE SAYS
I'M GOING TO KEEP MAKING THE ART THAT MAKES ME HAPPY...
SCULPTURES OF MY DEAD RELATIVES USING BUG CORPSES!
BUT EVERYONE LOVES YOUR DISTURBING ARTWORK!

CHARADES

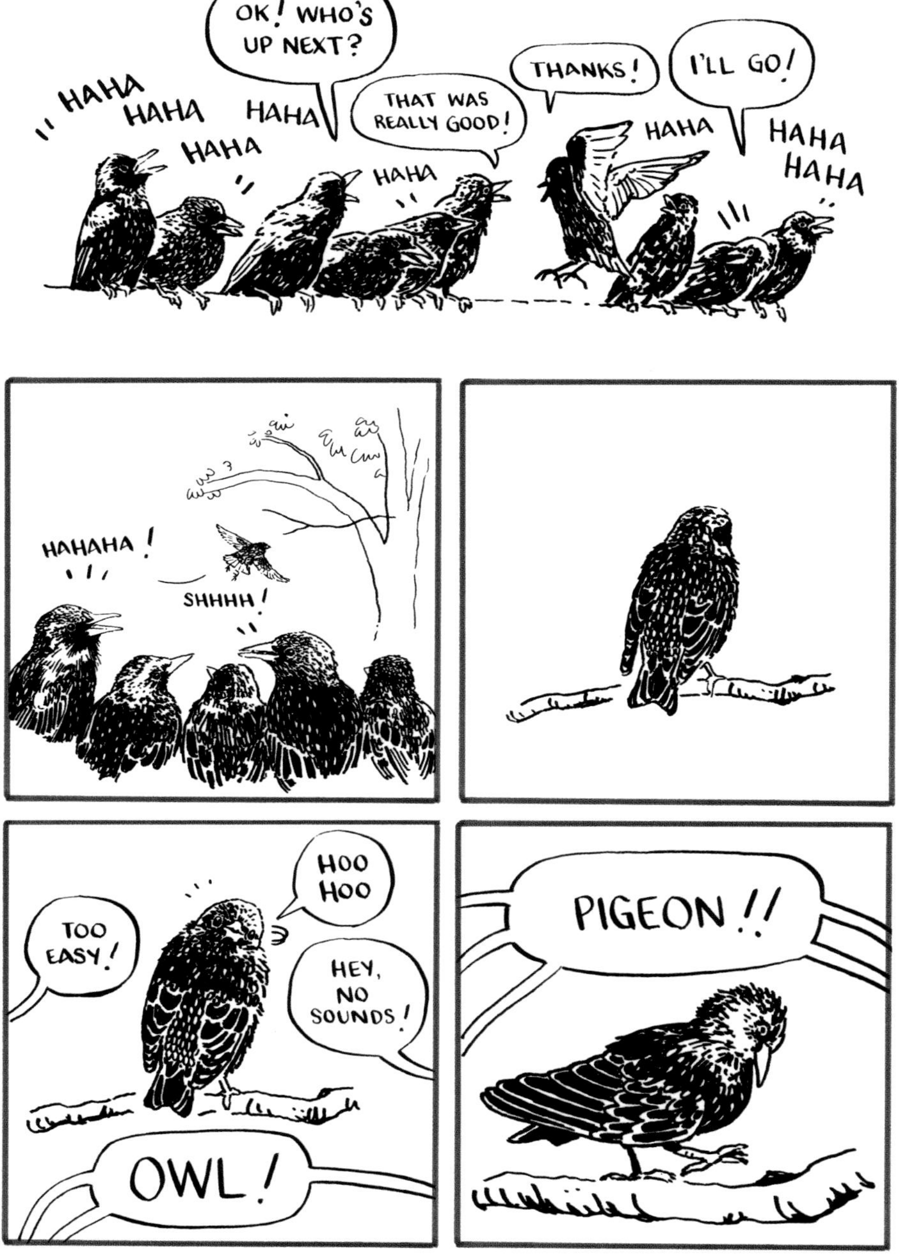
HAHA
HAHA
HAHA
HAHA
OK! WHO'S UP NEXT?
HAHA
THAT WAS REALLY GOOD!
THANKS!
HAHA
I'LL GO!
HAHA HAHA
HAHAHA!
SHHHH!
HOO HOO
TOO EASY!
HEY, NO SOUNDS!
OWL!
PIGEON!!

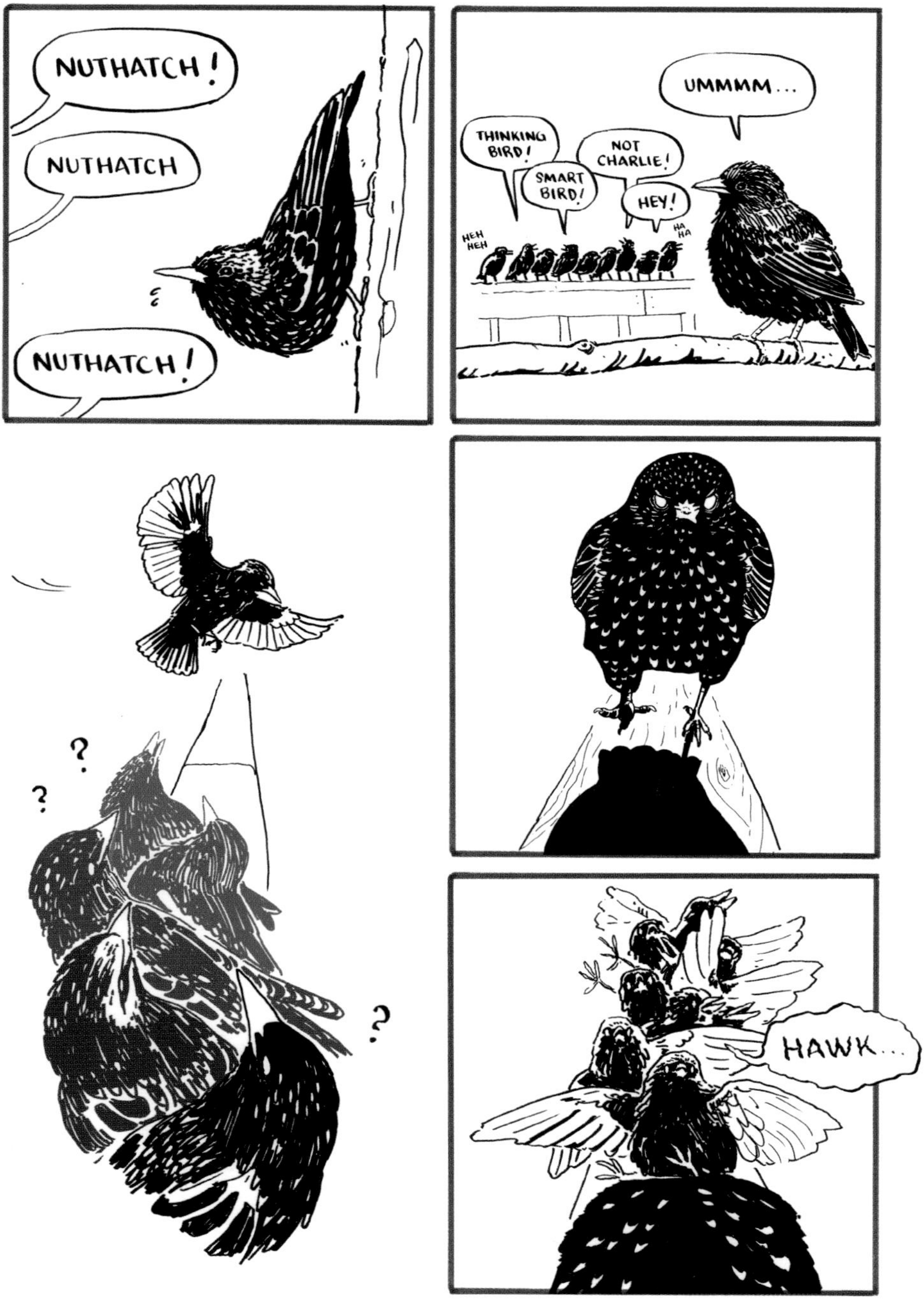
NUTHATCH!
NUTHATCH
NUTHATCH!
UMMMM...
THINKING BIRD!
SMART BIRD!
NOT CHARLIE!
HEY!
HEH HEH
HA HA
?
?
?
HAWK...

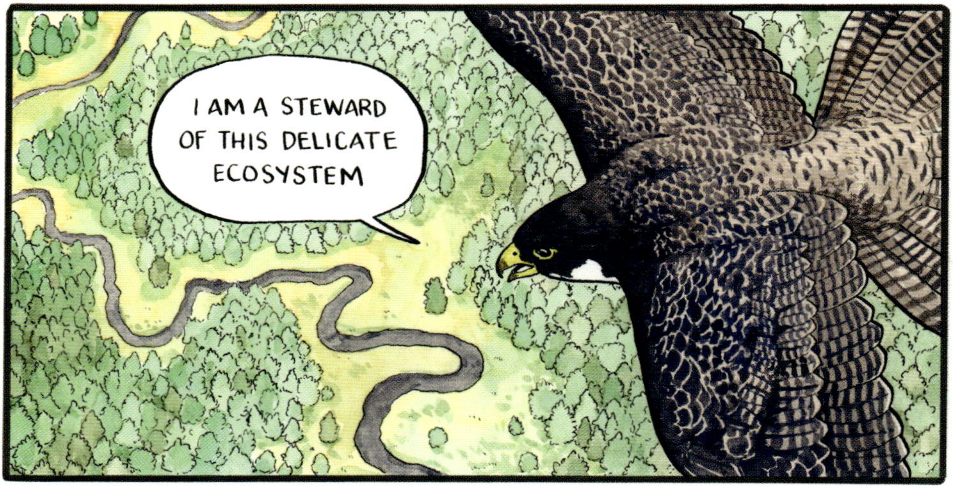
I AM A STEWARD OF THIS DELICATE ECOSYSTEM

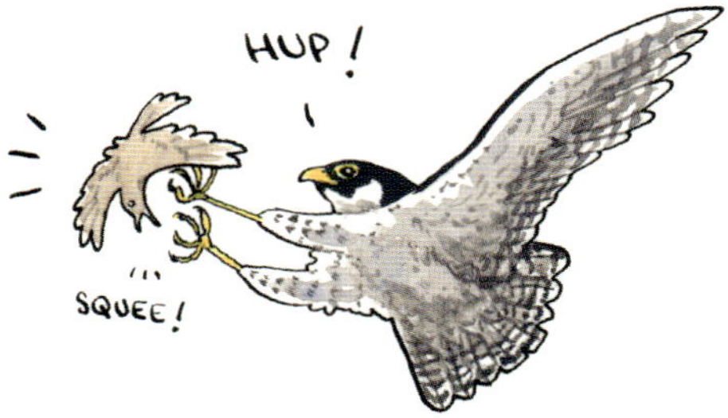
HUP!
SQUEE!

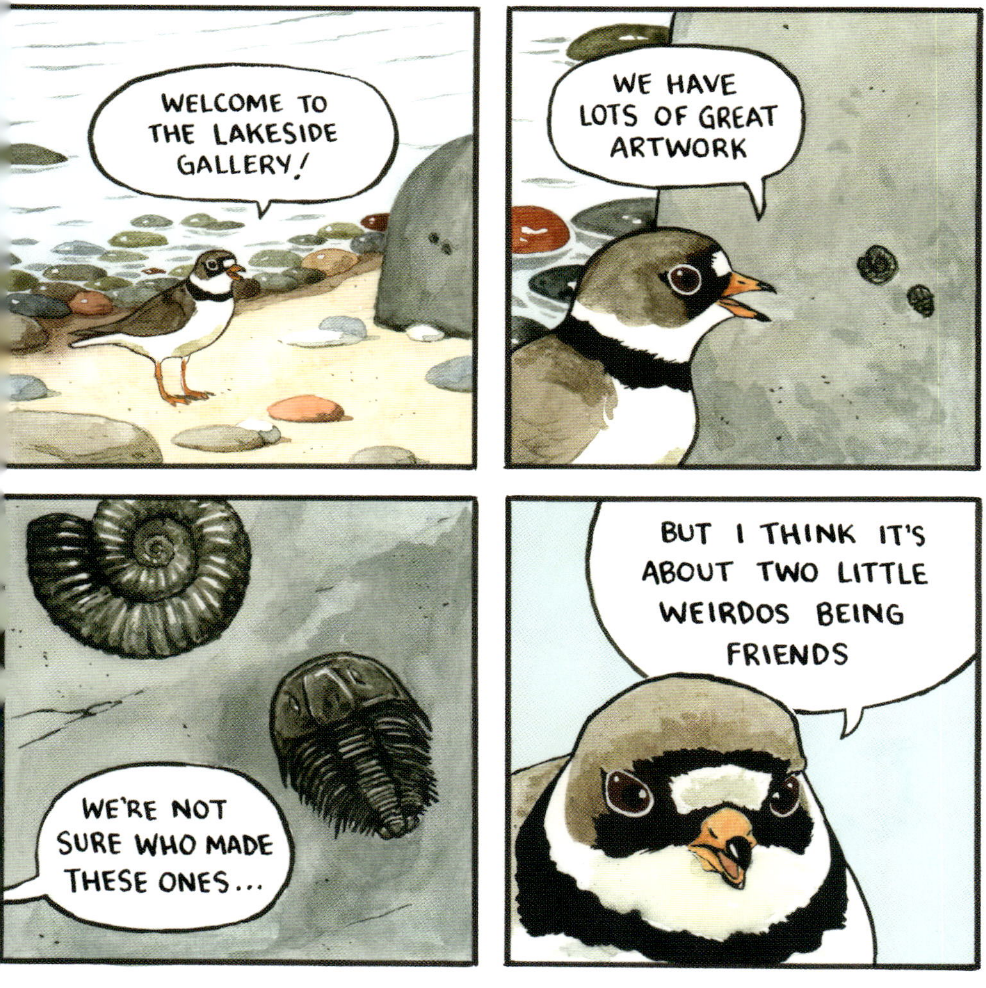
WELCOME TO THE LAKESIDE GALLERY!
WE HAVE LOTS OF GREAT ARTWORK
WE'RE NOT SURE WHO MADE THESE ONES...
BUT I THINK IT'S ABOUT TWO LITTLE WEIRDOS BEING FRIENDS

Fall

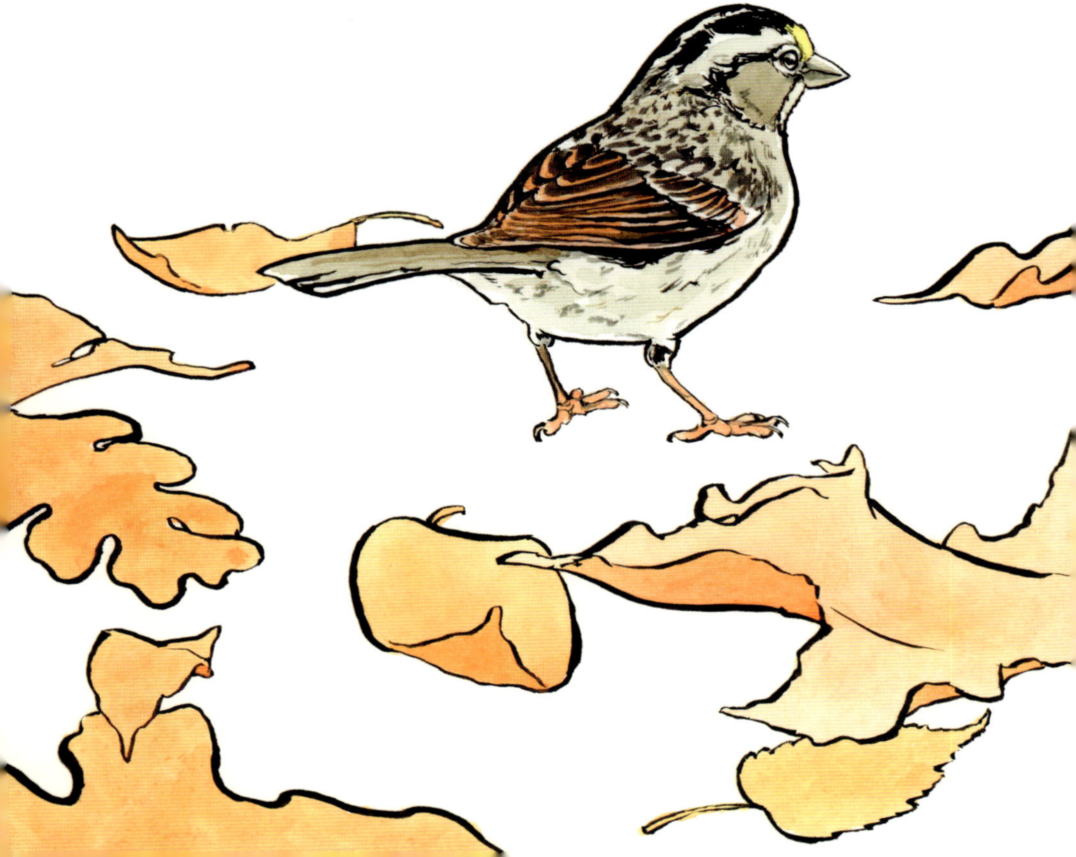

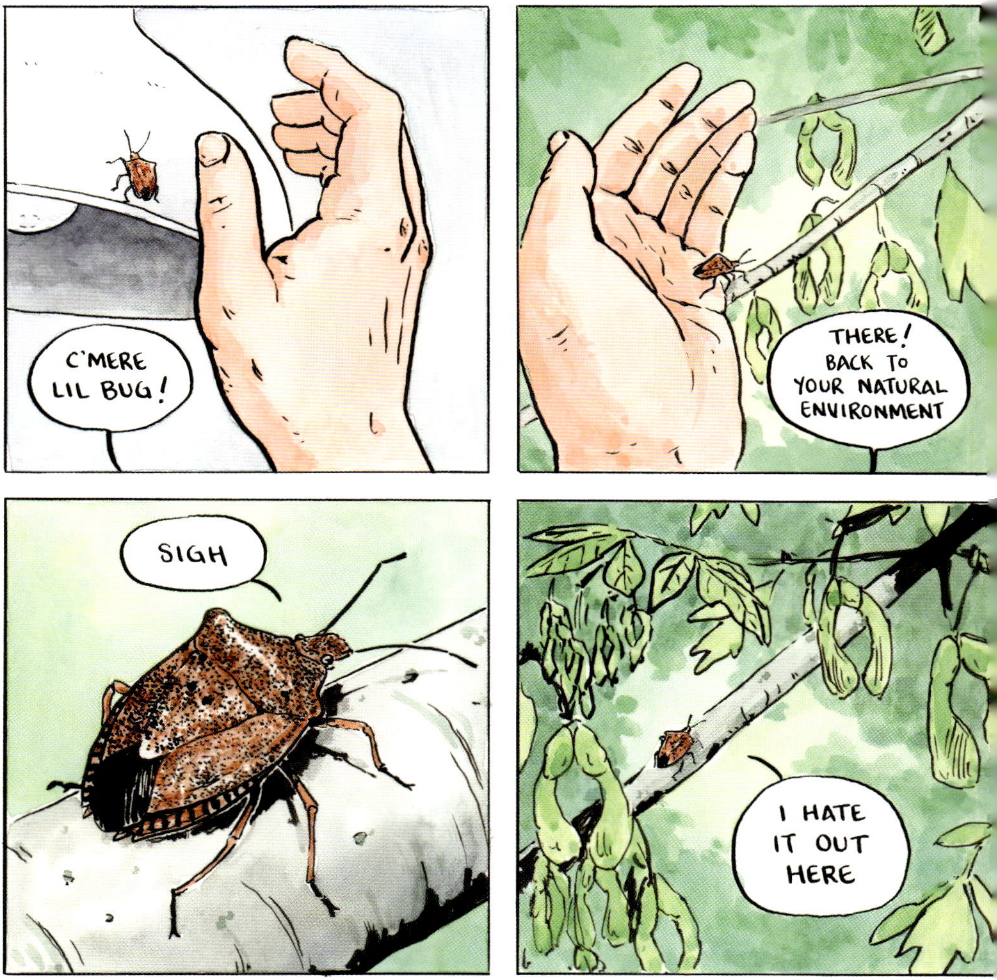
C'MERE LIL BUG!
THERE! BACK TO YOUR NATURAL ENVIRONMENT
SIGH
I HATE IT OUT HERE

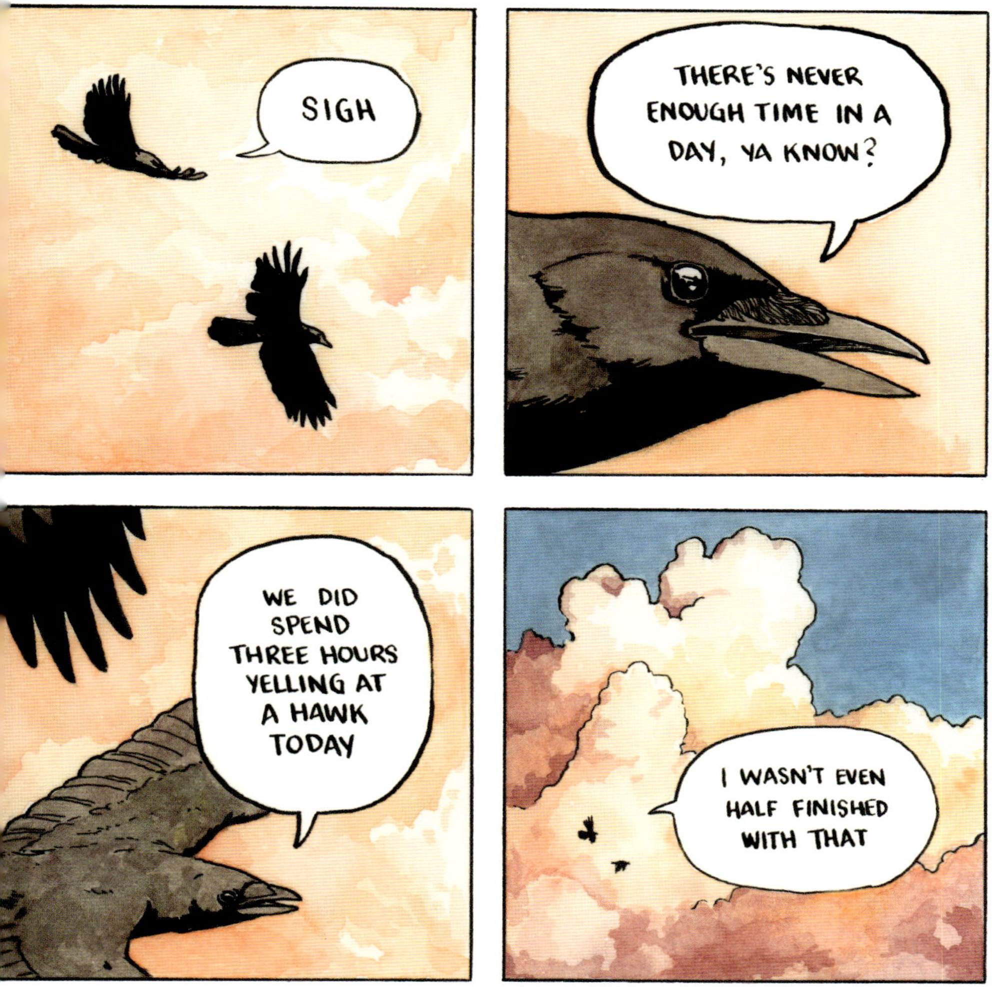
SIGH
THERE'S NEVER ENOUGH TIME IN A DAY, YA KNOW?
WE DID SPEND THREE HOURS YELLING AT A HAWK TODAY
I WASN'T EVEN HALF FINISHED WITH THAT

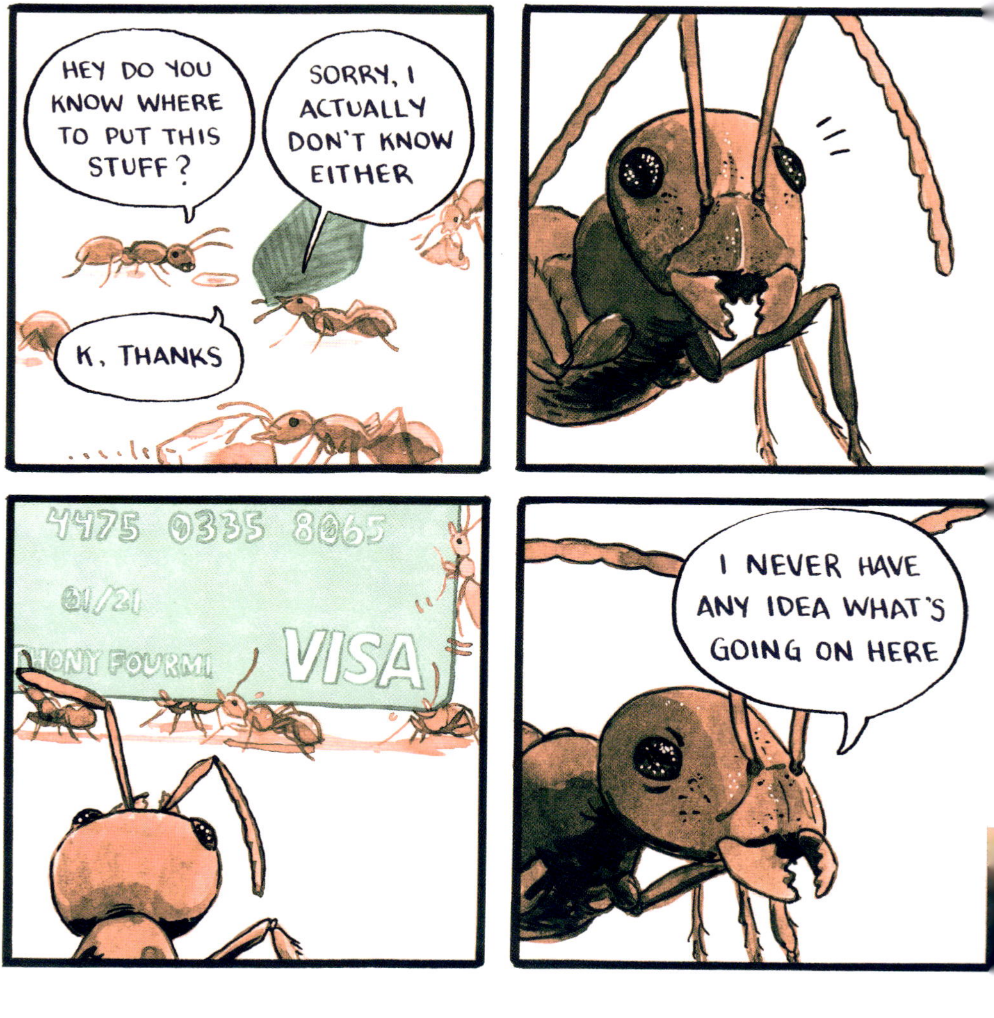
HEY DO YOU KNOW WHERE TO PUT THIS STUFF?
SORRY, I ACTUALLY DON'T KNOW EITHER
K, THANKS
4475 0335 8065
01/21
HONY FOURMI
VISA
I NEVER HAVE ANY IDEA WHAT'S GOING ON HERE

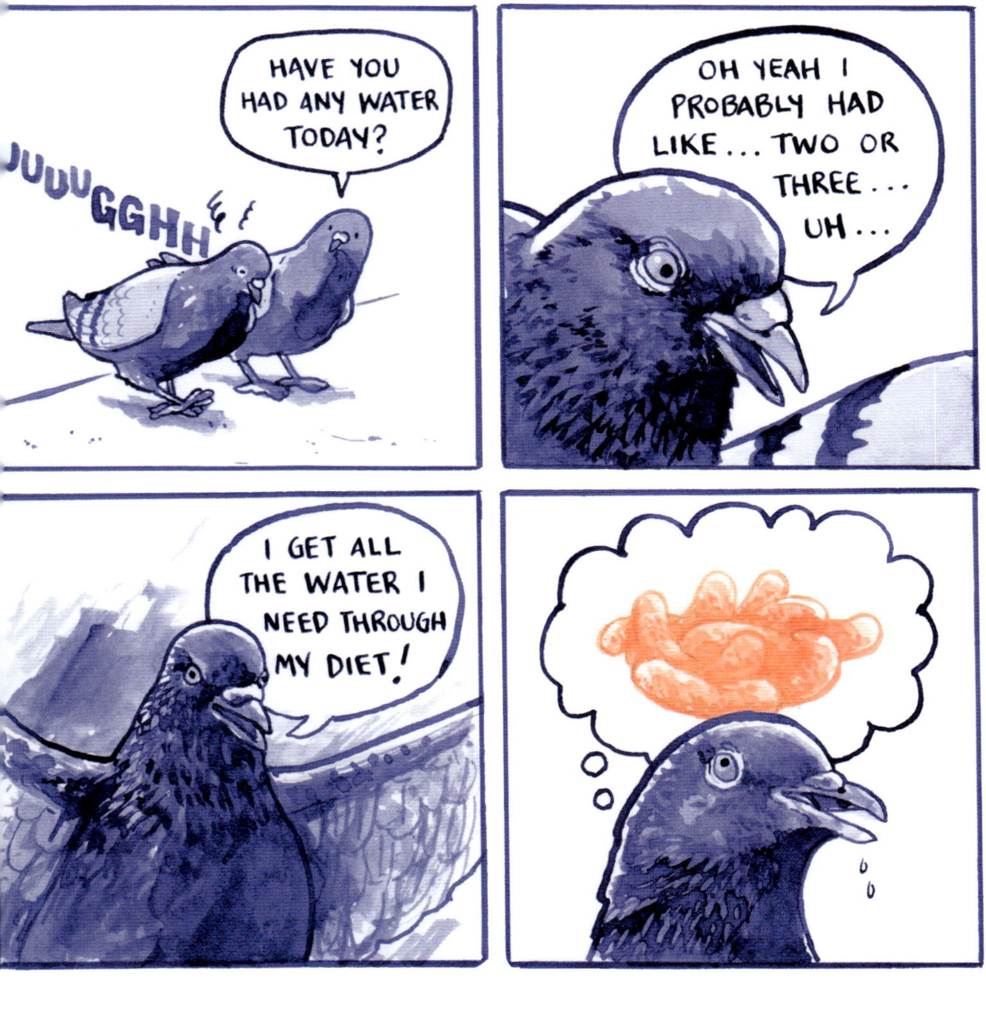
HAVE YOU HAD ANY WATER TODAY?
UUUUGGHH
OH YEAH I PROBABLY HAD LIKE... TWO OR THREE... UH...
I GET ALL THE WATER I NEED THROUGH MY DIET!

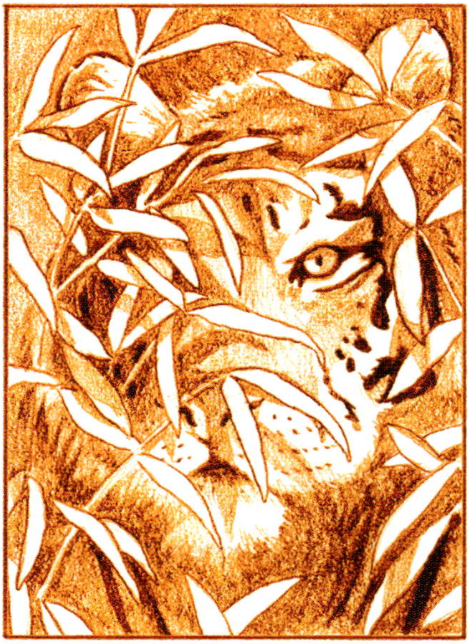

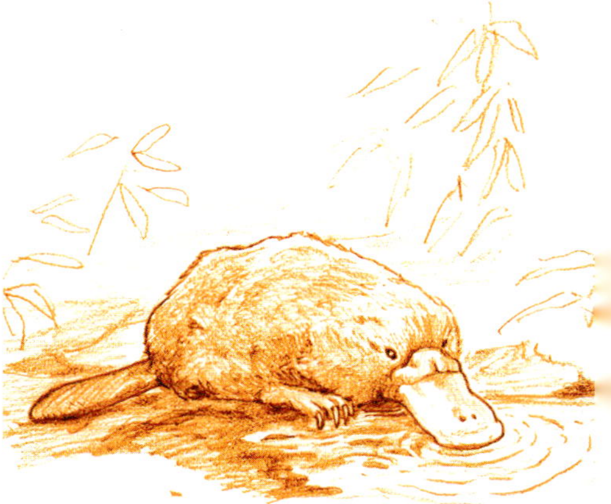

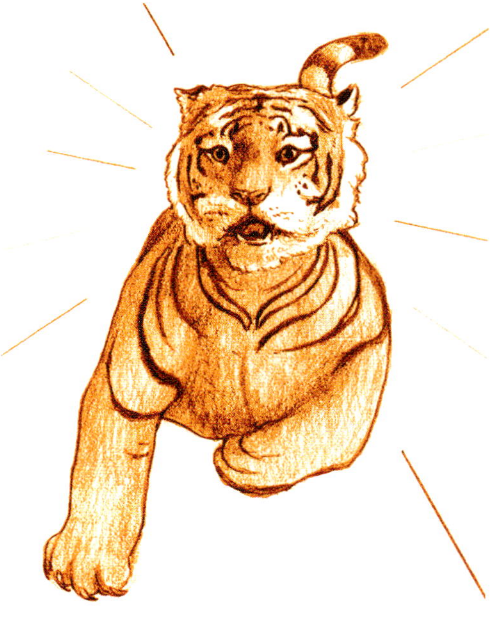

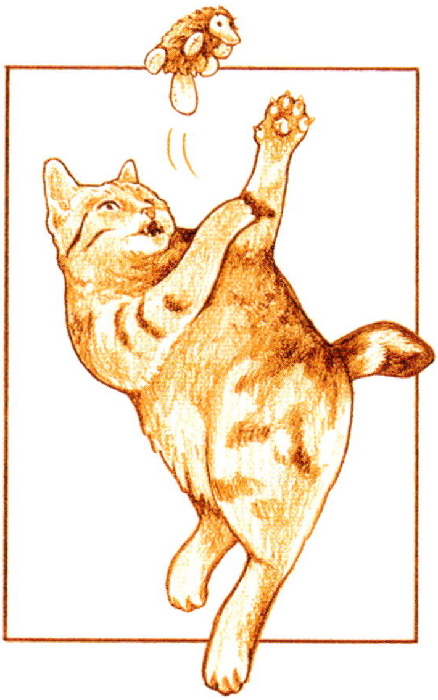

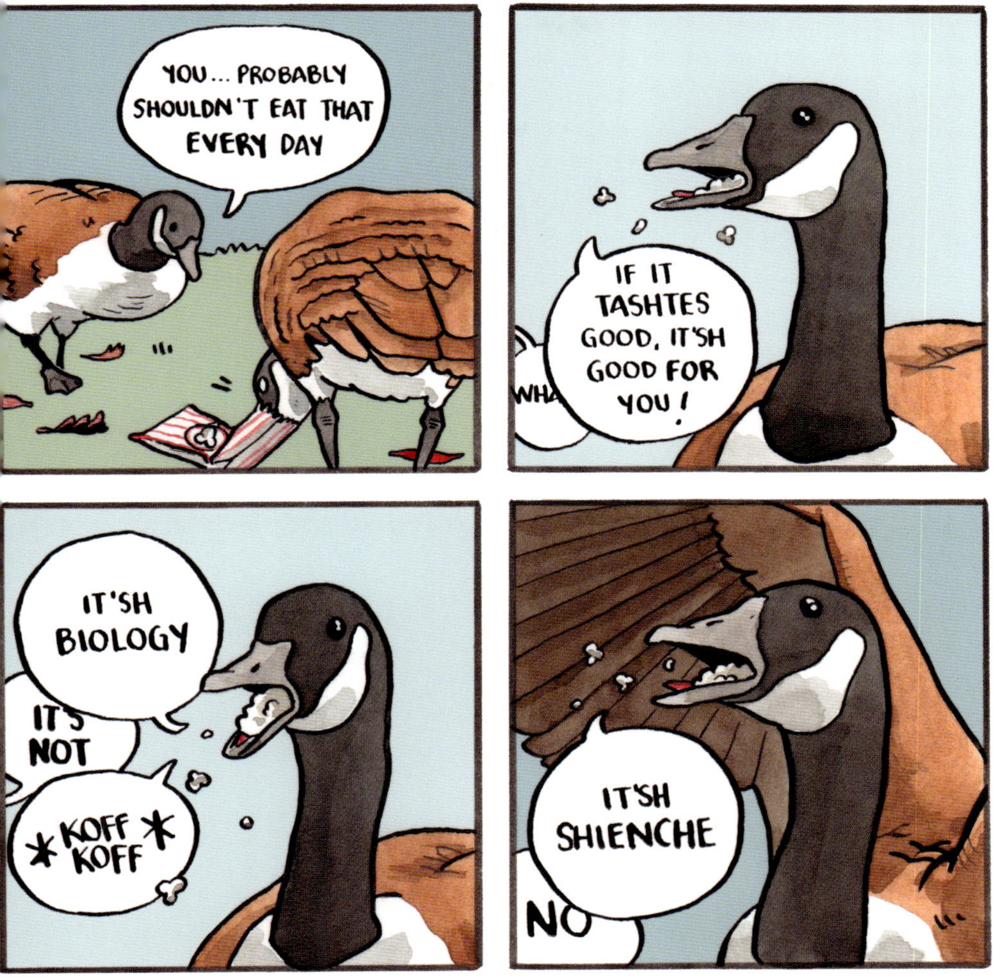
YOU... PROBABLY SHOULDN'T EAT THAT EVERY DAY
IF IT TASHTES GOOD, IT'SH GOOD FOR YOU!
WHA
IT'SH BIOLOGY
IT'S NOT
KOFF KOFF
IT'SH SHIENCHE
NO

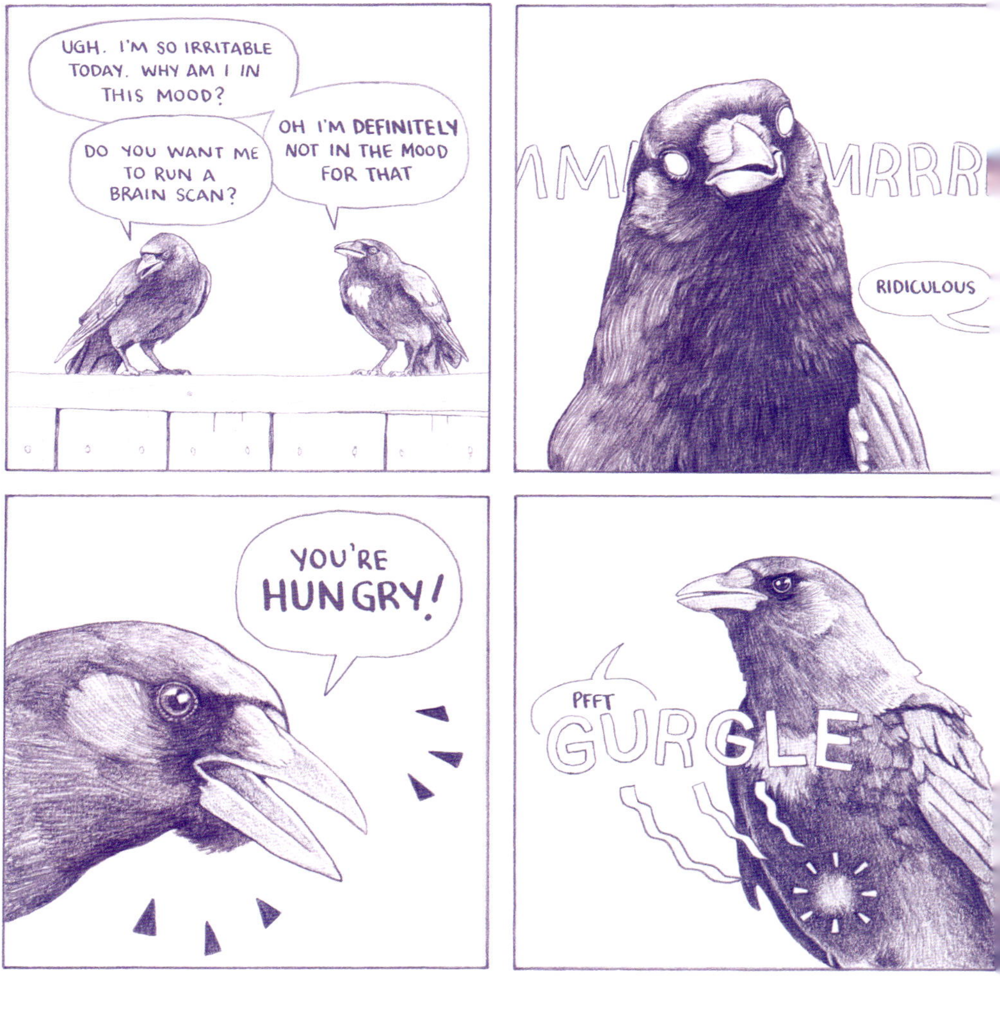
UGH. I'M SO IRRITABLE TODAY. WHY AM I IN THIS MOOD?
DO YOU WANT ME TO RUN A BRAIN SCAN?
OH I'M DEFINITELY NOT IN THE MOOD FOR THAT
MRRRR
RIDICULOUS
YOU'RE HUNGRY!
PFFT
GURGLE

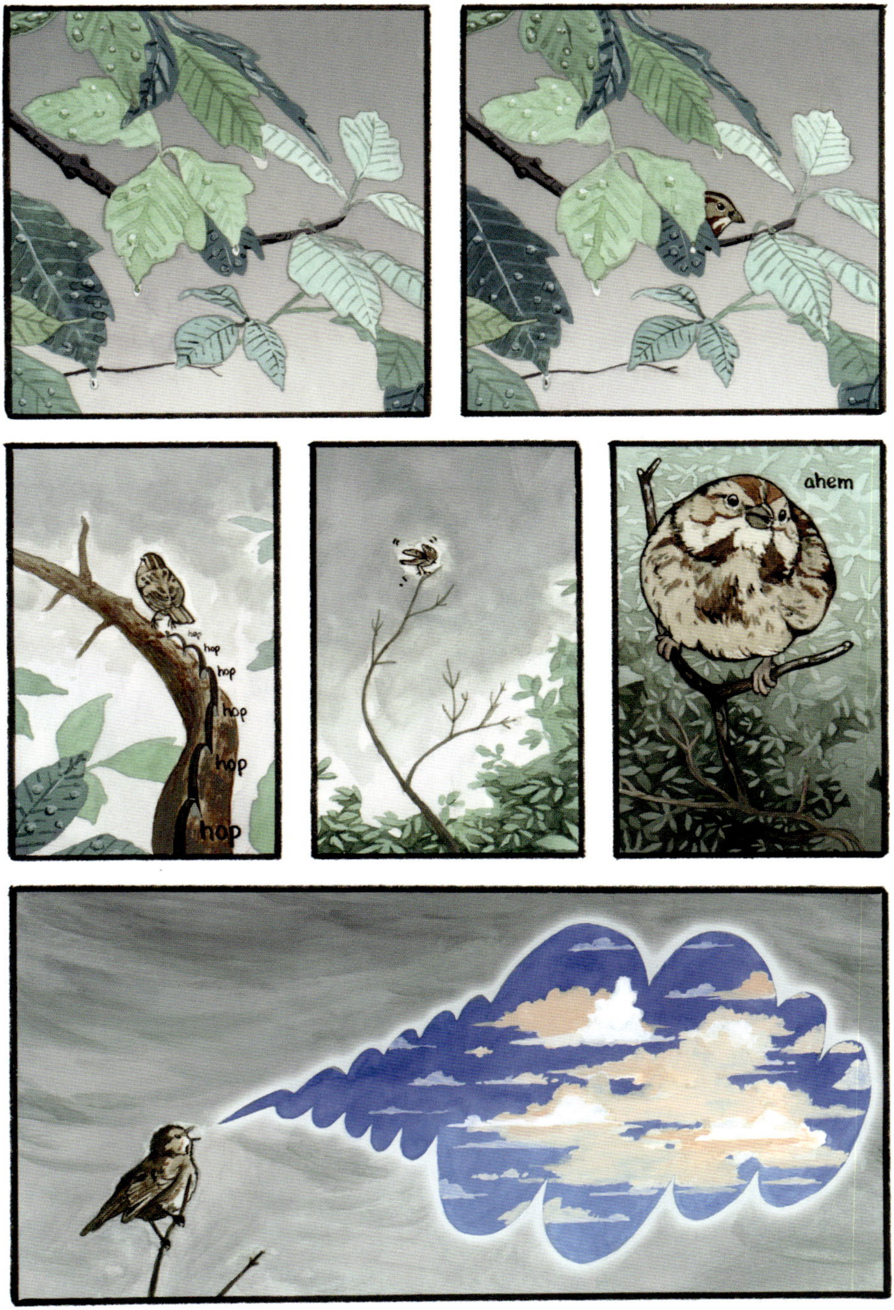
hop
hop
hop
hop
hop
hop
ahem

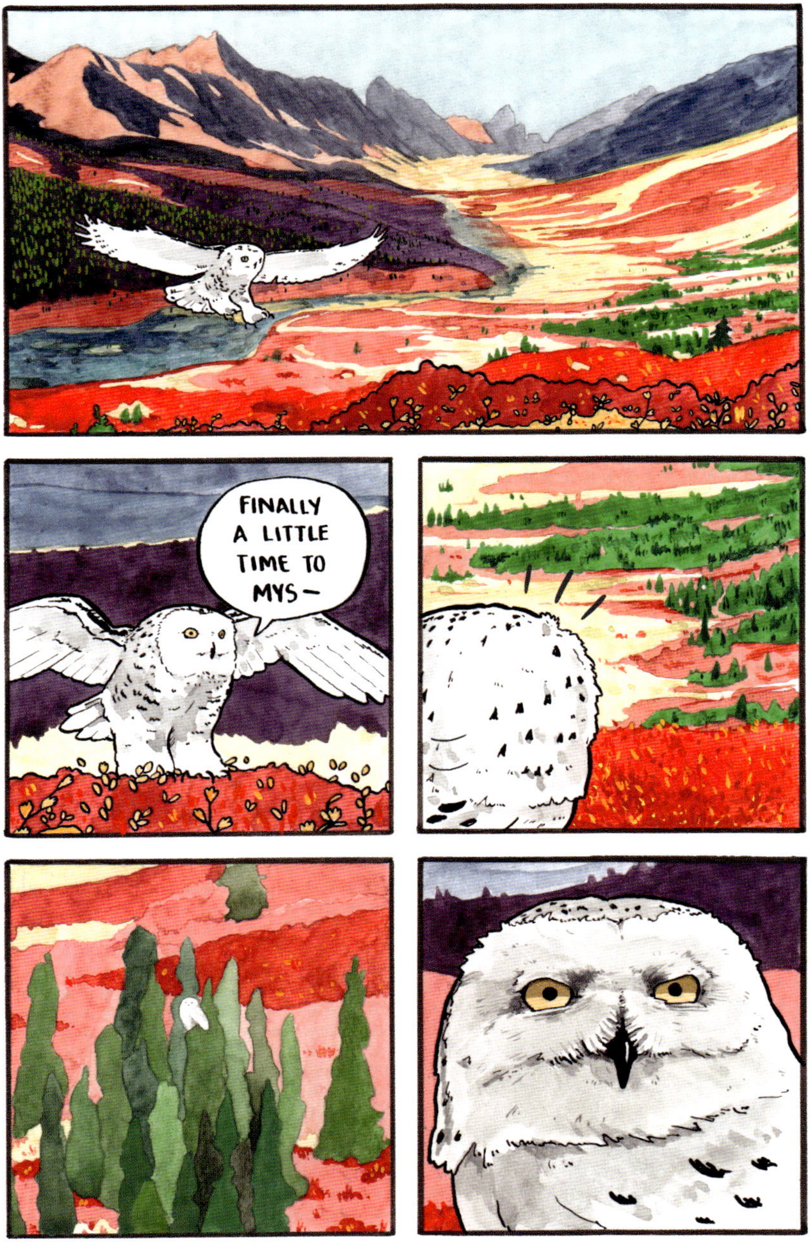
FINALLY A LITTLE TIME TO MYS—

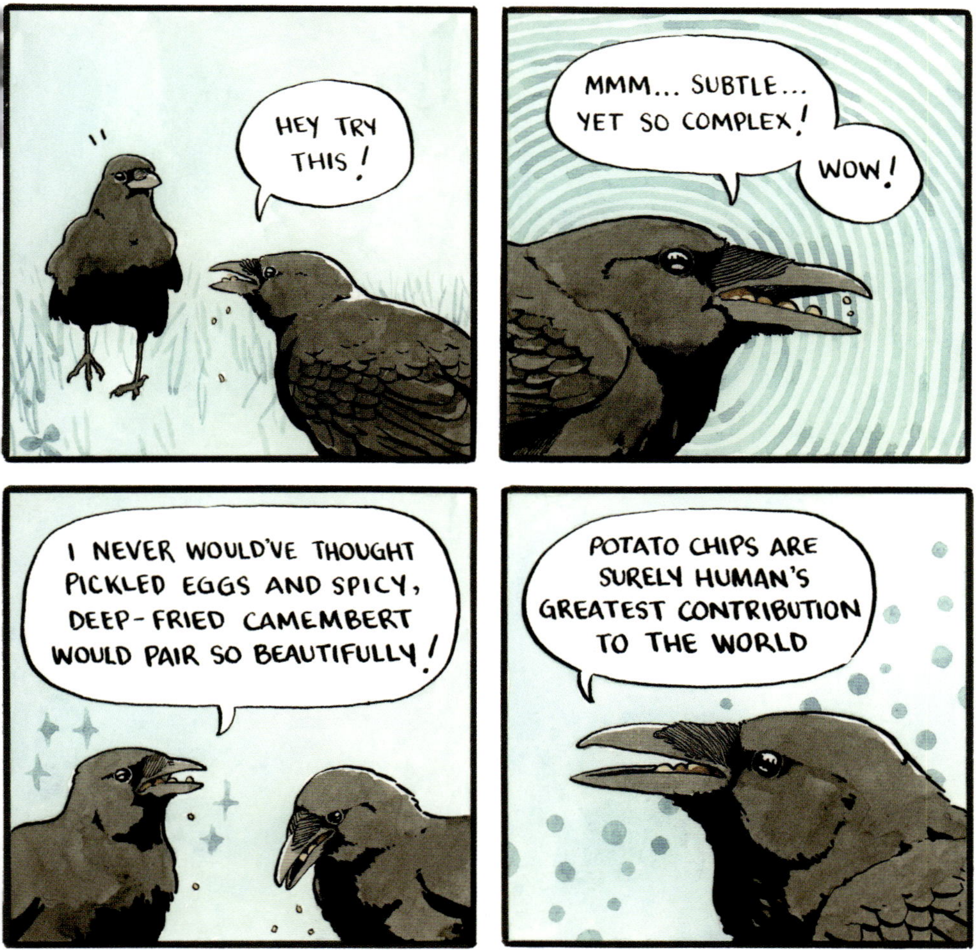
HEY TRY THIS!
MMM... SUBTLE... YET SO COMPLEX!
WOW!
I NEVER WOULD'VE THOUGHT PICKLED EGGS AND SPICY, DEEP-FRIED CAMEMBERT WOULD PAIR SO BEAUTIFULLY!
POTATO CHIPS ARE SURELY HUMAN'S GREATEST CONTRIBUTION TO THE WORLD

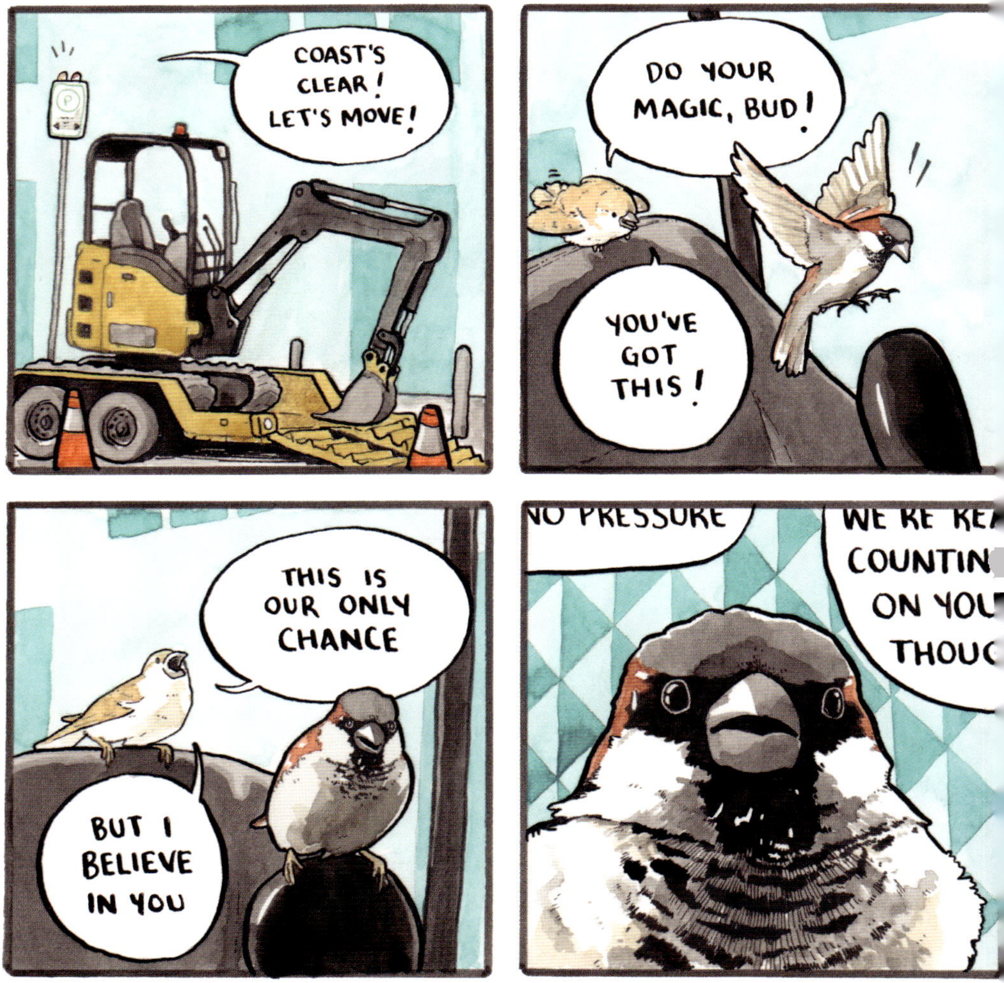
COAST'S CLEAR! LET'S MOVE!
DO YOUR MAGIC, BUD!
YOU'VE GOT THIS!
THIS IS OUR ONLY CHANCE
BUT I BELIEVE IN YOU
NO PRESSURE
COUNTIN ON YOU THOUG

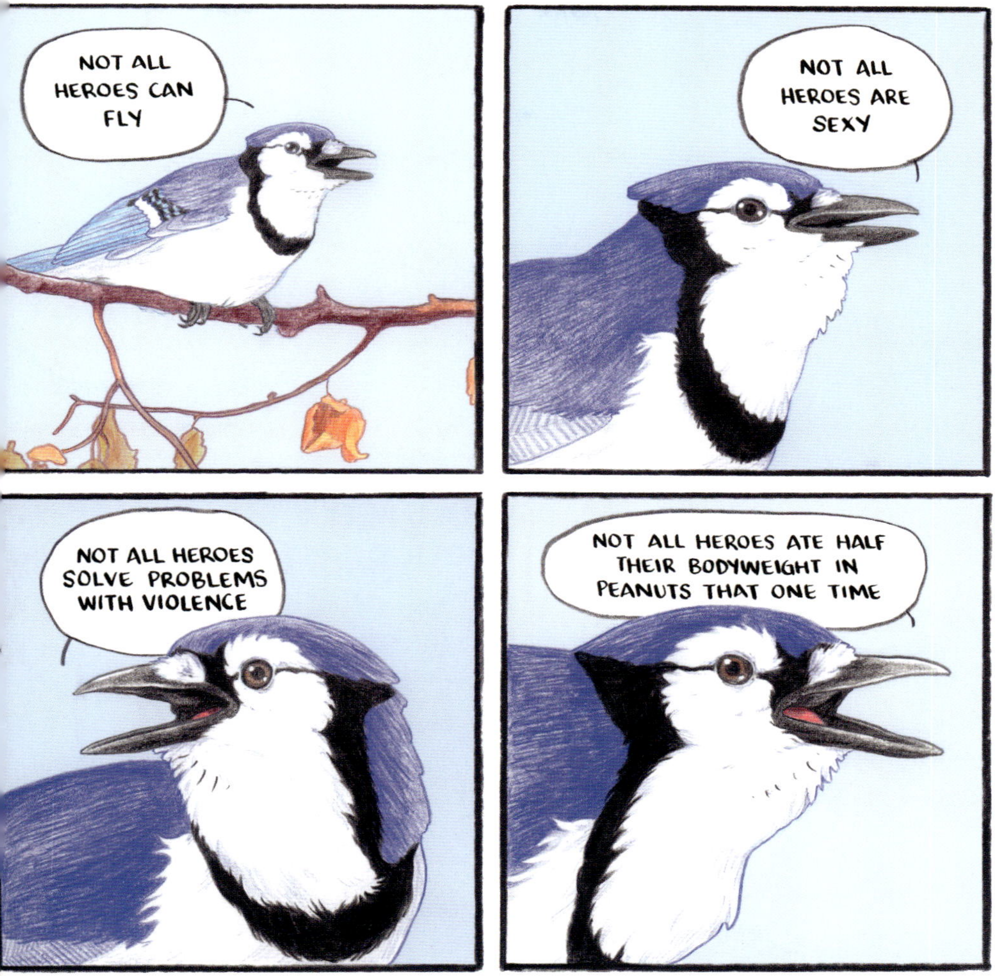
NOT ALL HEROES CAN FLY
NOT ALL HEROES ARE SEXY
NOT ALL HEROES SOLVE PROBLEMS WITH VIOLENCE
NOT ALL HEROES ATE HALF THEIR BODYWEIGHT IN PEANUTS THAT ONE TIME

HEY I GOT YOU A SNACK!
AWW, THANKS!
SORRY, IT'S PROBABLY NOT MY BEST CATCH...
OH NO, IS IT DRY? YOU DON'T HAVE TO EAT IT...
SHIT, IT LOOKS SUPER MEDIOCRE!
HAT IF IT'S GONE BAD? YO
OULD SPIT IT OU
IT'S FINE!

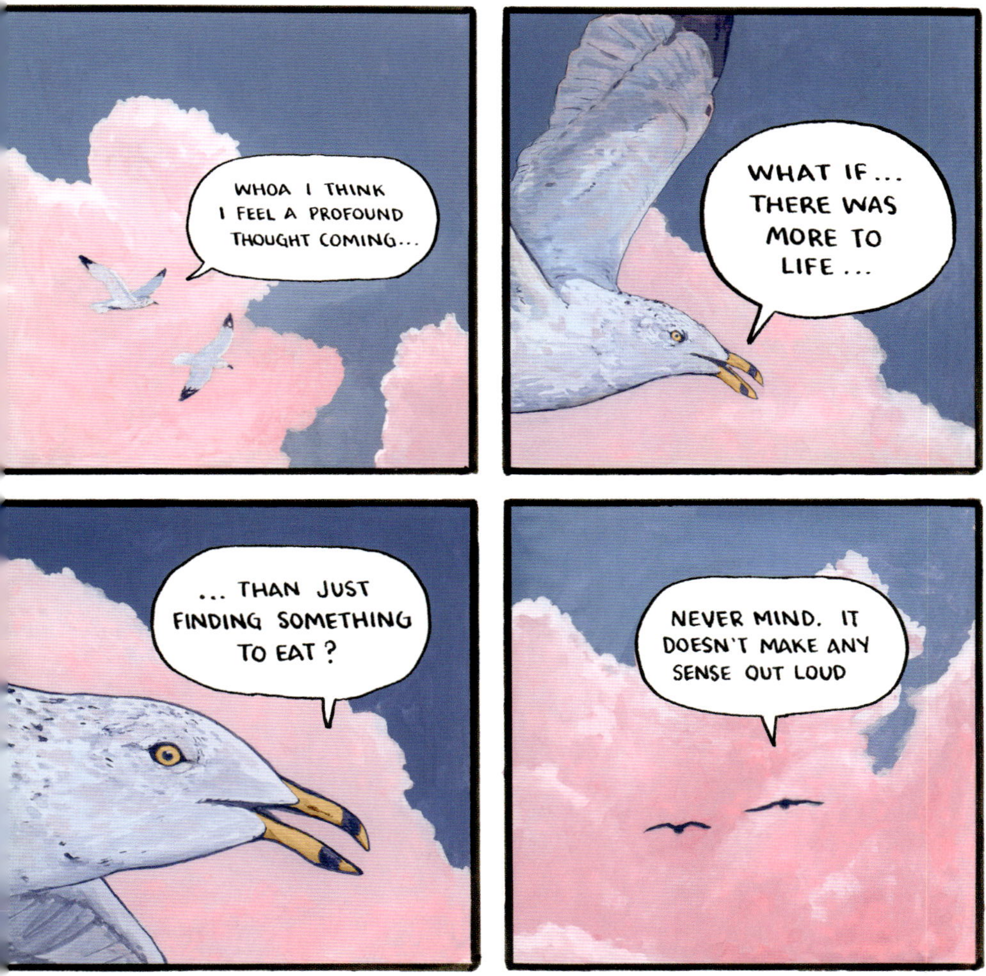
WHOA I THINK I FEEL A PROFOUND THOUGHT COMING...
WHAT IF... THERE WAS MORE TO LIFE...
... THAN JUST FINDING SOMETHING TO EAT?
NEVER MIND. IT DOESN'T MAKE ANY SENSE OUT LOUD

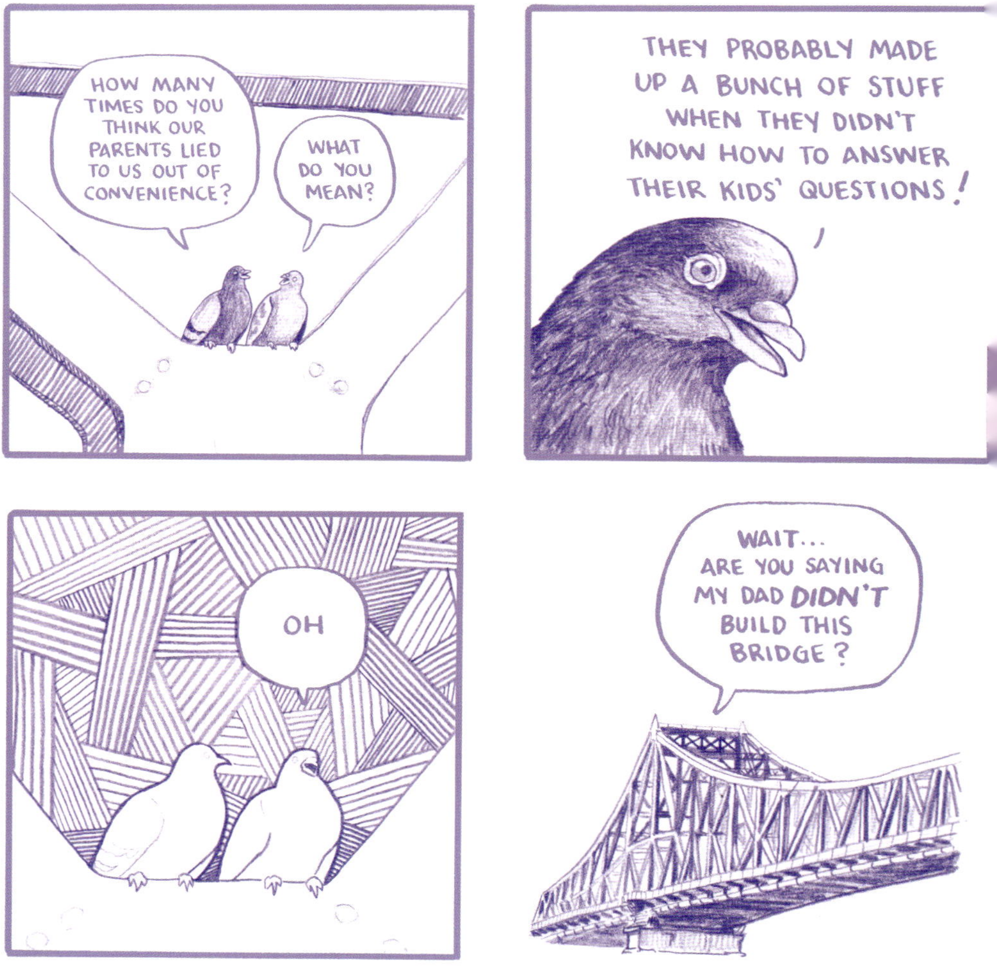
HOW MANY TIMES DO YOU THINK OUR PARENTS LIED TO US OUT OF CONVENIENCE?
WHAT DO YOU MEAN?
THEY PROBABLY MADE UP A BUNCH OF STUFF WHEN THEY DIDN'T KNOW HOW TO ANSWER THEIR KIDS' QUESTIONS!
OH
WAIT... ARE YOU SAYING MY DAD DIDN'T BUILD THIS BRIDGE?

DO YOU THINK WE'RE BEST FRIENDS IN OTHER UNIVERSES TOO?
UM
UM
UM
UM
WELL
UM
UM
UM
WELL
IT DOESN'T SEEM LIKELY

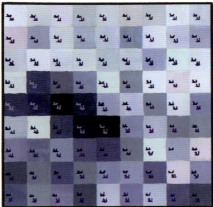

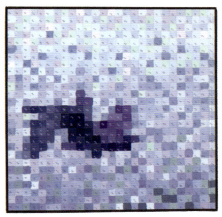

VERMILLION
GAMBOGE
CARNELIAN
ALL GREAT COLORS!
BUT MY FAVORITE IS BLORANGE
WHICH YOU CAN ONLY SEE ONE WAY...

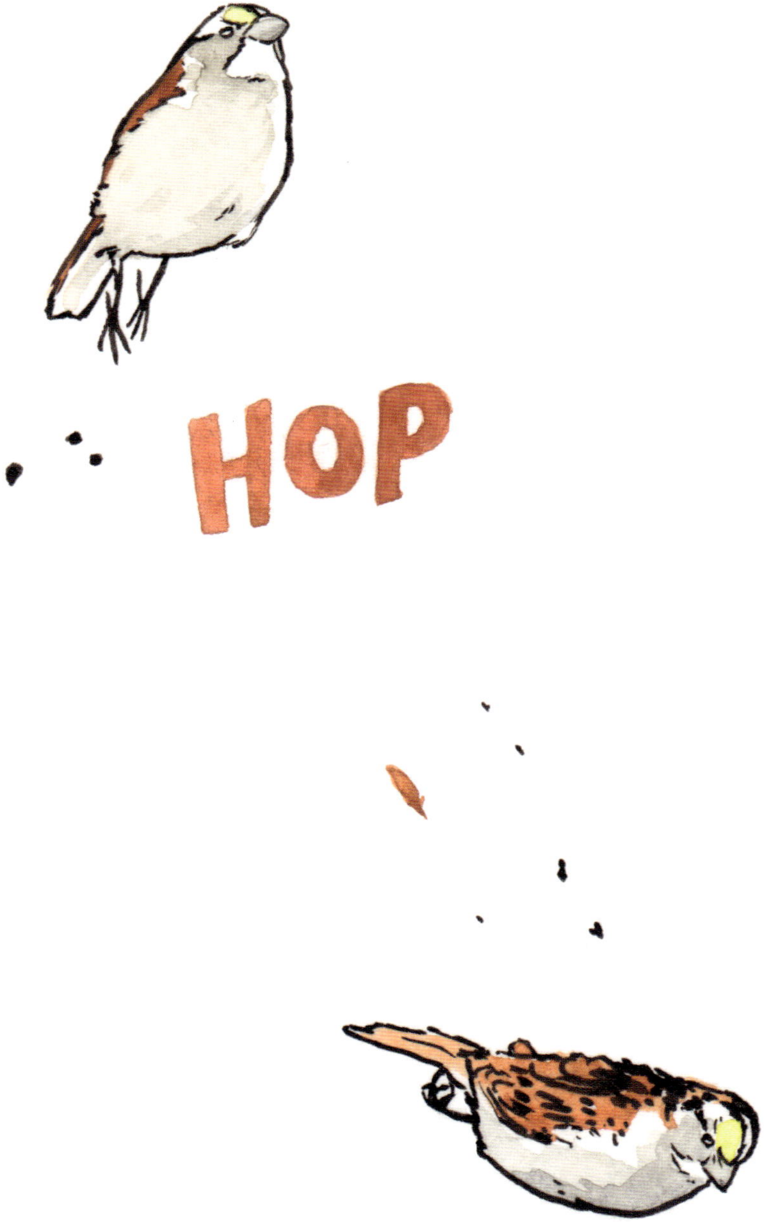
HOP

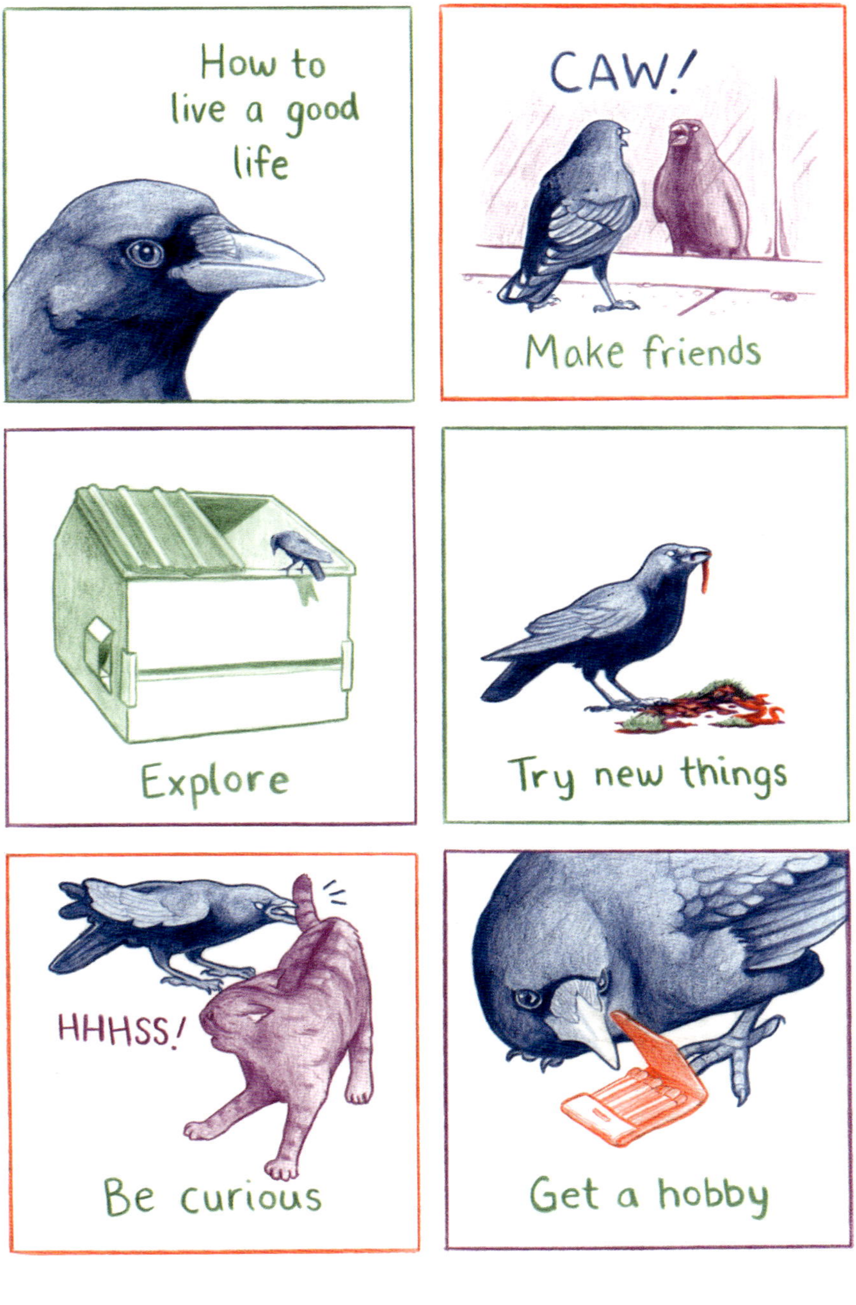
How to live a good life
CAW!
Make friends
Explore
Try new things
HHHSS!
Be curious
Get a hobby

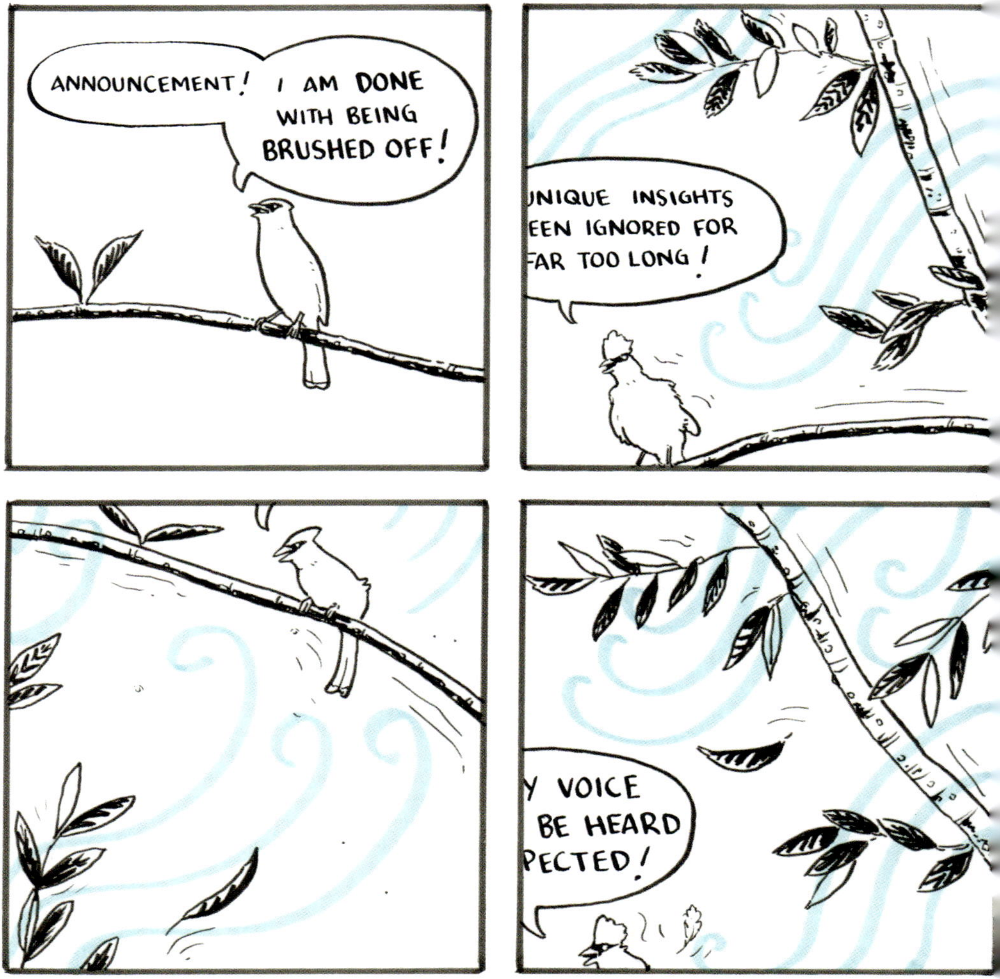
ANNOUNCEMENT!
I AM DONE WITH BEING BRUSHED OFF!
UNIQUE INSIGHTS
EEN IGNORED FOR
FAR TOO LONG!
Y VOICE
BE HEARD
PECTED!

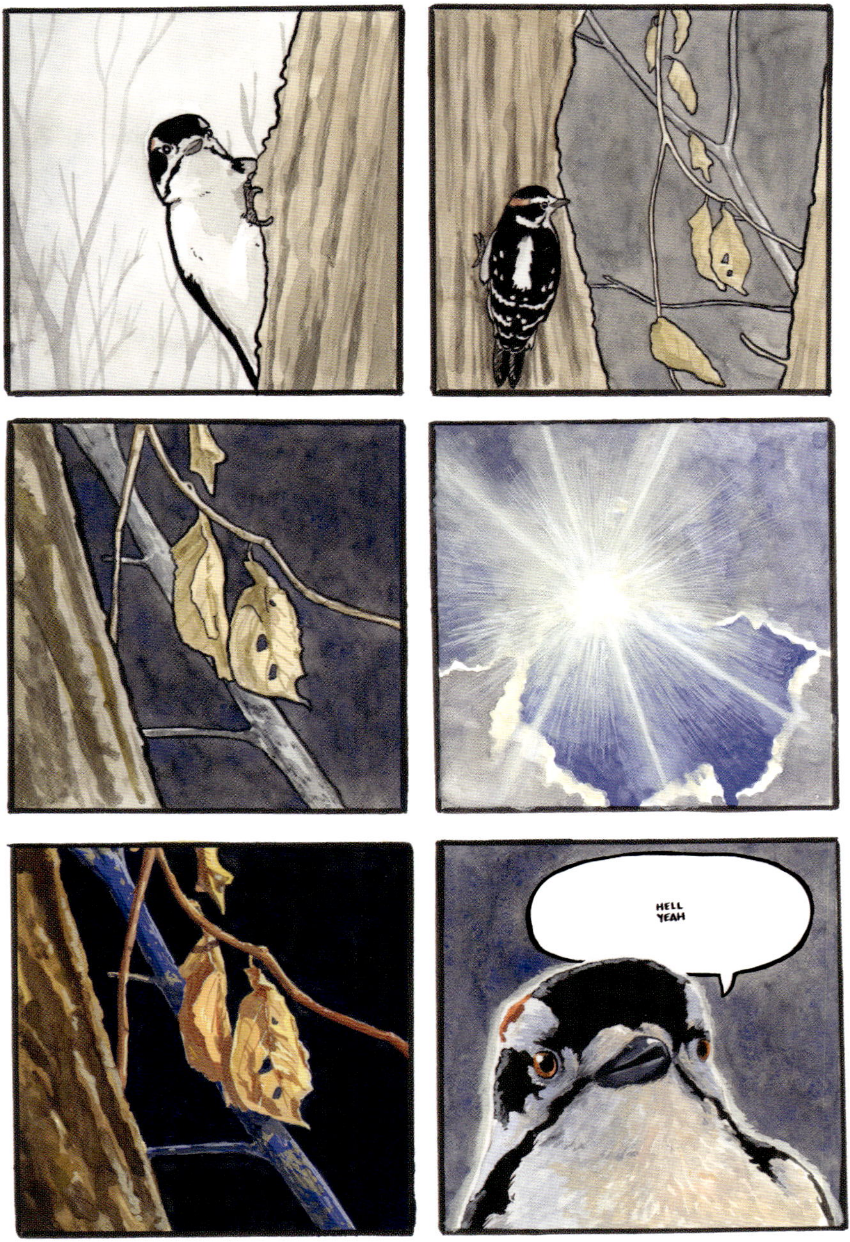
HELL
YEAH

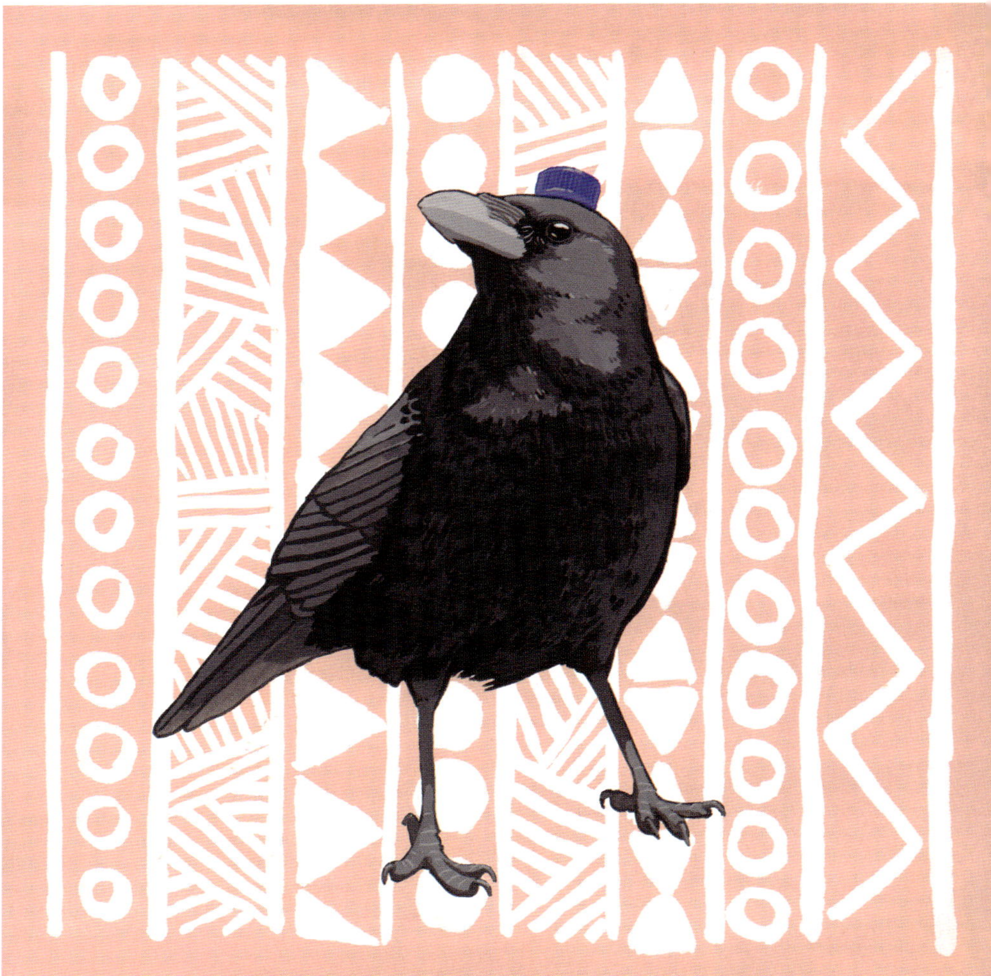

fashion is confidence

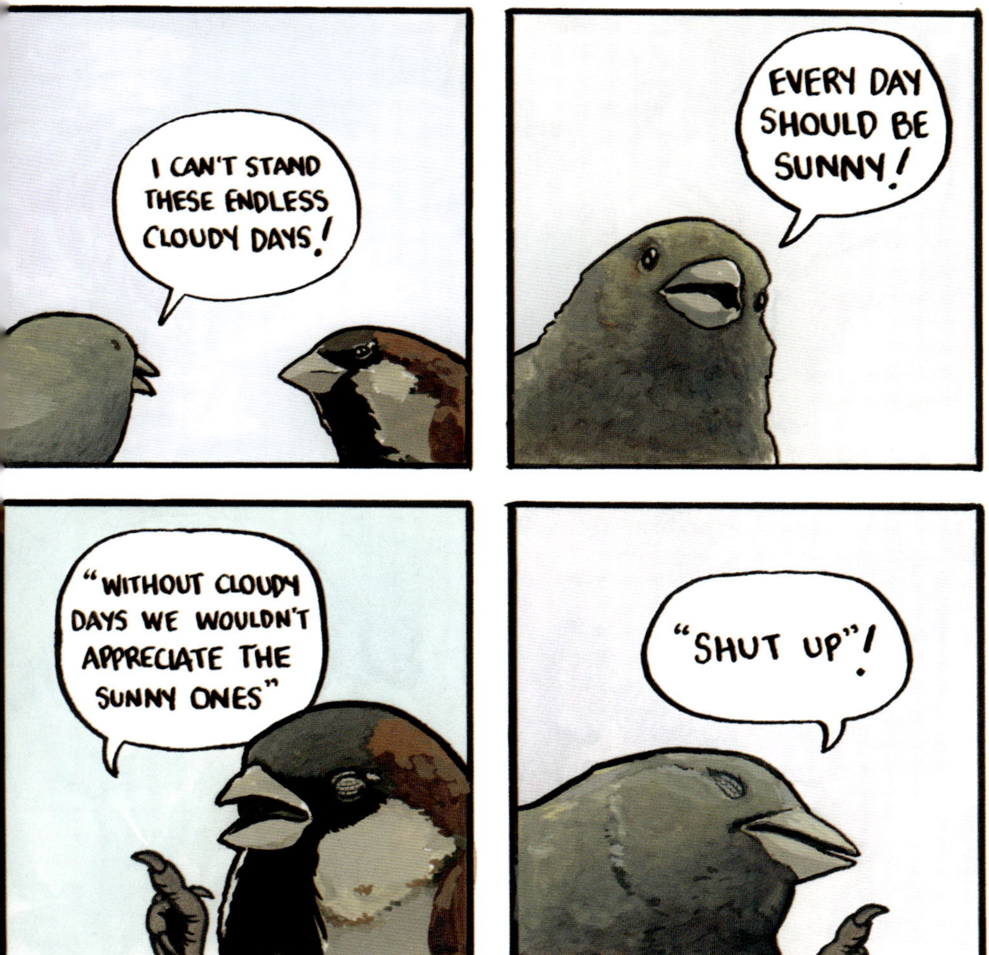
I CAN'T STAND THESE ENDLESS CLOUDY DAYS!
EVERY DAY SHOULD BE SUNNY!
"WITHOUT CLOUDY DAYS WE WOULDN'T APPRECIATE THE SUNNY ONES"
"SHUT UP"!

UM
...
HUH
...
HMM
THERE'S SOMETHING WRONG WITH THIS TREE

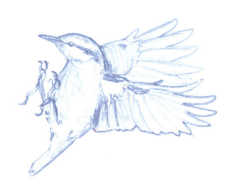

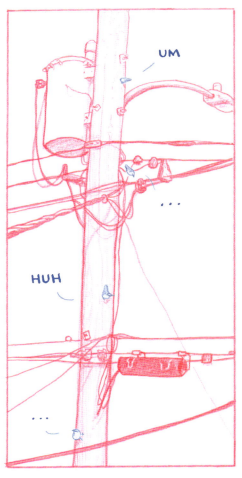

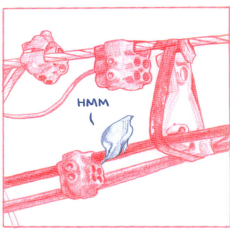

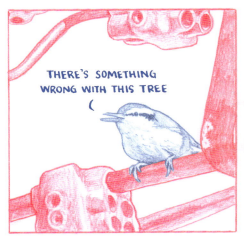

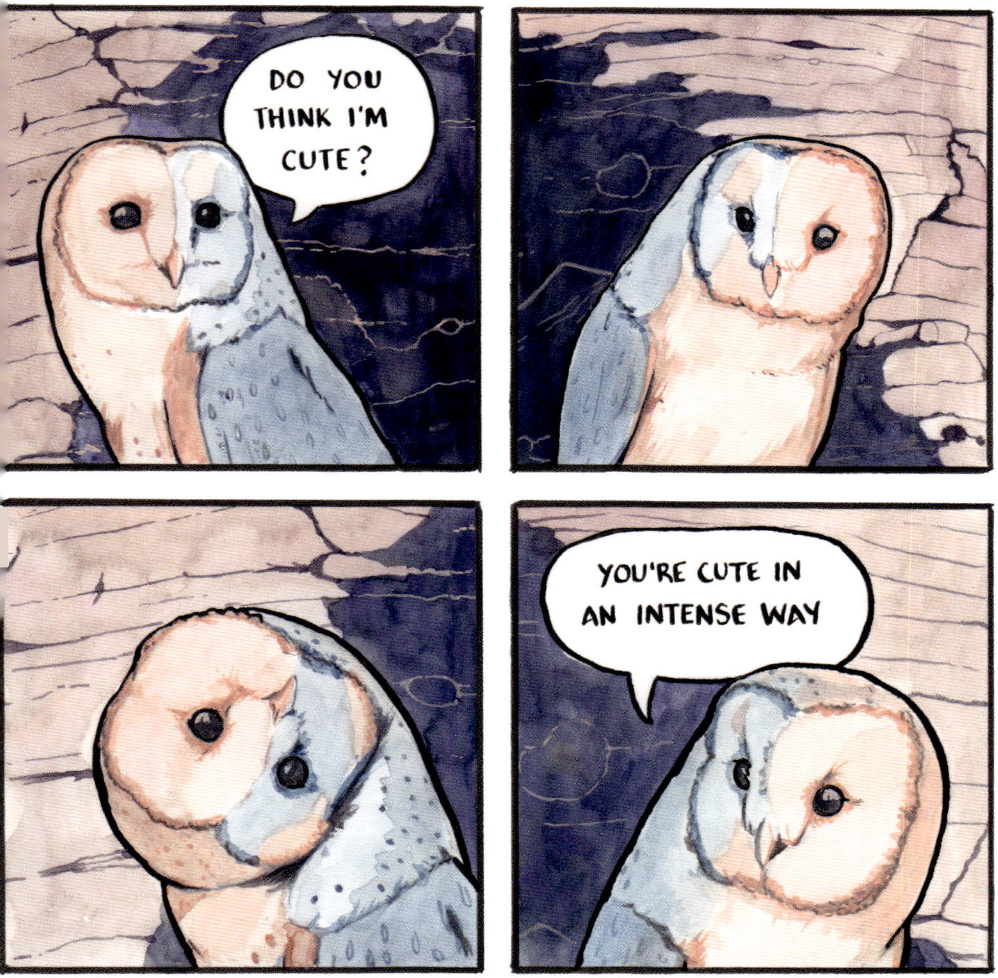
DO YOU THINK I'M CUTE?
YOU'RE CUTE IN AN INTENSE WAY

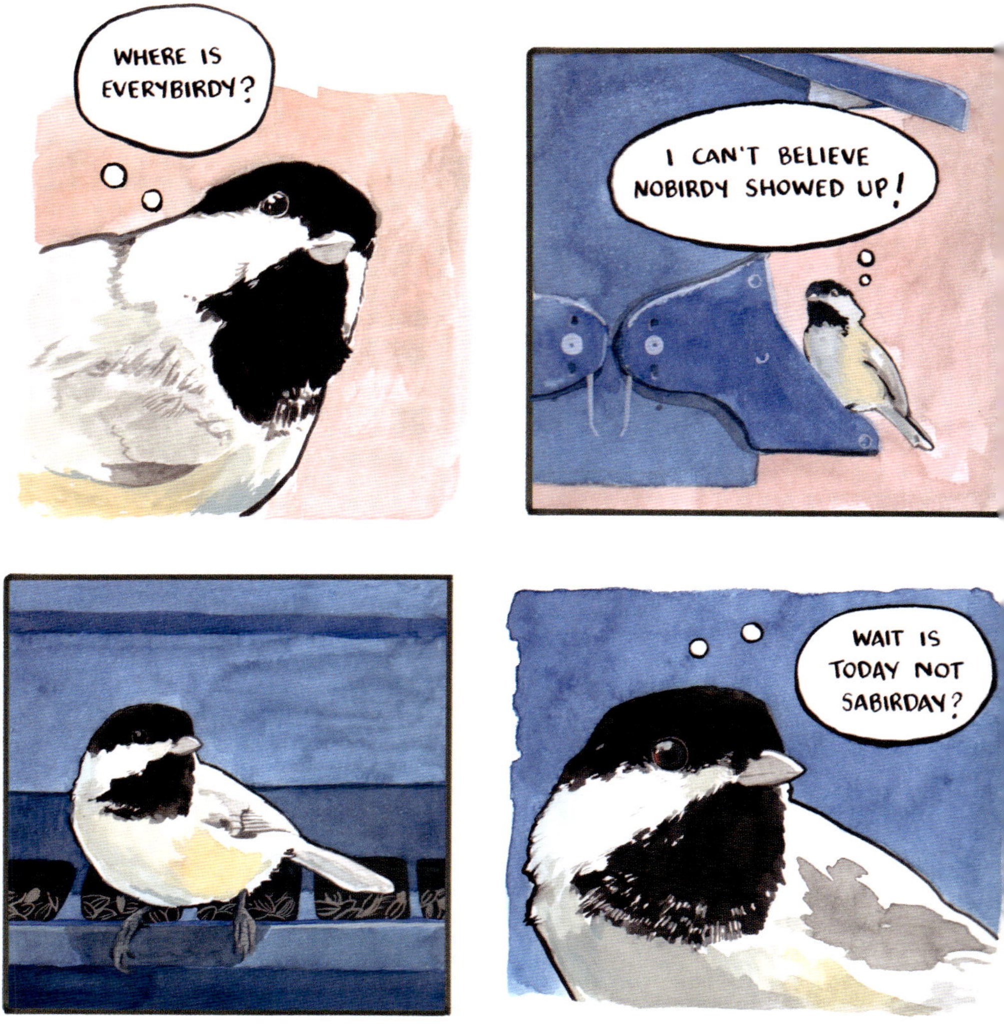
WHERE IS EVERYBIRDY?
I CAN'T BELIEVE NOBIRDY SHOWED UP!
WAIT IS TODAY NOT SABIRDAY?

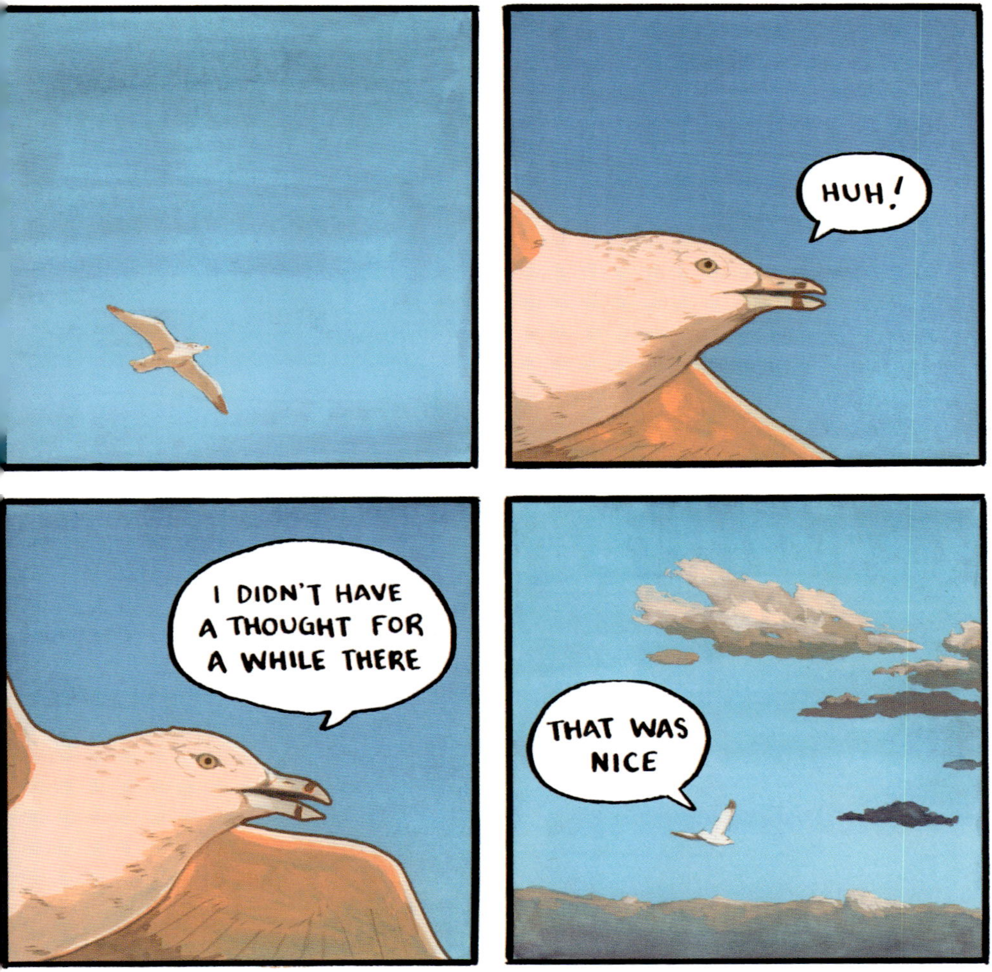
HUH!
I DIDN'T HAVE A THOUGHT FOR A WHILE THERE
THAT WAS NICE

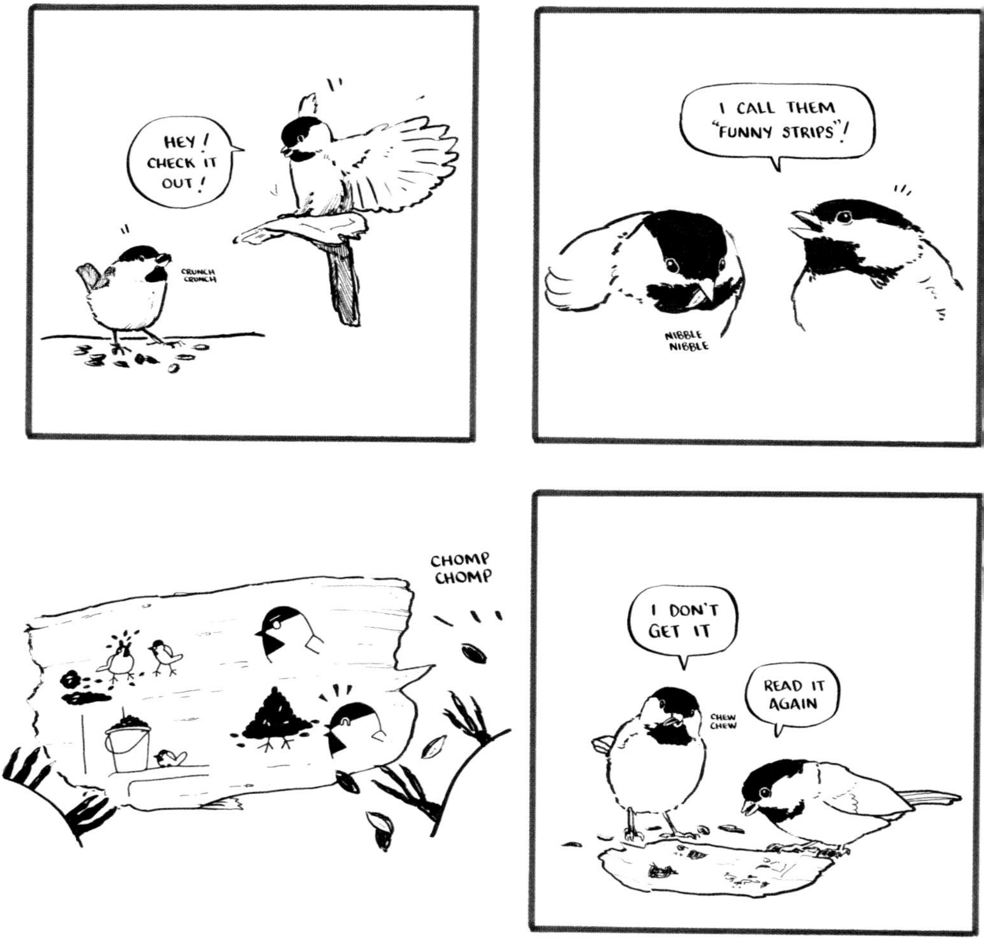
HEY! CHECK IT OUT!
CRUNCH CRUNCH
I CALL THEM "FUNNY STRIPS"!
NIBBLE NIBBLE
CHOMP CHOMP
I DON'T GET IT
CHEW CHEW
READ IT AGAIN

Ew, It's Beautiful: A False Knees Comic Collection
copyright © 2025 by Joshua Barkman. All rights reserved.
Printed in China. No part of this book may be used or reproduced
in any manner whatsoever without written permission
except in the case of reprints in the context of reviews.

Andrews McMeel Publishing
a division of Andrews McMeel Universal
1130 Walnut Street, Kansas City, Missouri 64106

www.andrewsmcmeel.com

25 26 27 28 29 TEN 10 9 8 7 6 5 4 3 2

ISBN: 978-1-5248-9764-2

Library of Congress Control Number: 2024950636

Editor: Melissa Rhodes Zahorsky
Art Director: Diane Marsh
Production Editor: Elizabeth A. Garcia
Production Manager: Tamara Haus

ATTENTION: SCHOOLS AND BUSINESSES
Andrews McMeel books are available at quantity discounts with
bulk purchase for educational, business, or sales promotional use.
For information, please e-mail the Andrews McMeel Publishing
Special Sales Department: sales@andrewsmcmeel.com.